# Negotiating Abolition

# Negotiating Abolition

## *The Antislavery Project in the British Straits Settlements, 1786–1843*

By Shawna R. Herzog

BLOOMSBURY ACADEMIC
LONDON • NEW YORK • OXFORD • NEW DELHI • SYDNEY

BLOOMSBURY ACADEMIC
Bloomsbury Publishing Plc
50 Bedford Square, London, WC1B 3DP, UK
1385 Broadway, New York, NY 10018, USA

BLOOMSBURY, BLOOMSBURY ACADEMIC and the Diana logo are trademarks of Bloomsbury Publishing Plc

First published in Great Britain 2021
Paperback edition first published 2022

Copyright © Shawna R. Herzog, 2021

Shawna R. Herzog has asserted her right under the Copyright, Designs and Patents Act, 1988, to be identified as Author of this work.

For legal purposes the Acknowledgments on pp. ix–x constitute an extension of this copyright page

Cover design: Terry Woodley
Cover image: Balinese slave in Batavia in 1700 from Cornelis de Bruin *Voyages de Corneille le Brun* 1718.

All rights reserved. No part of this publication may be reproduced or transmitted in any form or by any means, electronic or mechanical, including photocopying, recording, or any information storage or retrieval system, without prior permission in writing from the publishers.

Bloomsbury Publishing Plc does not have any control over, or responsibility for, any third-party websites referred to or in this book. All internet addresses given in this book were correct at the time of going to press. The author and publisher regret any inconvenience caused if addresses have changed or sites have ceased to exist, but can accept no responsibility for any such changes.

Every effort has been made to trace copyright holders and to obtain their permissions for the use of copyright material. The publisher apologizes for any errors or omissions and would be grateful if notified of any corrections that should be incorporated in future reprints or editions of this book.

A catalogue record for this book is available from the British Library.

Library of Congress Cataloging-in-Publication Data
Names: Herzog, Shawna, author.
Title: Negotiating abolition : the antislavery project in the British Strait Settlements, 1786-1843 / Shawna Herzog.
Description: New York : Bloomsbury Academic, 2021. | Includes bibliographical references and index.
Identifiers: LCCN 2020035894 (print) | LCCN 2020035895 (ebook) | ISBN 9781350073203 (hardback) | ISBN 9781350202481 (paperback) | ISBN 9781350073210 (ebook) | ISBN 9781350073227 (epub)
Subjects: LCSH: Antislavery movements–Straits Settlements–History–18th century. | Antislavery movements–Straits Settlements–History–19th century. | Abolitionists–Straits Settlements–History–18th century. | Abolitionists–Straits Settlements–History–19th century.
Classification: LCC HT1250.S73 H47 2021 (print) | LCC HT1250.S73 (ebook) | DDC 326/.809033–dc23
LC record available at https://lccn.loc.gov/2020035894
LC ebook record available at https://lccn.loc.gov/2020035895

| ISBN: | HB: | 978-1-3500-7320-3 |
|---|---|---|
| | PB: | 978-1-3502-0248-1 |
| | ePDF: | 978-1-3500-7321-0 |
| | eBook: | 978-1-3500-7322-7 |

Typeset by Integra Software Services Pvt. Ltd.

To find out more about our authors and books visit www.bloomsbury.com and sign up for our newsletters.

*[For the Richards and Friends]*

# Contents

| | |
|---|---|
| List of Maps | viii |
| Acknowledgments | ix |
| | |
| Introduction | 1 |
| 1   A Policy of Noninterference | 35 |
| 2   Negotiating Abolition in the Indian Ocean World | 57 |
| 3   Redefining Slavery and Servitude in the Straits | 75 |
| 4   The Politics of Abolition in the Straits | 91 |
| 5   Tolerance vs. Emancipation: Abolition in Malacca | 109 |
| 6   A Convenient Compromise | 125 |
| 7   An Illicit Trade to Penang and Singapore | 147 |
| 8   The Wild, Womanless East Indies | 175 |
| Conclusion: In the Wake of Abolition | 193 |
| | |
| Bibliography | 201 |
| Index | 215 |

# Maps

| | | |
|---|---|---|
| 1 | Map of Southeast Asia | 54 |
| 2 | Map of Global Trade/Slave Routes | 55 |

# Acknowledgments

The book began as a dissertation project and would not have been possible without the guidance, encouragement, and probing questions from Heather Streets-Salter. As both my mentor and friend, she has become my yardstick for world historians and I am incredibly thankful to have had the privilege of her encouragement and input at every step of the way. Jennifer Thigpen's meticulous eye for detail and impromptu counseling were also invaluable and helped keep this entire process in perspective. Comments and analysis from scholars like Candice Goucher, Sue Peabody, Pier Vries, Patrick Manning, and Adam McKowen—a scholar sorely missed—and Philippa Levine shaped the direction of this research and have all had a significant impact on my understanding of colonialism and its effects on our daily lives. I am also thankful to Washington State University, the encouragement and nurturing I received from its History Department, and financial support from scholarships like the Gillis Family Research Award and the Aiken Travel Grant, which funded the majority of the international travel for research and made time for writing possible.

The support of my family and friends carried me through this project. Dr. Tabitha Erdey, a scholar whom I admire immensely, gave crucial feedback on various drafts. A fellow "Shenanigans Enthusiast," I forced her to endure my incessant research-ramblings at every festival, bluegrass show, and trip to Missoula for nearly a decade. I am also eternally grateful for the critical input and extra set of eyes from Malcolm Purinton, Katy Whalen, Marianne Rhett, and Melanie Reimann. Of course, there are no words to express the debt of gratitude I feel for my best friend, loyal research assistance, partner in crime, and all-around soul sister, Jessica Riley. Thank you for hangin' out at the Lighthouse, Fashion Fair, the 80s, London riots, bad coffee, 3AM texts, and a litany of manic phone calls; you are the best, Bestie, and I would walk through fire for you.

The years 2017–19 were particularly difficult and punctuated by the deaths of several close friends, my nephew, father, and father-in-law. It is to them, "The Richards and Friends" that I dedicate this book. My father and I were very close, and I miss him every day; it is his wry, sarcastic sense of humor you hear echoing in my words. My mother, Jonna True, and brother, Flint Sweet, in spite of never really understanding my academic pursuits, have given unwavering support and are in large part responsible for the person I am today. Of course, my mother could not be prouder, and naturally, without her, none of this would have been possible. I love and appreciate her more than she will ever know. Finally, I would like to say thank you to the people who make my life better every day. My daughter Freyja has inspired me since the day she was born and my partner Brian has spent the past twenty-five years making my happiness his priority. They both have made unimaginable sacrifices to afford me the opportunity to accomplish so many personal and professional goals. Their love, patience, and resolute confidence have helped me persevere. I am so very thankful for my village.

# Introduction

One summer morning in 1823, Abdullah Kadir went walking through Singapore's harbors looking for a slave market he had discovered the day before. Not only had the British government banned the slave trade in all British territories in 1807, but both Parliament and the East India Company (EIC) had passed regulations in 1811 making slave trading a felony. Yet, within the British colony of Singapore, the young clerk had seen "fifty or sixty slaves being led by a Bugis man around the town."[1] In his autobiography, written a little more than a decade later, Kadir explained that he saw the slaves "herded along" and struck by the driver's cane as they walked through the streets.[2] Kadir followed the group to ask the Bugis man where the slaves had come from and their price. He wrote that the man told him the slaves in that group were between 30 and 40 dollars each, but the slaver suggested to him that if he were really interested, a boat had landed in the harbor the day before, "carrying three or four hundred." When he arrived on the docks the following morning, Kadir had no trouble finding what he was looking for.

As he reached the slave ship, Kadir saw hundreds of men, women, and children available for sale; some of the pregnant women looked as though they were about to give birth. He recalled seeing a "hundred Chinese men" looking through the merchandise and remembered, "watching this pitiful sight, seeing pregnant

---

[1] A. H. Hill, trans., *The Hikayat Abdullah* (London: Oxford University Press, 1970), pp. 181–5; Abdullah Bin Abdul Kadir was a "Malay scholar" who rose to a "position of importance as a member of the harbormaster's department under the Dutch" (6–7). Then, eventually, he became "the youngest of a number of scribes and copyists whom Raffles employed in his office" and wrote extensively about the negotiations and events surrounding the birth of British Malaya (9). The above story was taken from Kadir's writings. Barbara Watson-Andaya and Leonard Andaya's *A History of Malaysia* (Honolulu: University of Hawaii Press, 2001), p. 114, explains that Kadir was a noted teacher and became a scribe for Stamford Raffles after the British took possession of Malacca in 1825. William Evans, *Slave Trade (East India) Slavery in Ceylon: Copies or Abstracts of All Correspondence between the Directors of the East India Company and the Company's Government in India, since the 1st Day of June 1827, on the Subject of Slavery in the Territories under the Company's Rule: Also Communications Relating to the Subject of Slavery in the Island of Ceylon* (London: Great Britain Foreign Office, 1838), p. 1.

[2] Hill, *The Hikayat Abdullah*, pp. 182–4.

women gazing at [him] with tear-stained eyes." He noticed they were given "rice in coconut shells and water in bamboo scoops just as one gives food to dogs" and claimed the sight brought him to tears. When he went inside, Kadir explained that he found women and girls, young and old, "some fair, other[s] dark." He remarked that some were from surrounding islands but that he could tell that many had come from far away; some did not speak Malay, or had "fat stomachs and thick lips," while others had "frizzy hair and black faces." He asserted that the slave owner "behaved like a beast," and when one of the men wanted to buy a girl, the master opened "their clothing with all manner of gestures" that mortified him. According to Kadir, slavers had given the young girls that were in high demand a "piece of cloth to wear," but no other provisions were made for the weak or sick among them. The male slaves had been tied, "round the waist like monkeys, one to each rope, made fast to the side of the boats." The final blow came when Kadir saw the slave owner sell a woman to one man and her child to another. As he watched them take the two in opposite directions, "the mother wept and the child screamed and screamed when she saw her mother taken away." Outraged, he went back to town to describe to authorities what he had seen.

Upon returning to his post as a scribe and copyist for the EIC, Kadir told his supervisor, founding resident of Singapore Sir Stamford Raffles, about what he had seen. A man who had a complicated relationship with slavery, the EIC official told Kadir "[T]hat business will not last much longer for the English are going to put a stop to it." Raffles explained that many had petitioned Parliament "demanding that the slave trade shall cease." He told Kadir that slavery was not only in the East Indies, but that "to England too boatloads of people are brought from other countries, and thousands of black men are turned into slaves." Raffles insisted that these people were also "put up like goods for sale in all the countries of Europe." However, the optimistic official assured Kadir that "if we live to be old we may yet see all the slaves gain their freedom and become like ourselves." The official was full of authority and promise when he declared that the British would bring an end to such "wicked" practices. He believed they were bringing freedom—free trade and free labor—to Southeast Asia. Yet despite the fact that slave trading was at that moment altogether illegal in Singapore, and that Raffles had declared himself no friend of the trade, the official was not moved enough to go down to the harbor to stop it.

Indeed, the matter was much more complicated than Raffles had led his colleague to believe. In addition to lacking the authority to dispossess people of their private property and a clear understanding of their jurisdiction, inconsistent efforts and application of policies by a string of EIC administrative officials hobbled the enforcement of antislavery laws in the Straits Settlements.

In fact, as late as July of 1842 a concerned member of Parliament, reacting to recent public allegations by the Anti-Slavery League, asked EIC representative B. Baring, "[W]hat steps had been taken for the abolition of slavery and the slave-trade which had been proven to exist without sanction of law in the British settlements of Penang, Province of Wellesley, and Singapore?"[3] Mr. Baring's response not only encapsulated the primary obstacles colonial officials faced in the implementation of antislavery measures but also obfuscated a few of the intrinsic realities that had inhibited them. Baring explained to his awaiting audience that the details were best left to the official report presented to the government, but he assured them that the EIC "gave every security to individuals in enacting that no one should be dispossessed of their property on the ground that his predecessors, having been slaves, had no right to acquire it."[4] He wanted his critics to understand that the Company had to consider particularly delicate circumstances when confronting slavery in the Empire's Southeast Asian territories. Both Kadir's tale and Baring's statement provide important clues about the composition and complexities of slavery in the east and also how the EIC went about the task of abolishing slavery in the Straits Settlements.

The Company had certainly promulgated a variety of legislative measures to prohibit European slavery in their eastern territories between Parliament's 1807 Slave Trade Act that prohibited the transportation of and trading in slaves and the Emancipation Act enacted in 1834, which theoretically manumitted any person within British territory holding the status of slave. However, very few of the local governments had the manpower or the authority to enact or enforce the cessation of a trade that existed centuries before their arrival.[5] As Andrea Major explains in *Slavery, Abolitionism and Empire in India*, the EIC understood "slavery was recognized by both Hindu and Muslim law" and unless a case "impinged on colonial stability, or the rule of law," EIC Officials "preferred not to interfere."[6]

---

[3] *Hansard's Parliamentary Debates, William IV, Vol. LXV*, July 12 to August 12, 1842 (Vol.VI) (London, 1842), pp. 1074–5.
[4] Ibid., p. 1075.
[5] For more about the duration and interconnectivity of Indian Ocean, Southeast Asian, and Chinese maritime trading relationships see Andaya and Andaya, *A History of Malaysia*, pp. 10–37; Himanshu Pragha Ray and Edward A. Alpers, eds., *Cross Currents and Community Network: The History of the Indian Ocean World* (Oxford: Oxford University Press, 2007), pp. 286–306; Carl A. Trocki, *Prince of Pirates: The Temenggongs and the Development of Johor and Singapore, 1784-1885* (Singapore: Singapore University Press, 1979), pp. 1–20; Anthony Reid, *Charting the Shape of Early Modern Southeast Asia* (Chiang Mai: Silkworm Books, 1999), pp. 39–55; Eric Tagliacozzo and Wen-chin Chang, *Chinese Circulations: Capital, Commodities, and Networks in Southeast Asia* (Durham: Duke University Press, 2011), pp. 21–101; David Killingray, Margarette Lincoln, and Nigel Rigby, *Maritime Empires* (Suffolk, UK: Boydell Press, 2004), pp. 48–66.
[6] Andrea Major, *Slavery, Abolitionism and Empire in India, 1772-1843* (Liverpool: Liverpool University Press, 2012), pp. 8–9.

Aside from his compellingly dramatic prose, Kadir's writings provide a number of clues about the slave trade in Southeast Asia during this period. First, contrary to existing legislation and official reports, even as late as 1823 there were clearly still slaves—men, women, and children—openly sold on the docks in Singapore. As Kadir's description illustrates, after the 1807 Act the slave trade was primarily dominated by Malay and Chinese who purchased and procured both enslaved and indentured labor to work on pepper plantations or in tin mines all along the peninsula.[7] However, we also know that the Chinese generally imported debt-slaves from China to work on their plantations and in their mines, rather than purchasing slaves outright from open markets.[8] Perhaps these people were meant to labor for one of the surrounding Malay leaders who still owned many slaves; *owning* slaves was not yet illegal. The problem here was that, in spite of official prohibition, slaves were being *sold in front of a Company official*, without reproach, in Singapore—a place established well after passage of the Acts and slavery was unequivocally illegal. Moreover Kadir, a Company employee who must have known slavery was prohibited at the founding of the colony in 1819, made no attempt to inquire with the Harbor Master at the dock or interrupt the market himself, nor did Raffles make any effort to send a police force to stop it. As we will see, there was often more pomp in EIC antislavery rhetoric than any real change in the circumstance of slaves. Finally, the scene as a whole also summarizes what we know about the slave trade in Southeast Asia during this period: women and girls made up the bulk of the cargo—they filled the hull and spilled out on to the deck—and, depending on their perceived beauty, were also the most valuable.[9] It is also worth noting that,

---

[7] Geoff Wade, "An Early Age of Commerce in Southeast Asia, 900–1300 CE," *Journal of Southeast Asian Studies* 40, no. 2 (June 2009): p. 249.

[8] Adam McKeown, "The Social Life of Chinese Labor," in *Chinese Circulations: Capital, Commodities, and Networks in Southeast Asia*, eds. Eric Taggliacozzo and Wen-Chin Chang (Durham: Duke University Press, 2011), pp. 62–5.

[9] Evans, *Slave Trade (East India) Slavery in Ceylon*, p. 239. The following articles in *The Singapore Chronicle* offer examples of the issue about local demographics and populations: *The Singapore Chronicle*, March 1, 1827; *The Singapore Chronicle*, February 26, 1829; *The Singapore Chronicle*, November 15, 1829; *The Singapore Chronicle*, June 23, 1831; *The Singapore Chronicle*, November 8, 1932; *The Singapore Chronicle*, February 7, 1833; Reid, *Charting the Shape of Early Modern Southeast Asia*, pp. 181–212; Anthony Reid, "The Decline of Slavery in Nineteenth-Century Indonesia," in *Breaking the Chains: Slavery, Bondage, and Emancipation in Modern Africa and Asia*, ed. Martin A. Klein (Madison: University of Wisconsin Press, 1993), pp. 64–80; Barbara Watson Andaya, *Other Pasts: Women, Gender and History in Early Modern Southeast Asia* (Honolulu: University of Hawai'i Press, 2000), pp. 174–94; James Francis Warren, *The Sulu Zone, 1768–1898: The Dynamics of External Trade, Slavery, and Ethnicity in the Transformation of a Southeast Asian Maritime State* (Singapore: Singapore University Press, 1981), pp. 215–51; Eric Tagliacozzo, "Ambiguous Commodities, Unstable Frontiers: The Case of Burma, Siam, and Imperial Britain, 1800–1900," *Comparative Studies in Society and History* 46 (2004): pp. 354–77.

unlike the claims of many Company officials, none of the women, according to Kadir's descriptions, appeared to be happy with their circumstance. At the same time, while Kadir seemed quite disturbed by the spectacle, as we will see, many officials maintained that most of these women were destined to be the "wives of wealthy Chinese merchants" and, even if they were made domestic servants, their lot was better simply by their good fortune of being brought within the protective sphere of His Majesty's (HM) territories.

While Kadir's story gives us a glimpse, even if a bit biased and after the fact, of the slave trade to Singapore in the 1820s, Baring's statement helps us understand the Company's primary focus: profits and protection of property. Indeed, an examination of the Company's official reports on slavery, contemporary public discourse, and published monographs from retired administrators demonstrates that the Company's oath to the protection of private property and the primacy given to the preservation of political and economic relationships were key inhibitors to the full implementation and enforcement of British imperial antislavery legislation in the East Indies during the first half of the nineteenth century. Local authorities throughout the Empire were strategic in their use of legal ordinances and enforced or ignored imperial policy, as necessary, to negotiate for power and influence in their respective regions. The EIC were first and foremost a business venture; it would be naive to believe that administrators were not selective in their application of the law. Moreover, slaves were an elemental component of most Asian societies during this period, so Company officials had to look for ways to accommodate the demands of Parliament without disrupting important political and economic relationships.

By the 1820s, many colonial officials and eastern planters had constructed slavery in the east in opposition to western systems in the Caribbean and the Americas, which they described as "frightful abuses of power" to protect profits and deflect the attention of abolitionist critics (for a time) focused on the horrors of the Atlantic system.[10] Many feminized and mitigated the eastern systems arguing, as one official did, that most slaves were "employed generally for domestic services," leaving some the impression that slavery in the East Indies was akin to some benevolent form of social welfare.[11] Apologists used stories about women and children sold as wives, concubines, and domestic servants into wealthy households of the Chinese and Arab elite to illustrate the banality of the system, but these images obfuscated the violence, depredation,

---

[10] John Hobhouse, *Returns: Slavery (East Indies)* (London: Great Britain Foreign Office, 1838), p. 188; Major, *Slavery, Abolitionism and Empire in India*, pp. 293–315, asserts that the EIC constructed the image of benevolent eastern slavery to reframe perceptions of East India labor and stabilize sugar profits suffering from the abolitionist campaign on the trans-Atlantic trade.

[11] Evans, *Slave Trade (East India) Slavery in Ceylon*, p. 245.

and exploitation experienced by the enslaved and ignored all those working in the mines, on plantations, or on the docks. The belief that the trade was more of a marriage or employment service, rather than *true* slavery, kept abolitionist fervor at bay for more than a decade; Malacca's registry lasted until 1841.

This work is a small contribution to a much larger conversation about the historical legacies embedded within the modern problem of slavery, and the domestic and sexual exploitation of women in particular. Of course, it is ludicrous to insinuate that it was "easier" for men to be enslaved than women— suffering is not a contest and slavers meted out unimaginable tortures to millions of people around the world, regardless of gender. Nonetheless, as this book demonstrates, Britain's conception of slavery in the Indian Ocean World rested on inherently gendered perceptions of domestic labor, which tempered the implementation, interpretation, and enforcement of antislavery legislation in the east. More importantly, those same attitudes helped colonial officials justify the enslavement of women, providing they performed some form of domestic service: wife, concubine, or household servant. This meant that the status of "slave," including any legal protections or financial compensatory measures that came with emancipation, was dependent upon their relationship to a man—not the labor they performed or the conditions under which they performed their duties. This, of course, highlights a striking presumption made by both contemporaries and modern scholars alike: freeing women meant for the purposes of marriage, concubinage, or domestic servitude (with exception of those unknowingly prostituted) was never part of the deal.

The following analysis of slavery and abolition in the British Straits Settlements looks at the EIC's efforts to implement antislavery ordinances in their eastern territories from the first ordinance passed in 1795 at Prince of Wales Island to 1843, when the status of slave was no longer recognized within the British Straits Settlements.[12] I argue that in addition to a dogmatic adherence to the protection of personal property, real limits to colonial authority and legal disputes within many of the EIC's outposts complicated and prolonged efforts to eliminate the status of "slave" in its colonies. At the same time, British perceptions of race and class shaped the way colonial officials perceived eastern slave systems, while gendered understandings of a patriarchal domestic order and orientalist constructions of eastern sexualities influenced how authorities understood and responded to the illicit trade they encountered. Ultimately, this work demonstrates the folly in Raffles's statement to Kadir: the EIC was not

---

[12] Major, *Slavery, Abolitionism and Empire in India*, pp. 8–9.

focused on the abolition of the slave trade in the East Indies, their power and jurisdiction far too limited during this period, and orientalist preconceptions about slavery, combined with gendered concepts undergirding domestic labor, prejudiced those meant to enforce the law. As a result, the institution persisted within EIC territories long after Britain claimed to have abolished it.

## Establishing a Foundation

Before progressing any further, it is important to clearly articulate the contributions this research seeks to make. This book is about the process of abolition and the ways practical limitations, cultural bias, and colonial policy hobbled the enforcement of British law in the Straits of Malacca. It seeks to expose the conflicts, nuance, and consequences of the Company's procedures and practices, which were not readily visible from the imperial center. It is not a comparison of abolitionism in British colonial spaces in the Atlantic and Indian Ocean World (IOW), nor does it offer statistical data and analysis for the slave trade in the region. For that, we look to Richard Allen's comprehensive work. Adding to a long list of publications about Indian Ocean slavery, *European Slave Trading in the Indian Ocean* is the first to make the herculean effort to quantify and analyze Europe's pre-abolition slave trading in this region. However, as he explains, there is a "relative paucity of archival sources on slavery and slave trading in this part of the world," and EIC records are "brief and scattered."[13] While we can get a general idea of the outlines by looking at the disparate accounts of pre-abolition numbers, scholars examining slavery and abolition in the IOW simply do not have the cache of data that historians of the Atlantic enjoy.

Allen's most recent article about slavery to one of the Company's earliest factories at Bencoolen on the island of Sumatra posits that "the company acquired at least 10,000 and perhaps as many as 15,000 to 20,000 African, Indian, Malagasy, and Southeast Asian slaves between the 1620s and the late eighteenth century."[14] Company slaves, he asserts, came from "a global catchment area," containing "'Coffrees' from eastern Africa and Madagascar, 'Malabars' from Southern India, and 'Malays' from Southeast Asia, as well as men, women, and children identified specifically as coming from Angola, Bali, Bengal, Java,

---

[13] Richard Allen, *European Slave Trading in the Indian Ocean, 1500–1850* (Athens, OH: Ohio University Press, 2014), p. 7.
[14] Richard Allen, "Slavery in a Remote but Global Place: The British East India Company and Bencoolen, 1685–1825," *Social and Education History* 7, no. 2 (2018): p. 153.

Madagascar, Mozambique, Nias, and Siam."¹⁵ Guided by preconceived notions of African and Asian behavior, he explains that EIC officials showed a preference for the Malagasy of Madagascar, believing them to be "more intelligent and harder working than their Asian counterparts."¹⁶ Unfortunately, his thorough history does not include the indigenous and Chinese slave trades we know also thrived during this period. Nonetheless, there is ample evidence demonstrating that there was a robust slave trade in which the British participated before antislavery measures, and there were illegal markets importing and exporting slaves throughout the IOW in ports from Mauritius to the Straits even after the Felony Act in 1811.¹⁷

However, this story is not about the numbers of slaves flowing through the Straits, nor is it about where they came from. Instead, this micro history uses Britain's published Parliamentary Papers, EIC correspondence, public discourse, and publications from past administrators and local officials to expose the policies, attitudes, and behaviors that shaped the Company's response and inhibited the implementation of antislavery laws in a small colonial space—far from the metropole's gaze, during a time of heightened abolitionist tensions. The myopic and arguably structured discourse within this collection of documents makes them admittedly problematic. Indeed, drawing from this same archive in her examination of abolitionism in India, Andrea Major describes the Parliamentary Papers as "a record of a 'triangulated conversation' between EIC officials, the Presidency and Supreme Governments and the home authorities, around issues of colonial governance, slavery, and abolition."¹⁸ Like Major, this book's use of these papers is not for any "empirical reality," but "for the insight they offer" into the ways Company officials in the East Indies "interpreted slavery there and their own relationship to it, as rulers, administrators and, occasionally, reformers."¹⁹ The records used within the first parts of this book are meant to highlight the perceptions, attitudes, and accepted behaviors that facilitated a slave trade after abolition.

Letters of complaint, legal filings challenging colonial legal authority, and failing to register all of their slaves provide a clear picture of the impertinence that the wealthy slave-owning elite felt and are examples of small ways they resisted Dutch and British antislavery ordinances. Moreover, while these documents certainly reveal the value that the local non-European elite placed on their slaves,

---

¹⁵ Allen, "Slavery in a Remote but Global Place," p. 156.
¹⁶ Ibid.
¹⁷ Allen, "Slavery in a Remote but Global Place," p. 153; Allen, *European Slave Trading in the Indian Ocean*, pp. 143–55.
¹⁸ Major, *Slavery, Abolitionism and Empire in India*, p. 11.
¹⁹ Ibid.

and in some ways how they perceived British power in the region, their insistence upon legal and political guarantees for the return of runaways is also telling. If circumstances for slaves in the Straits were so "mild," if domestic servitude—for either men or women—was so bucolic and banal as many insinuated, then why were slave owners so adamant for laws that required EIC officials to return any who absconded? If it were such an easy and pampered existence, why would anyone leave?

Like any other subaltern population, to find the stories of slaves in the Straits required "reading against the grain," and this study looked for the experiences and voices of the enslaved in brief statements made by runaways found in police records and witness testimony copied into the transcripts of criminal cases. Although direct quotes are rare, the stories of physical and sexual violence, isolation, emotional abuse, and forced prostitution that do emerge are powerful reminders of the dehumanizing nature of slavery as an institution—in the Indian and Atlantic Oceans. Chapters 7 and 8 in particular, even if it is nearly two hundred years late, bear witness to the enslavement, rape, and exploitation of women whose experiences were reconstructed and minimized by a simple, yet deliberate choice of words. Together, correspondence between colonizers and fragments of statements from the enslaved reveal how slippery definitions, cultural bias, and a "want for laboring people" facilitated the persistence of a trade in slaves, regardless of what officials chose to call them, in one of the most geopolitically relevant waterways in Asia.[20]

Far more impactful than their initial settlements at Priaman and Bencoolen—even with their vast pepper resources—the factories in Straits Settlements were critically disruptive to indigenous economic and power structures. As we know from Craig Lockard's analysis *Southeast Asia in World History* (2009) those states able to gain control of the Straits of Malacca often held the most power in the region. While the Portuguese and Dutch Empires had each occupied Malacca, the British were the first European power to take the Straits. This book is interested in what happened when the British EIC attempted to develop and enforce antislavery legislation in a place where slaves were the equivalent of money, the majority of slaveholders were not European, and the Company's bottom line guided British imperial policy.

There are many definitions for the term "slave" within current academic discourse. Chattel slavery is the basest form of enslavement and what most people think of when they hear the word. As Joel Quirk explains, the term "slavery,"

---

[20] Richard Allen, "Satisfying the 'Want for Labouring People': European Slave Trading in the Indian Ocean, 1500–1850," *Journal of World History* 21, no. 1 (March 2010): p. 45.

both in contemporary and modern scholarship, inherited a specific historical projection in which contemporaries and modern scholars use Atlantic slavery as "an unofficial yardstick" to evaluate various forms of human bondage.[21] A chattel slave, which David Turley believes is the more complete term, is a person viewed as "inanimate property."[22] The physical and mental endurance of the individual is the only limit to the masters' expectations of their chattel slaves. However, we know from scholars like Anthony Reid that broader terms are necessary when discussing slaves in Southeast Asia.[23] The relatively sparse and interspersed polities made the power over people and labor more important than jurisdiction over land in Southeast Asia.[24] Debt was a primary form of bondage, and most indigenous societies did not differentiate between debt bondsmen and captured slaves. Since this study focuses on the slave trade in insular Southeast Asia, Reid's definition of a slave, as someone obligated to "labor for a patron without direct recompense," is most suitable.[25] It reminds us that by the middle of the nineteenth-century poverty and desperation had supplanted capture and transportation as a method of exploiting vulnerable populations for labor.

Until the last half of the twentieth century, the bulk of scholarship about slavery and abolition generally ignored systems in the east.[26] However, over the past two decades several studies have expanded beyond the Atlantic and offered more inclusive descriptions of the size, scope, and primary characteristics of the Indian Ocean slave trade and connecting networks, including those in Southeast Asia.[27] As several works have demonstrated, slavery and personal indenture were endemic in Asian societies; Europeans categorized and assigned western moral associations and values on this eastern system that forever transformed

---

[21] Joel Quirk, *The Anti-Slavery Project: From the Slave Trade to Human Trafficking* (Philadelphia: University of Pennsylvania Press, 2011), p. 5.
[22] David Turley, *Slavery* (Oxford: Blackwell Publishing, 2000), p. 6.
[23] Reid, "The Decline of Slavery in Nineteenth Century Indonesia," p. 65.
[24] Ibid., p. 67.
[25] Ibid., p. 65.
[26] Gwyn Campbell, Suzanne Miers, and Joseph Calder Miller, eds., *Women and Slavery: The Modern Atlantic* (Columbus: Ohio University Press, 2007); David Brion Davis, *The Problem of Slavery in the Age of Revolution, 1770-1823* (Oxford: Oxford University Press, 1999); David Brion Davis, *Inhuman Bondage: The Rise and Fall of Slavery in the New World* (Oxford: Oxford University Press, 2006); Seymour Drescher, *Abolition: A History of Slavery and Antislavery* (Cambridge and New York: Cambridge University Press, 2009); Stanley L. Engerman, Seymour Drescher, and Robert L. Paquette, *Slavery* (Oxford: Oxford University Press, 2001).
[27] Gwyn Campbell, ed., *The Structure of Slavery in Indian Ocean Africa and Asia* (Portland: Frank Cass, 2004), pp. 83-129; Reid, *Charting the Shape of Early Modern Southeast Asia*, pp. 181-212; Alain Testart, "The Extent and Significance of Debt Slavery," *Revue Française de Sociologie* Annual English Selection 43, no. 1 (2002): pp. 173-204; Markus Vink, "'The World's Oldest Trade': Dutch Slavery and Slave Trade in the Indian Ocean in the Seventeenth Century," *Journal of World History* 14, no. 2 (June 2003): pp. 131-77; B. D. Hopkins, "Race, Sex and Slavery: 'Forced Labour' in Central Asia and Afghanistan in the Early 19th Century," *Modern Asian Studies* 42, no. 4 (July 2008): pp. 629-71.

indigenous labor in the region.[28] In precolonial Southeast Asia, social structures depended on systems of what Reid describes as "vertical bonding," and personal indebtedness was endemic to society.[29] Here, slavery and servitude operated as part of an intricate web of social debt and obligation and often functioned as way to care for the poor and destitute.[30]

Debt was a primary reason for enslavement in the IOW, which further blurred the boundaries between slavery and other forms of servitude.[31] This was incredibly problematic and, at times, made some slaves seem less destitute. Consequently, in the eyes of many in the EIC courts during this period, debtors were not truly slaves because they at least had the option—however unlikely—of purchasing their freedom.[32] Most urban, commercial centers during the sixteenth and seventeenth centuries, such as Malacca, Aceh, Banten, Patani, and Makassar, were populated with former slaves brought by the wealthy men who immigrated to the region or as merchandise on a commercial expedition.[33] Slavery was embedded within Southeast Asian culture and society, was a primary source of labor, and played an essential role in local and regional economies. Indeed, both Reid and James Warren argue that the lives of indigenous populations were disrupted by European abolition.[34] Warren's unique and intricate analysis of slave markets, escape routes, and the strategies of pirates and slave traders within the Sulu archipelago provides a road map of the various ways indigenous traders circumvented colonial authority.[35] The breadth and depth of his study is still unmatched and, frankly, is the most profound illustration that in Southeast Asia imperial regimes had an easier time conceiving laws than they did enforcing them.

One of the most distinguishing features of slavery in the IOW was the large numbers of women and girls within the Southeast Asian networks during the late eighteenth and early nineteenth centuries.[36] This was particularly true in the Straits. Since many of those circulating within the region were from the

---

[28] Anthony Reid and Jennifer Brewster, eds., *Slavery, Bondage, and Dependency in Southeast Asia* (New York: St. Martins, 1983), pp. 25–30.
[29] Reid, "The Decline of Slavery in Nineteenth Century Indonesia," p. 65.
[30] Bruno Lasker, *Human Bondage in Southeast Asia* (Chapel Hill: University of North Carolina Press, 1950), p. 30; Vink, "The World's Oldest Trade," pp. 136–8.
[31] Reid and Brewster, *Slavery, Bondage, and Dependency in Southeast Asia*, p. 10.
[32] Hobhouse, *Returns*, pp. 189–90.
[33] Ibid., p. 69.
[34] Reid, "The Decline of Slavery in Nineteenth Century Indonesia," p. 71; Warren, *The Sulu Zone*, pp. xv–xxi.
[35] Hobhouse, *Returns*, pp. 25–30; Warren, *The Sulu Zone*, pp. 198–9.
[36] Reid, *Charting the Shape of Early Modern Southeast Asia*, pp. 181–212; Reid, "The Decline of Slavery in Nineteenth-Century Indonesia," pp. 64–80; Andaya, *Other Pasts*, pp. 174–94, p. 1; Warren, *The Sulu Zone*, pp. 215–51; Tagliacozzo, "Ambiguous Commodities, Unstable Frontiers," pp. 354–77.

Indonesian archipelago, specifically Bali, Rhio, Nias, and the eastern coasts of Sumatra, the dominance of women and girls in the slave trade could be an interesting example of the increased autonomy and mobility of Southeast Asian women so frequently discussed by scholars of the region.[37] It is possible that some women came of their own volition and sold themselves to a slave trader or ship's captain to look for more lucrative opportunities in the region. However, as of yet, I have encountered no evidence of this and, as we will see, none of them seemed as though they had that amount of control in their situation.

As previously mentioned, some scholars have asserted that these women and girls were primarily intended to supply a "marriage market," as seen elsewhere in the latter half of the nineteenth century, however others find such a benign purpose highly unlikely.[38] It is certainly true that the flood of "free" male labor, convicts, and sailors that arrived in the Straits Settlements during this period created a strong demand for women to care for and support them. However, cultural prohibitions against interracial intimacies and their lack of financial security make it doubtful that large numbers of men moved abroad in search of brides.[39] Moreover, the notion that large populations of women were so eager to abandon everything they knew and barter their freedom in order to marry the nearest available man is incredibly sexist and based on the predilection that the value of women is measured by their relationship with men. By these standards, wealthy women were meant for marriage, the poor and beautiful became concubines, and the rest were expected to serve the lot. A valuable commodity, slave traders and their intermediaries brought women into this region to sell as wives, concubines, domestic servants, or prostitutes, which is what the bulk of limited slave testimonies indicate. Most (if not all) were expected to labor, like any other slave, in a multitude of ways; women and girls were not, as many believed, limited

---

[37] Reid, *Charting the Shape of Early Modern Southeast Asia*, p. 189; Campbell, *The Structure of Slavery in Indian Ocean Africa and Asia*, pp. x–xiii; Craig Lockard, *Southeast Asia in World History* (Oxford: Oxford University Press, 2009), pp. 32, 71.

[38] Carl A. Trocki, "Opium as a Commodity in the Chinese Nanyang Trade," in *Chinese Circulations: Capital, Commodities, and Networks in Southeast Asia*, eds. Eric Taggliacozzo and Wen-Chin Chang (Durham: Duke University Press, 2011), pp. 88–94; Philippa Levine, *Prostitution, Race, and Politics: Policing Venereal Disease in the British Empire* (New York: Routledge, 2003), p. 25; James Francis Warren, *Pirates, Prostitutes and Pullers: Explorations in the Ethno- and Social History of Southeast Asia* (Crawley: UWA Press, 2008), pp. 148–50.

[39] Reid, *Charting the Shape of Early Modern Southeast Asia*, pp. 212–15; Warren, *The Sulu Zone*, p. 198. For convict labor see Anand Yang, "Indian Convict Workers in Southeast Asia in the Late Eighteenth and Early Nineteenth Centuries," *Journal of World History* 14, no. 2 (June, 2003): pp. 179–208; Clare Anderson, *Subaltern Lives: Biographies of Colonialism in the Indian Ocean World, 1790–1920* (Cambridge: Cambridge University Press, 2012); Con Costello, *Botany Bay: The Story of the Convicts Transported from Ireland to Australia, 1791–1853* (Cork: Mercier Press, 1987).

to household or *domestic* chores. Unlike their male counterparts, satisfying the sexual and domestic needs of their masters, as Kathleen Wilson describes, was "part and parcel for an enslaved woman."[40] At the same time, in many cases racial prejudice and orientalist perceptions about Asian sexuality gave EIC officers an excuse to overlook what they knew to be trafficking in slaves; simply calling a woman "wife" or "concubine" could erase her status as a slave.[41] As Reid explains, the British "turned a blind eye to the importation of the predominantly female slaves," since it was "an immense advantage" to the development and stability of the settlements.[42]

In addition to using the Atlantic system as a standard, both contemporary activists and current scholarship about slavery have focused on the concept of "ownership" as a key requirement for defining a slave's status.[43] Accordingly, if a person was a debtor, officials generally believed they had entered into their contract willingly. By this standard, "slave-debtors" were not, in the strictest sense of the word, "owned" because they, technically, had an expedient way to freedom (repaying their debt). However, most officials quickly recognized that these debtors were fast becoming a "new" group of slaves in a system of perpetual debt-bondage from which most were unable to escape. Raffles made early attempts to regulate the practice in 1823, but Singapore officially prohibited the importation and employment of persons under "the denomination of 'Slave Debtor,'" within the colony of Singapore on March 9, 1830.[44] Early attempts at regulation, and the proclamation's clear assertion that this arrangement was "in reality [...] a cover to actual slave dealing," are evidence that colonial officials understood the system's rampant abuse. Yet, as the following study reveals, throughout this period officials regularly used the term "debtor" to differentiate populations of exploited labor from what they believed were *true* slaves, which were entirely illegal. By 1842,

---

[40] Kathleen Wilson, "Gender, Empire, and Modernity," in *Gender and Empire*, ed. Philippa Levine (Oxford: Oxford University Press, 2004), p. 30.
[41] Ann Laura Stoler, *Carnal Knowledge and Imperial Power: Race and the Intimate in Colonial Rule* (Berkeley: University of California Press, 2002); Jean Gelman-Taylor, *The Social World of Batavia: Europeans and Eurasians in Colonial Indonesia* (Madison: University of Wisconsin Press, 2004); Tamara Loos, "A History of Sex and the State in Southeast Asia: Class, Intimacy and Invisibility," *Citizenship Studies* 12, no. 1 (February 2008): pp. 27–43; Anne McClintock, *Imperial Leather: Race, Gender, and Sexuality in the Colonial Contest* (New York: Routledge, 1995); and Tony Ballantyne and Antoinette Burton, eds., *Bodies in Contact: Rethinking Colonial Encounters in World History* (Durham: Duke University Press, 2005).
[42] Reid, "The Decline of Slavery in Nineteenth Century Indonesia," p. 72; John Anderson, *Mission to the East Coast of Sumatra: In M.DCCC.XXIII, under the Direction of the Government of Prince of Wales Island: Including Historical and Descriptive Sketches of the Country, an Account of the Commerce, Population, and Customs of the Inhabitants, and a Visit to the Batta Cannibal States in the Interior* (London: W. Blackwood, 1826), p. 26.
[43] Quirk, *The Anti-Slavery Project*, pp. 10–12.
[44] "Slavery in the Eastern Settlements," IOR/F4/1960/85815, p. 52.

most Company officials vehemently claimed slavery, in all its forms, had been eliminated in their provinces.[45] This research does not differentiate between whether or not the (primarily) women and children in these reports were captured slaves, sold by their families, or debtors; they were all part of an international system providing cheap labor, controlled by the wealthy and powerful of societies, who were bought, sold, or unfairly contracted, and distributed through imperial trading centers around the world to work for little or no direct compensation.

In addition to placing nineteenth-century abolitionism within the context of world history, Joel Quirk's *The Anti-Slavery Project* offers an important theoretical framework within which these characters perform. He contends that while legal abolition occurred in 1833, various forms of slavery persisted. Therefore, rather than abolitionism, the British simply began an "anti-slavery project" or "the ongoing task, or undertaking, which has gone through a number of phases."[46] As explained above, Quirk also argues that the term has gone "through a distinctive form of historical projection, which has seen an inherited image of transatlantic slavery invoked as an unofficial yardstick against which various forms of bondage has been evaluated."[47] A common phase of the Anti-Slavery Project is the period of "delay, deflection, and dilution," in which officials were able to delay the effects of abolition, "maximize gain and minimize loss."[48] As we will see, in the first thirty-five years after Britain's government prohibited the trade in 1807, debt-slavery became a convenient compromise to total abolition and gave all interested parties time to redefine and cultivate a supply of "new" laborers that now included debtors, convicts, and enlisted men. Still, while both the Dutch and the British organized systems to differentiate between slave and slave-debtor, most Southeast Asian societies did not, and by the 1820s, slave traders had figured out which term they needed to use within British territories. The only difference seemed to be that slave owners had essentially become loan sharks who charged exorbitantly high interest rates and made personal freedom practically unattainable.

Britain's endeavor to abolish slavery was not one singular task, mounted by a group of morally outraged social reformers in the 1770s and completed with

---

[45] IOR/F4/1960/85815, pp. 34–54.
[46] Quirk, The Anti-Slavery Project, p. 5.
[47] Ibid.
[48] Ibid., p. 12.
[49] Christopher Brown and the Omohundro Institute of Early American History & Culture, *Moral Capital: Foundations of British Abolitionism* (Chapel Hill: University of North Carolina Press, 2006); Robin Blackburn, *Overthrow of Colonial Slavery, 1776–1848* (London: Verso, 1988); Thomas Bender, *The Antislavery Debate: Capitalism and Abolitionism as a Problem in Historical Interpretation* (Berkeley: University of California Press, 1992); Drescher, *Abolition*.

criminalization in 1843.[49] Rather, the Anti-Slavery Project is the ongoing efforts of abolitionists around the world, over the past century and a half, working to eliminate slavery in modern society. This book examines the first phase of this process in the British Straits Settlements to better understand how Britain and the EIC went about implementing antislavery legislation in the east. It unpacks the particular challenges officials faced in Asia's vibrant and cosmopolitan societies, filled with and dependent upon slaves, and perhaps more importantly, at a time when Europeans were not at the top of the food chain.[50] It adds evidence to Andrea Major's assertions in *Slavery, Abolitionism and Empire in India*, that in the beginning EIC officials were not interested in inhibiting the sale or transfer of slaves altogether.[51] Like in India, Company officials in the Straits were more concerned with maintaining stable trade relationships; they concentrated on ending European slave trading and protected slaves from excessive violence or from being unwillingly transported across territorial boundaries.[52] Otherwise, until Parliament's Emancipation Act in 1834, local authorities generally honored existing slaves status, enforced indigenous slave laws, and tolerated local markets.[53]

Not only does this project expand the academic discourse by offering the example of Britain's antislavery efforts in the British East Indies, but this work also forces us to consider the racist and gendered foundations upon which antislavery policies were built. While recognizing the importance of the trans-Atlantic trade within an overall global system, there has been an abundance of research about western slavery in the Caribbean. We have suffered from what Edward Alpers has coined "the tyranny of the Atlantic" or the myopic preoccupation with the analysis of Europe's transportation and systematic dehumanization and exploitation of millions of slaves to the Americas.[54] Yet, in the past twenty-five years more scholars have begun to look east.[55] Still, even the bulk of this research has been focused on the northwestern littorals of the Indian Ocean and, other than Indonesia, has generally neglected anything farther east

---

[50] Quirk, *The Anti-Slavery Project*, p. 5.
[51] Major, *Slavery, Abolitionism and Empire in India*, p. 164.
[52] Ibid.
[53] Richard Allen, "Suppressing a Nefarious Traffic: Britain and the Abolition of Slave Trading in India and the Western Indian Ocean, 1770–1830," *The William and Mary Quarterly* 66, no. 4 (2009): pp. 873–94, 888.
[54] Edward A. Alpers, "The African Diaspora in the Northwestern Indian Ocean: Reconsideration of an Old Problem, New Directions for Research," *Comparative Studies of South Asia, Africa, and the Middle East* 17, no. 2 (1997): pp. 62–81; Allen, *European Slave Trading in the Indian Ocean*, p. 4.
[55] Some important works, which focus on the trans-Atlantic system are Campbell, Miers, and Miller, *Women and Slavery*; Davis, *The Problem of Slavery in the Age of Revolution, 1770–1823*; Davis, *Inhuman Bondage*; Drescher, *Abolition*; Seymour Drescher, *Econocide: British Slavery in the Era of Abolition* (Pittsburgh: University of Pittsburgh Press, 1977); Engerman, Drescher, Paquette, *Slavery*.

than India.[56] After providing a picture of Indian Ocean slavery as a whole, the remaining chapters move to Southeast Asia to examine the impact of British abolitionism in the Straits of Malacca. As one of the most geopolitically diverse and strategic regions in the world, stopping the flow of any trade commodity, particularly one as culturally entrenched and profitable as slaves in this region, proved to be an herculean task that the British colonial government was only half-heartedly committed to undertaking.

## A Strategy for the Straits

A highly desirable waterway at the far east of the Indian Ocean World, the Straits of Malacca have served as a central node between the Indian and Pacific Ocean trading networks since at least the tenth century.[57] A significant slave trade flowed throughout, and between, the two intra-regional systems of the Indian and Pacific Oceans, and by the end of the eighteenth and beginning half of the nineteenth century, Britain's Anti-Slavery Project became a significant part of their expansion into and colonization of their Asian territories. By this point, Europeans had categorized and assigned moral associations and values to the institution of slavery, which forever transformed indigenous systems of labor and vertical bonding. Both legitimate and illegitimate networks operated on the Malayan Peninsula and in the Sulu archipelago and the lives of indigenous maritime populations were significantly disrupted by Britain's attempt to abolish slavery as a lawful system to control people and acquire labor.[58] Nonetheless, pirates and slave traders within the archipelago maintained flourishing slave markets and escape routes to circumvent colonial authority when necessary.

The EIC's acquisition of Singapore in 1819 immediately put the British in competition with these indigenous maritime societies, many of which colonial authorities subsequently labeled pirates. These groups easily negotiated the region's complex topography and were already in controlled of the bulk of illegitimate commerce.[59] Britain's cessation of the legal trade in slaves afforded

---

[56] Several recent works (written within the past twenty-five years) describe the size and scope of the western portions of the Indian Ocean slave trade: Campbell, *Structure of Slavery in Indian Ocean Africa and Asia*, pp. vii–xxvi; Allen, "Satisfying the 'Want for Labouring People,'" pp. 45–73; William Gervase Clarence-Smith, *The Economics of the Indian Ocean Slave Trade in the Nineteenth Century* (London: Frank Cass, 1989), pp. 1–60; Patrick Manning, *Slavery and African Life: Occidental, Oriental, and African Slave Trades* (Cambridge: Cambridge University Press, 1990), pp. 60–100; Deryck Scarr, *Slaving and Slavery in the Indian Ocean* (London: Macmillan Press, 1998), pp. 14–53.
[57] Andaya and Andaya, *A History of Malaysia*, pp. 7–10.
[58] Warren, *The Sulu Zone*, p. xix.
[59] Ibid., pp. 66–74.

Southeast Asian networks new opportunities to prosper from the reduction of foreign competition. This period of indigenous conflict ultimately left many societies exposed to European advancement but also made the enforcement of antislavery legislation nearly impossible; the persistence of underground trade persistently dogged the colonial state in this region.[60] A variety of waterways and escape routes provided ample opportunity for smugglers to avoid detection and import illicit commodities into British ports. Authorities were simply not able to control all avenues of trade and woefully ill-equipped to have much effect on ceasing the flow of something so profitable as young women and girls. The implementation of antislavery legislation inspired a number of societies and cartels to circumvent imperial policy and supply colonies with whatever type of labor in demand: coolies, wives, concubines, servants, and/or prostitutes.[61]

It is important to understand that the first phase of antislavery policies was enacted during wha C. A. Bayly's "imperial meridian," between 1780 and 1830, when Europeans used colonial expansion to extend their national rivalries into Africa and Asia in ways that mimicked centuries of religious and ideological conflict.[62] Furthermore, these new types of domination "were characterized by a form of aristocratic military government" and "emphasized hierarchy and racial subordination, and the patronage of indigenous landed elites."[63] Eighteenth-century Enlightenment Liberalism also initiated a transition in British imperial objectives. When the Company received its first charter in 1600 and arrived in Bantam, their objective was to establish trading centers and control markets, intervening with native politics or culture only when necessary. By the end of the eighteenth century, others, like Raffles, came to believe that empire should take a new, more aggressive form, move out of the trading centers, conquer the countryside, and civilize the native populations.

This shift was epitomized in the conflicting approaches to leadership and governance between the aforementioned expansionist Stamford Raffles (1781–1826) and the colonial minimalist, John Crawfurd (1783–1868). According to his biographer, Gareth Knapman, in addition to the examination of race in human history, Crawfurd devoted his life to "the promotion of democracy, universal suffrage, free trade and limiting European colonialism, as solutions to

---

[60] Eric Tagliacozzo, *Secret Trades, Porous Borders: Smuggling and States along a Southeast Asian Frontier, 1865–1915* (New Haven: Yale University Press, 2005), pp. 2–15.
[61] Ibid., pp. 27–100, 185–230.
[62] C. A. Bayly, *Imperial Meridian: The British Empire and the World, 1780–1830* (London: Longman Group, 1989), p. 8.
[63] Ibid., p. 9.
[64] Gareth Knapman, *Race and British Colonialism in Southeast Asia, 1770–1870: John Crawfurd and the Politics of Equality* (New York: Routledge, 2017), p. 1.

the problems he defined in 1820."[64] A Scotsman from the Highlands, Crawfurd was born in 1783 and, after attending medical school in Edinburgh, started with the EIC in 1803 as a physician serving in northwest India. He was promoted quickly, then, the Company appointed him resident to Penang in 1808 where he "threw himself into acquiring 'knowledge of the language and manners of the native tribes.'"[65] In true academic fashion, Crawfurd sought to thoroughly understand the people with whom he was about to do business.

Raffles, on the other hand, was a part of, and perhaps even the figurehead for, an emerging group of Company officials who favored a more aggressive style of expansionism that included a comprehensive civilizing mission. As Knapman explains, "Raffles and his followers advocated maximum engagement and occupation of territory in Asia," while Crawfurd encouraged the Company to follow a policy of "controlled minimalist colonialism."[66] Raffles's biographer, Tim Hannigan, tells us that he was born in 1781 on the slave ship *Ann* and grew up in a lower-middle-class family. His father worked for a "firm of Glasgow slave brokers," Hibberts & Co.[67] Unlike Crawfurd, Raffles was not an academically educated man and, with the help of his uncle Mr. Hammond, began his tenure with the Company as a temporary clerk in the secretary's office at the age of fourteen.[68] Apparently, Raffles's lack of formal education perpetually vexed him, and one of his biographers, C. E. Wurtzburg, claimed that "as late as 1824 he described himself as being 'as ignorant as a Hottentot.'"[69]

Nonetheless, after a decade of menial transcription in London, Raffles acquired a promotion and arrived in Penang in 1805 as a young, upwardly mobile clerk looking for the opportunity for personal and professional advancement. Hannigan explains that a significant amount of intrigue and gossip surrounded his "remarkable and exotic promotion" that increased his salary "by a factor of *two thousand per cent*."[70] Raffles's supporters asserted that his quick wit and "pen-pushing" abilities brought him to the notice of his superiors. On the other hand, those more critical of his epic acclaim posit that his marriage to the thirty-four-year-old Mariamne Fancourt (née Devenish) was the impetus for his lofty new position—although Raffles himself vehemently denied this. Nonetheless, he was clever enough that by 1811, he had managed to convince Lord Minto to appoint him Lieutenant-Governor of Java, which, Hannigan explains, put

---

[65] Ibid., p. 22.
[66] Ibid., p. 35.
[67] Tim Hannigan, *Raffles and the British Invasion of Java* (Singapore: Monsoon Books, 2012), pp. 40–1.
[68] C. E. Wurtzburg, *Raffles of the Eastern Isles* (London: Hodder and Stoughton, 1956), p. 18.
[69] Ibid., p. 17.
[70] Hannigan, *Raffles and the British Invasion of Java*, p. 40.

him "in absolute charge of an island the size of England with a population of some 5 million people."[71] Wurtzburg asserts that "the very fact that time and opportunity might be short encouraged embezzlement on a large scale."[72] Far away from the prying eyes of the Company's Board of Control, Raffles was made "oriental despot of the Land of Promise" at the age of thirty.[73]

However, it was Crawfurd's detailed knowledge of local custom and history, combined with an understanding of the culture and cultivated relationships with indigenous leaders, that facilitated Raffles's successes in Java from 1811–1816 and gave him the idea for Singapore.[74] However, it was in their experiences together in Java, and their subsequent interactions that we see their ideas most at odds. When Raffles wanted to assert Company authority in a dispute over the appointment of indigenous leaders, Crawfurd advised an avenue more accustomed to local traditions; Raffles wanted to assert Indian land tax policy on Javanese elites; Crawfurd suggested they follow a method guided by Javanese custom.[75] Although Raffles generally acquiesced to Crawfurd's more studied perspective, the two clearly represented a changing of the guard. Although ultimately resolved, Raffles returned to England amid controversy and scandal and died on July 5, 1826, a day before his forty-fifth birthday.[76] This left Crawfurd, not Raffles, to lobby against aggressive expansion and advise the EIC board of directors on how best to proceed in Asia. In fact, Knapman argues that "it was Crawfurd's lone advocacy of limited colonialism that influenced policy makers in the first half of the nineteenth century."[77] Crawfurd's respect of indigenous customs and rigid adherence to the Company's policy of non-intervention set the tone for the administration of colonial policy in the Straits.

Regardless of what he felt about the institution of slavery (although his biographer asserts he was a life-long opponent of the institution), Crawfurd believed that they should interfere in native affairs as little as possible and antislavery reform put the EIC at odds with indigenous economic, political, and social norms. It was under his direction that the Company advised its officials in the East Indies to proceed in the most unobtrusive way possible. Yet, by the 1830s (three years before Britain's Abolition Act), Crawfurd's influence had waned. Despite his success in the 1840s at holding James Brooke at bay in Sarawak,

---

[71] Ibid., p. 130.
[72] Wurtzburg, *Raffles of the Eastern Isles*, p. 186.
[73] Hannigan, *Raffles and the British Invasion of Java*, p. 130.
[74] Ibid., pp. 35–49.
[75] Ibid., pp. 204–5, 43.
[76] Wurtzburg, *Raffles of the Eastern Isles*, p. 186.
[77] Knapman, *Race and British Colonialism in Southeast Asia*, p. 35.

Emrys Chew's research on Malay resistance to British colonialism demonstrated that the Naning War (1831–2) was a clear illustration of the Rafflesque type of aggressive expansionism that Crawfurd spent his career fighting.[78] The old official died in 1868, and by the 1880s the British had taken control of the Malay Peninsula and had their eyes on the surrounding islands.[79] Nonetheless, the non-interventionists were at the helm during the first phase of Britain's Anti-Slavery Project and that was not a battle they were interested in fighting. Most would have had no issue preventing Europeans from slaving in Asian waters, but few were willing to include the Chinese or Malay slave trades within their jurisdictions. Although the first few years of the project in the Straits created an incredible inconvenience for European slavers, the Malay, Sulu, and Chinese trades continued relatively unimpeded. This is particularly noteworthy, since we also know from Allen's study that by the mid-eighteenth century, the EIC's Court of Directors began to consider indentured Chinese as a potential source of agriculture and plantation labor for their settlements as far away as Trinidad.[80]

In 1811, Parliament passed the Felony Slave Trade Act and the Company's government passed Regulation X, making slave trading a felony within British territory. However, as Major explains, although each presidency had a version of this regulation by 1813, none of these measures "could have been entirely successful," because they enacted "re-enforcing" legislation in 1826 and 1827.[81] Nonetheless, in order to monitor the number of slaves in their settlements, officials in the Straits went about the task of developing systems to identify and classify the slaves that were there. This initiated a liminal phase in which slaves, debtors, and free laborers legally coexisted within British territories and they were nearly impossible to differentiate. Traffickers benefited from uncertainty and exploited the loose definitions and limited authority of early EIC antislavery policies. Moreover, the Company's vague directives and legal disagreements between colonial officials meant that the enforcement of policy depended upon the zeal or apathy of individual officers. This led to haphazard enforcement of unclear legislation. The cases discussed here illustrate that regardless of professed disdain and contempt for the institution of slavery, the actual implementation of antislavery measures placed the Company officials at odds with existing policy and local elites, threatened to strain economic and political relationships, and required delicate negotiations in which the interests of slaves were generally not the first priority.

---

[78] Emrys Chew, "The Naning War, 1831–1832: Colonial Authority and Malay Resistance in the Early Period of British Expansion," *Modern Asian Studies* 32, no. 2 (1998): p. 352.
[79] Knapman, *Race and British Colonialism in Southeast Asia*, pp. 233–4.
[80] Allen, *European Slave Trading in the Indian Ocean*, p. 201.
[81] Major, *Slavery, Abolition, and Empire in India*, p. 175.

## The Gender of Abolition

There is a common presumption that the Emancipation Act legally and effectively abolished slavery in the British Empire. However, we must be cautious about how we interpret this accomplishment. While The British did indeed abolish traditional forms of the "enduring social order" of slavery, if there is evidence that its more heinous characteristics, such as kidnapping and the prostitution of women and girls have persisted, as Quirk suggests, "under different designations or through illicit activities," then it is not correct to assume that the institution was fully eradicated.[82] This examination of the first phase of Britain's Anti-Slavery Project in the Straits Settlements exposes the foundations of modern human trafficking in Southeast Asia. It was British antislavery ordinances that generated a transition from slave to "free" labor in the region and reduced the demand for male slaves. The Straits were quickly teaming with migrant labor—indentured and free—looking for their piece of this new colonial enterprise. There were plenty of workingmen; but, cultural prohibitions on the immigration of Chinese, Muslim, and Hindu women meant there were few available women to keep them mollified.[83] Women's bodies became an incredibly valuable commodity that initiated an illicit trade in women and girls for the purpose of domestic and sexual labor, which not only persisted, but prospered and developed into what is now the third most profitable commodities in the modern black market economy.[84] Defining the non-European women and girls they saw as potential wives, or concubines, or servants relieved colonial officials of the responsibility to emancipate the slaves they encountered. Most women were considered the property of some man or another—their fathers or husbands—but as long as they were not identified as slaves, the law did not require officials to act.

British constructions of gender, patriarchal responsibility, and domestic order also had a significant impact on the policing of bodies and enforcement of antislavery ordinances in the EIC's eastern settlements. British historian Susan Kingsley Kent argues that for the British, "patriarchal rule-whether it

---

[82] Quirk, *The Anti-Slavery Project*, p. 7.
[83] Evans, *Slave Trade (East India) Slavery in Ceylon*, p. 239.
[84] Quirk, *The Anti-Slavery Project*, p. 7; Evans, *Slave Trade (East India) Slavery in Ceylon*, p. 68; Dr. Louise I. Shelley, Hearing before the Subcommittee on International Terrorism, Nonproliferation and Human Rights of the Committee on International Relations House of Representatives, *Trafficking in Persons Report* on June 25, 2003, 108th Cong., 1st session, Serial No. 108–53, p. 55, accessed May 20, 2013, http://democrats.foreignaffairs.house.gov/archives/108/87997.pdf; Sarah E. Mendelson, *Barracks and Brothels: Peacekeeping and Human Trafficking in the Balkans* (Washington, DC: The Center for Strategic & International Studies (CSIS) Press, 2005); Sally Stoecker and Louise Shelly, eds., *Human Trafficking and Transnational Crime: Eurasian and American Perspectives* (Lanham: Rowman & Littlefield Publishers, Inc., 2002), p. 14; Victor Malarek, *The Natashas: Inside the New Global Sex Trade* (New York: Arcade Publishing, 2003); Kathryn Farr, *Sex Trafficking: The Global Market in Women and Children* (New York: Worth Publishers, 2005).

be of master to man or man to woman—prevailed."[85] Women were, "in fact if not by law," men's property within British cultural and social ideology until the twentieth century. She explains that "patriarchy in state and society rested on the ancient presumption that the male head of household held property not simply in his land and his animals, but in his wife and his children as well." Echoing Kent, Kathleen Wilson asserts that patriarchy, "in the form of supreme authority of the white, predominantly property-holding male heads of household was the building block and organizing principle," and "the household was the main unit of social order and indigenous reclamation."[86] During the late eighteenth and early nineteenth centuries, British gender constructs placed men in control of the public sphere of commercial life, while moral purity could only be achieved in the domestic sphere of women. While British colonial officials likely saw the importation of non-European women and girls as a travesty, they were more concerned about the potential social chaos resulting from the overwhelmingly male populations arriving in their ports daily. Allowing the sale of slave-women and girls in the Straits was a convenient compromise of Britain's professed moral agenda in exchange for the promise of a female civilizing force who also provided a tremendous amount of unpaid labor.

Unfortunately, rather than emancipating and employing women as free and fully autonomous laborers, as they hoped to do for men, British antislavery efforts reinforced the existing patriarchal order with the Empire's men placed at the top of it and indigenous women and the bottom. Discussions about abolition insisted on the preservation of men's property rights and for almost half a century excluded the domestic realm all together. Wealthy patriarchs labeling the women in their *zinanas*, or harems, and households (many of whom they purchased from slavers) as wives, concubines, or domestic servants, shielded them from the jurisdiction of the law. Moreover, Muslim, Hindu, and Chinese religious and cultural practice prohibited women from freely immigrating, so only men were able to capitalize on the newly available wage labor. The result was that accumulating crowds of "free," migrant male laborers, far from their wives and families, created an insatiable and overwhelming demand for domestic and sexual services and not enough local women willing or available for the task. Consequently, it should not be surprising that the majority of those trafficked within this region were women and children.

As Carol Pateman has theorized, there is a "sexual contract" between men that functioned as an unofficial pact, which protected the rights of fathers and heads of households from the interference of the state. This implicit, sometimes explicit

---

[85] Susan Kingsley Kent, *Gender and Power in Britain, 1640–1990* (London: Routledge, 1999), p. 6.
[86] Wilson, "Gender, Empire, and Modernity," p. 25.

contract, is about women, but between men, and secures the transformation of man's "natural right over women into the security of civil and patriarchal right."[87] In this instance, antislavery legislation gave the colonial state the right as patriarch and, after the 1830s, it began to interfere more completely in the intimate lives of its native subjects. Nonetheless, Company officials considered the non-European women and girls circulating within eastern slave markets as the property of the men they were with—wives, concubines, or otherwise. Local authorities were willing to make pragmatic compromises because antislavery efforts in the Straits had, essentially, interrupted men's access to women's bodies. The brutal and horrific images of Africans, treated like beasts on plantations in the West Indies were repugnant to most EIC officials, but the trade in women and children for the purpose of domestic and sexual labor was what some officials considered an "important system of social welfare."[88]

There is significant scholarship demonstrating the ways colonial officials gendered and racialized bodies, which facilitated the subjugation of native populations and legitimized imperial conquest and expansion. Indeed, as Wilson explains, "the 'gender frontier' was the first line of offence of British imperial power."[89] Within the context of the African slave trade, Jennifer Morgan contends that the British needed a substantial amount of "intellectual work" to rationalize the enslavement of other human beings and argues that the British "laid out the discursive groundwork on which the 'theft of bodies' could be justified."[90] The same was true in the Straits; racialized discussions of women's sexuality and reproductive abilities naturalized their subjugation. Company officials arrived with a collection of predilections about civilization, race, class, gender, and sexuality that not only shaped their behavior in general, but also impeded the first phase of their Anti-Slavery Project.[91] Perhaps, if they had been less preoccupied with the financial obligations of these women, and more with the nature of their employment—regardless of sex—legislation might have been more effectively, and certainly equitably, enforced.

However just as Philippa Levine has demonstrated that Empire was an inherently gendered process, British Abolitionism was also, at its core, a gendered process that focused on the liberation and self-determination of men,

---

[87] Carol Pateman, *The Sexual Contract* (Stanford: Stanford University Press, 1988), p. 6.
[88] Hobhouse, *Returns*, pp. 191–203.
[89] Wilson, "Gender, Empire, and Modernity," p. 35.
[90] Jennifer Morgan, "Male Travelers, Female Bodies, and Gendering of Racial Ideology, 1500–1700," in *Bodies in Contact: Rethinking Colonial Encounters in World History*, eds. Tony Ballantyne and Antoinette Burton (Durham: Duke University Press, 2005), pp. 56–7, 65.
[91] Ibid., p. 64.

not women. The emancipation of women from patriarchal authority was not part of the debate and the assertion by some modern scholars that this trade was primarily a "marriage market" indicates that current conceptions of gender equality are not much farther along. Clearly, marriage into a well-positioned family was an avenue to emancipation for a very small number of slave women. However, it is highly unlikely that very many wealthy and powerful men had need to find wives in such markets. Moreover, term suggests that the public and indiscriminate sale of women (we assume to those willing and able to pay), for the purpose of marriage, was not as egregious as the enslavement of those meant for non-domestic labor. Either literally or figuratively, such claims overlook demographic realities and employ a fictitious, patriarchal, and bucolic image of western matrimony that required service and subservience from women that even early modern proto-feminists like Aphra Behn compared to slavery.[92] Whether or not these women were eventually married to the men who purchased them did not erase their experience of being sold and treated as slaves. We know that the arrival of Chinese, Muslim, and European colonialism in Southeast Asia after 1500 initiated what Barbara Watson-Andaya called an "attitudinal shift," which increasingly condemned women who exchanged sex for material gain.[93] She argues that before Europeans arrived on the scene, "it was widely accepted that a foreign trader could establish a sexual relationship with a local woman who would act as his wife and economic partner for as long as required."[94] These arrangements were purely economic and the labor and business connections they provided were more important than their individual status as princess or slave. Andaya explains that "by receiving valuable or unusual gifts from foreign traders, women and their families acquired prestige items that could be displayed or exchanged, significantly enhancing their status within the community." As a result, well-placed village women and the wives and daughters of elite households, looking to strengthen the trading power of their families, sought these "temporary marriages" with arriving traders.

In addition to facilitating and monitoring the accumulation of wealth, temporary wives also attended to the domestic comforts of their foreign spouses. This included cooking, washing, and mending laundry, as well as sexual

---

[92] Aphra Behn, "The False Count; or, A New Way to Play an Old Game," in *The Plays, Histories, and Novels of the Ingenious Mrs. Aphra Behn, Volume III* (London: J. Pearson, 1700), pp. 150–1.
[93] Barbara Watson-Andaya, "From Temporary Wife to Prostitute: Sexuality and Economic Change in Early Modern Southeast Asia," *Journal of Women's History* 9, no. 4 (1998): p. 12. Andaya expands her analysis of this subject in *The Flaming Womb: Repositioning Women in Early Modern Southeast Asia* (Honolulu: University of Hawai'i Press, 2006), pp. 104–33.
[94] Andaya, "From Temporary Wife to Prostitute," p. 28.

intimacy. The relationship was mutually dissolvable at any time; the men in such relationships were expected to abide by local norms, and as Andaya clarifies, the woman's family "acted as a safeguard to ensure her marital rights were honored and that she was not ill-treated."[95] However, in addition to growing restrictions on elite women's sexual autonomy and changing economic structures, Andaya contends that by the eighteenth century there were so many foreign traders in the region that merchants ceased relying on "princess-emissaries" and began instead to "marry" concubines and slaves connected to local households who had fewer protections. In an increasingly monetized economy, non-elite women unconcerned with "premarital chastity" commonly exchanged sex for money or goods as income for the family, and if "particularly pressed, daughters could be mortgaged as debt-slaves" and "domestic servants who were also available for sex." Eventually, European and Chinese traders preferred more transactional relationships without the obligation of a marriage contract and began paying local slave women for domestic and sexual services. Not only had the social capital and economic authority been taken from these temporary wives, as Andaya demonstrates, in this colonial patriarchy, they became a "disposable asset."[96] Yet, Southeast Asian trading economies and the expansion of global trade within the region depended on the labor of women—slave women in particular—and the profit and position gained from it.

According to Jean Gillman Taylor, since the beginnings of the Dutch presence in Batavia in the early seventeenth century, "there was the freest intercourse with slave women," and officials and servants of the Dutch East India Company (VOC) were known to choose wives from among local women and slaves imported as concubines.[97] Through marriage and personal cunning, some of these women were able to make their way into the colonial elite. However, the great majority of the slaves purchased by the Dutch worked as household servants who were totally under their masters' control. As Taylor notes, the harsh reality for most of these domestic slaves was that they faced abuse and "lurid tortures" within the privacy of the household.[98] In the Dutch fortress of Batavia, patterns of cohabitation and marriage were inherently linked to systems of slavery, bondage, and debt within this flourishing multicultural society; physical proximity and sexual availability were the primary factors determining the extent to which the city's Dutch émigré residents married

---

[95] Ibid., p. 15.
[96] Ibid., p. 23.
[97] Jean Gelman Taylor, *The Social World of Batavia: European and Eurasian in Dutch Asia* (Madison: University of Wisconsin Press, 1983), pp. 69–71, 15. On Dutch colonialism's effect on women's status, see also Stoler, *Carnal Knowledge and Imperial Power*.
[98] Ibid., p. 70.

local women.[99] Moreover, Hendrik Niemeijer observed that these sexual encounters "often reflected relationships of status and power in which women were subordinate."[100] A domestic slave, for example, had less control over her life than a concubine, but perhaps more than did a local prostitute. Nonetheless, even when women were not slaves, they certainly did not have the rights and protections of free men, which in many cases made them vulnerable to slave-like living and working conditions. So while some might argue that the dominance of women and girls within Southeast Asian slave markets was due to their increased autonomy and mobility, we see that by the eighteenth century they had largely lost that fabled autonomy to the rigidly patriarchal Chinese, Muslim, and European merchants who now saw them as commoditized assets that provided domestic and sexual services.

While we know that the status and lives of free and slave women could be quite similar, we cannot automatically conflate all women with enslavement and servitude, a point that Eric Jones makes in his *Wives, Slaves and Concubines* (2010), which places women at the center of a world history about slavery in Dutch Asia.[101] Jones draws upon the voices of underclass women to explain how the increased presence of European women, the construction of the Suez Canal, and the use of anti-malarial drugs changed the nature of colonialism in eighteenth- and nineteenth-century Southeast Asia. The resulting increase in the commodification of labor motivated slave owners to begin to value "their underlings" less in terms of the prestige or status that slave ownership could convey and more in terms of the economic return they provided as laborers.[102] Like Taylor and Niemeijer, Jones shows that "economic pragmatism often took precedence over matters of race in the mixed ethnic societies of the early modern world."[103] More importantly, he demonstrates how the imposition of Dutch law and European slave structures on Asian systems "erected a firm partition between free and slave status" that initiated a devaluation of Southeast Asian women as a whole.[104]

The reality was that the slave women who did marry wealthy Muslim and Chinese merchants in the Straits did not have the life of luxury and protection implied. In fact, we know that women moving into these households were more likely to be the third or fourth wife, situated within a rigid and aggressively

---

[99] Hendrik Niemeijer, "Slavery, Ethnicity and the Economic Independence of Women in Seventeenth-Century Batavia," in *Other Pasts: Women Gender and History in Early Modern Southeast Asia*, ed. Barbara Watson-Andaya (Honolulu: University of Hawaii Press, 2000), p. 175.
[100] Ibid., p. 178.
[101] Eric Jones, *Wives, Slaves, and Concubines: A History of the Female Underclass in Dutch Asia* (DeKalb: Northern Illinois University Press, 2010).
[102] Ibid., p. 145.
[103] Ibid., p. 5.
[104] Ibid., p. 7.

maintained hierarchy, and whose acceptance was dependent upon her fertility.[105] In most cases she would have been purchased and brought into the household specifically for her reproductive abilities, regardless of her personal hopes or aspirations. Her husband/master may or may not (more likely not) have allowed her to leave their home unattended and would most likely have expected her to provide some additional domestic and/or sexual service for the household. Or, if her lot was to become a concubine, she was likely one among many, expected to provide sexual labor and reproduce for their master and subject to the disdain of his existing wives and concubines. Becoming the wife or the concubine of a wealthy merchant in Southeast Asia was not always the Cinderella story Company officials and subsequent scholars have intimated. We might also challenge the assumption that just because these women were unfortunate (without the protections of money or family influence) they were happy to marry any man willing to pay a price. Regardless of social status, forced marriage was, and continues to be, slavery.

Even those purchased for the specific purpose of domestic servitude were subject to the sexual demands of their masters. In spite of explicit cultural and legal prohibitions throughout Asia against it, slave masters controlled the bodies of their slaves and bountiful evidence has demonstrated that many slave-masters, and the powerful around them, took advantage of this authority. If the master did not make demands themselves, they could offer their slave's body to someone as a gift and/or compensation for a service or deed. Slaves purchased as household servants were without the legal protections of a marriage or business contract, expected to attend to the unending demands of the wives, concubines, and other family members within the household, and subject to indiscriminate emotional, psychological, sexual and/ or physical harassment, and violence. Although their material circumstances may have varied significantly, and there are a variety of works exploring this, neither the wives, concubines, nor the household slave women were truly free.[106] Their masters acquired each of them to fulfill some domestic and/or sexual need. If we assume that those who assimilated into this system happily and voluntarily were no longer enslaved, does this mean that those who were unhappy with

---

[105] Hsieh Bao Hua, *Concubinage and Servitude in Late Imperial China* (London: Lexington Books, 2014), pp. 41–8, 96–104, 198–201, 209–48; Johanna S. Ransmeier, *Sold People: Traffickers and Family Life in Northern China* (Cambridge: Harvard University Press, 2017), pp. 2–7; William Gervase Clarence-Smith, *Islam and the Abolition of Slavery* (Oxford: Oxford University Press, 2006), pp. 60–3, 80.

[106] Jones, *Wives, Slaves, and Concubines*, pp. 5–7; Gelman-Taylor, *The Social World of Batavia*, pp. 69–71; Andaya, *Other Pasts*, pp. 174–94.

their situation remained slaves? What happened to them? If regulations insisted slaves sexually violated or used for the purpose of prostitution be freed, why were the wives and concubines, purchased as slaves and forced to provide sex and bare children not entitled to emancipation? Historically, marriage has not brought a lot of "freedom" to women in either the east or the west, and any assertion supposing that a marriage market somehow made their enslavement better, or more acceptable, remains mired in those same nineteenth-century constructs. These sexist presumptions and gendered expectations about women's role in society, combined with geopolitical pressures, legitimized the demand for their bodies and services but made the slave status of females conveniently soluble when necessary.

## The Sources

This research relies heavily upon three volumes of assembled correspondence between EIC local officials and their superiors in India and London. On April 13, 1826, motivated by rumors of slavery in Britain's eastern dominions, members of the House of Commons (HoC) ordered the EIC to collect and deliver "copies or abstracts of all correspondence" between the EIC's Court of Directors and their governments in India pertaining to the slave trade, the Company's orders and regulations, or any criminal proceedings relative to the subject.[107] The first of what would be three separate efforts, with submissions spanning from the Gulf of Oman to the Pacific, was completed in May of 1827. An enormous endeavor, this first submission primarily offered Britain's government summaries from local governors about slave status in their areas, an explanation of how they implemented the government's legislation, and offered a few exemplary cases as evidence of their proactive application of the legislation.

The second volume, *Slave Trade (East India)—Slavery in Ceylon*, was part of a more robust survey (it is sixteenth among seventeen) and ordered by the HoC in November 1837. William Evans presented the papers to the government on 1 March, and they ordered them printed in July of 1838. These "accounts and papers" beginning from "the 1st day of June 1827 on the subject of slavery in the territories of the Company's Rule" expose the varying perceptions and inconsistent applications of the law that plagued this period.[108] This report

---

[107] *Slavery in India: Return to an Address of the Honorable House of Commons, Dated 13th April 1826* (London: House of Commons, 1828), p. 1.
[108] Evans, *Slave Trade (East India) Slavery in Ceylon*, p. i.

was indisputable evidence that the EIC still tolerated slavery within British territories even after the Abolition Act of 1833. Consequently, Sir John Hobhouse presented a third volume to the HoC in April of 1841 that contained copies of Company dispatches between the governor-general of India to the EIC Court of Directors and a "Report and Appendix furnished by the Indian Law Commissioners."[109] Some officials wanted to clear up "misapprehensions" about the status of slavery under EIC governance. The 1841 report explained that the EIC was more interested in first preparing "a complete criminal code for all parts of the British Indian Empire, and for every class of people, of whatever religion or nation, resident within its limits."[110] Slavery, they asserted, was not their priority. Most valuable for its copy of the law commissioner's report and their summary analyses, these papers expose just how truly wrought with obstacles such an objective truly was for an international corporation with anxious stockholders, during a time of tremendous economic, political, and social change.

These volumes afford us valuable information about the ideas and perceptions of local authorities and EIC officials about abolishing slavery in the east. Reading somewhat like the transcribed minutes of a protracted board meeting, these letters and reports documented the efforts of the Company's local officials to negotiate the implementation of antislavery measures in their districts. Some officers included copies of treaties with local leaders, while others described their struggles combating debt-slavery and the myriad entrenched networks maintaining their "clandestine importation of slaves."[111] Although the 1838 submission did establish that the EIC had, to some degree, attempted to implement antislavery measures throughout its territories long before its deadline of April 12, 1837, Parliament was dissatisfied with their first report because the Company had not provided the organized, in-depth, and systematic investigation of slavery in the East Indies that it was looking for.[112] Thus, rather than a compilation of case studies, the 1841 report provided much more detailed histories of slavery from the perspective of British officials. This last report was divided into sections dedicated to each presidency, "Bengal,"

---

[109] Hobhouse, *Returns*, p. 3.
[110] Ibid., p. 4. The beginning letter of the 1841 submission contains a lengthy discussion about what the EIC believed the expectations of the House of Commons were and why their previous report had been such action-centered account. The letter also tells the government that slavery was not the EIC's primary focus and, should they need any further analysis, "they would suggest that some of their members should be detached for the purpose of local inquiry," p. 5.
[111] Ibid., pp. 12, 28–9.
[112] Major's, *Slavery, Abolitionism and Empire in India*, explains that this was the deadline Parliament inserted into the EIC's 1833 Charter after they "removed the Company's trade monopolies, divested its commercial functions and transferred greater authority to the Parliamentary Board of Control" (3).

"Madras," and "Bombay," and included sections on the "African and Arabian" trades, as well as a "Copy of the Report from the Indian Law Commission."[113] As previously mentioned, the EIC included an additional 372 pages of accompanying documents within its Appendix. Generally, the individual EIC residents subdivided their areas by ethnicity, culture, or even tax boundaries in each of the district reports. In the case of the Madras Presidency at Fort St. George, it was "convenient to follow the division of the country observed by the Madras board of revenue."[114] Within these histories, colonial officials listed local ordinances, relayed their understandings of cultural practice, and defined the varying forms of slave labor they witnessed.

Although the 1841 submission was comprehensive, quantitative, and offered an historical account of slavery for each constituency, which was accompanied by summary "observations" by the Indian Law Commission, like the others, these reports were highly selective and subjective.[115] Each of these volumes was part of a compendium of correspondence on the subject, collected between 1771 and 1843, and among the most detailed for their time.[116] Moreover, the disparate boundaries these reports incorporated make it likely that they remain the most comprehensive accounts of eastern slavery to the east of Africa during this period. Still, they are not without limitations. It is important to note that in spite of their breadth and detail, these volumes were all selectively collected copies and extracts of correspondence and thus, subject to editing before presentation and publication. While this project, out of convenience, relied heavily on these volumes, this was with the assumption that they were not comprehensive collections. They are bolstered by a thorough examination of published and private papers, government minutes, correspondence, factory records, Company and military dispatches within the British Library's India Office of Records collection. Collectively, with a critical lens, these sources provide an important window into the EIC's approach to the complex and controversial task of abolishing slavery in the East Indies.

The first two chapters of this book offer context for the EIC's colonial policies in the IOW, Southeast Asia's connection to the region, and the Company's legislative approach to antislavery in both. They illustrate the size and scope of the pre-abolition slave trade in the east that, after the sixteenth century, connected Asia to the Americas via the Pacific and Indian Ocean trade routes. In the late eighteenth century, these systems met in the Straits of Malacca and

---

[113] Hobhouse, *Returns*, pp. 173, 188, 223–595.
[114] Ibid., p. 113.
[115] Ibid., p. 188.
[116] Major, *Slavery, Abolitionism and Empire in India*, p. 10.

fueled the development of ports like Bencoolen and Penang. These chapters contextualize antislavery measures in this region and illustrate the pragmatic necessity of the Company's policy of noninterference. At the same time, they reveal the common strategies, struggles, and resolutions local officials employed in their efforts to comply with what they understood to be British law, in places where the slave trade was a lucrative component of local economies.

Chapter 3, "Redefining Slavery and Servitude," narrows the field of study and turns our attention specifically to the British Straits Settlements as a whole; a collection of trading ports that secured Britain's control of the Straits of Malacca at the beginning of the nineteenth century.[117] An important part of negotiating control of the labor force in Southeast Asia the Company's first steps toward eradicating slavery was to identify who the slaves were and what labor they provided. Then, chapter 4 draws on popular discourse and official correspondence to unpack the implementation of antislavery measures in Southeast Asia. This chapter demonstrates the ways both Dutch and British colonial authorities were particularly narrow with their definitions of a slave and excluded all but a distinct few in order to preserve hard-won economic and political partnerships with slave-owning merchants and local elites. According to EIC reports, Company officials had been particularly proactive with early implementation of antislavery measures and had eliminated most slaves in the region. Of course, the reality was something quite different.

The remainder of the book provides a micro history for each settlement and draws comparisons between the ancient city of Malacca and the relatively new settlements of Penang and Singapore. Using popular discourse found in local media, police reports, witness testimony, and EIC correspondence these chapters illustrate the differences in the ways colonial officers dealt with slavery in each of the three communities. Possessing the largest slave population at the dawn of abolition, the ancient entrepôt of Malacca was a center of trade since at least the early fifteenth century and part of an historic and entrenched slave trade that formed the foundations of its indigenous population. Slaves represented wealth and prestige in most Southeast Asian societies until the nineteenth century, and the affluent and powerful citizens and merchants in Malacca had many of them. More importantly, the British were relative latecomers in the Straits and, until the middle of the nineteenth century, were

---

[117] In 1826, the formerly independent colonies of Singapore, Penang—which included the Province Wellesley—and Malacca were annexed as an administrative group to the presidency of Bengal and formed the Straits Settlements; this unified status remained until its transfer to the colonial office in 1867. From that point, officials attempted to unify colonial legislation in the settlements; Hobhouse, *Returns*, p. 107; Andaya and Andaya, *A History of Malaysia*, p. 122.

not the most powerful residents in Malacca. Their drive to eradicate slavery was circumscribed by Dutch, Portuguese, Chinese, and Malay residents who challenged the EIC's right to deprive them of legal property. The registries described in Chapter 5 and the disagreement between Garling and Lewis in Chapter 6 illustrate that local administrators from both the British and Dutch governments accommodated Malacca's established wealthy elite even as they attempted to implement significant prohibitions on their lifestyles.

The case was much different for Penang and Singapore. British officials considered these new settlements and contended that there could not yet be any established slave systems in these colonies. Using a registration system similar to Malacca's, during the 1820s colonial authorities in Penang believed it would be simple and expedient to register or manumit the existing slave population. Since the trade in slaves to the island was prohibited in 1795, colonial authorities maintained that the death of all the slaves on the register would bring an end to all slavery on the island. EIC officials asserted disingenuously that Singapore, established eight years after Regulation X and Parliament's Felony Act, had no slaves. However, the local testimony and correspondence in Chapter 7 challenge this assertion and demonstrate that administrators in both settlements were more than aware of the slave traffic flowing through these port cities. In fact, as Chapter 8 illustrates, Singapore quickly became a center for a trade in both enslaved and indentured women and girls. During this period, there were boat loads of laboring men—free and otherwise—arriving in Penang and Singapore, and the lack of available women caused concern among some local European residents, who believed that the lack of women threatened the stability of the settlement. As a result, we see evidence that authorities regularly "turned a blind eye" to the importation of women and girls they encountered, many of whom were without question enslaved.

Officials did not have to negotiate antislavery measures with established and powerful local slave owners in Penang and Singapore, but their rapid growth as colonial centers created a pressing demand for the domestic and sexual labor, or women and girls, which motivated authorities to overlook situations they knew to be illegal. Together, moving from a macro analysis of slavery in the Indian Ocean World and its connections to a wider, global system, to micro-studies of Malacca, Penang, and Singapore, these chapters tell the story of the EIC's negotiation of antislavery measures on its eastern frontier between 1795 and 1843. Layers of political and ideological forces were at play during this period of colonial development, but as the Company vied for trading power in the region, Britain's moral imperative to abolish slavery took a back seat to the Company's mandate to preserve political and economic relationships and desire to establish a prosperous and civilized settlement. In the Straits, abolition was generally not the first priority for EIC officials and, while many may have supported the cause against the Atlantic trade, most believed that slavery in the east was fundamentally different from the abhorrent, "inhumane" systems in the Americas.

Finally, the following story about Britain's antislavery efforts in the Straits demonstrates how the inconsistencies incompetence, and prejudice that plagued the enforcement of antislavery laws in this region not only shaped how many viewed the effort itself, but also how these failures irrevocably hindered the efficacy of the project as a whole. Limits to colonial authority and the Company's faithful adherence policies of noninterference certainly prolonged the implementation of Britain's Anti-Slavery Project in the Straits, however, and perhaps more importantly, the Company's concern over the protection of personal property and political relationships, combined with individual assumptions about race, class, and gender, shaped the way officials and local authorities perceived and reacted to the illicit trade they encountered.

1

# A Policy of Noninterference

On October 17, 1827, the EIC's Board of Control in London sent a dispatch to its officials in Bombay "relating to the existing treaties with the imaum [sic] of Muscat and to the slave trade off the eastern coast of Africa."[1] The board explained that they agreed with the India Office's "resolutions respecting the proper construction of existing treaties of alliance" and were aware of the significant concessions that the imam had already made the previous year by prohibiting the slave trade "within Christian states" in his African territories. They believed Mr. Warden, a member of the EIC Council at Bombay, had "undervalue[d]" the economic and political sacrifice of the local leader and praised the imam for "cessation of the great traffic which the French carried on with Zanzibar." Officials knew that the French, Portuguese, and Spaniards continued "an extensive traffic in slaves on the eastern coasts of Africa" and were pleased to have such an influential associate there. As they understood, Captain Moresby's 1822 treaty with the Omani government had given His Majesty's cruisers the authority to seize "all Arab vessels having slaves on board found to the eastward of a line drawn from Cape Delgado to Diu Head Cambay (passing 60 (sixty) miles to the east of Socotra)."[2] Based at Suez with the Bombay Marine (later the Indian Navy) and commissioned by the EIC to chart the Red Sea, Moresby possessed intimate knowledge of the region's coastline and cultures and is lauded by Jeremy Jones for negotiating "the first specifically anti-slave treaty with a Muslim power."[3] Correspondence between officials revealed the board concurred with Mr. Warden's assessment that such an "unpopular concession in the imaum's [sic] dominions, where power depend[ed] on popularity" would have come with significant political costs.[4] Both the board and local EIC officials

---

[1] Evans, *Slave Trade (East India) Slavery in Ceylon*, p. 12.
[2] ibid.; Jeremy Jones, *Oman, Culture and Diplomacy* (Edinburgh: Edinburgh University Press, 2013), p. 126.
[3] Sarah Searight, "The Charting of the Red Sea," *History Today* 53, no. 3 (March 2003): pp. 40–6; Jones, *Oman, Culture and Diplomacy*, p. 127.
[4] Evans, *Slave Trade (East India) Slavery in Ceylon*, p. 12.

recognized that if they pushed any further their ally might lose his power, which would have ultimately threatened British influence in the region.

The board also agreed with Warden's decision to stop short of entering into a more intimate alliance in exchange for the promise to completely abolish slavery in his territories. Officials explained that they had "on several occasions," reminded the imam about how important "the justice and expediency of suppressing the slave trade in all its branches" was to the Empire. However, he continually told officials that "slavery [was] permitted by the Mahomedan [*sic*] law; that the attempt on his part to suppress it would make his own subjects and all Musselmans [*sic*] his enemies." He asserted he "would do anything for the English" but could not promise a total prohibition of the slave trade, "without some measures to secure his safety." The imam insisted that if they wanted him to do as they asked, the EIC "should bind themselves to defend him" from all enemies or provide him with money and land to escape. Warden believed such an agreement involved the British "too deeply in an alliance with Muscat" and would have had complicated and costly political consequences he felt were not worth the effort. He and the EIC Board understood that there was a significant traffic in slavery throughout Britain's territories in the east, outside the reach of this leader's authority, and that any negotiation with one chief was likely to create conflict or set a precedent for others. They thought it far more prudent to preserve existing political and economic relationships rather than press for abolition. Indeed, evidence in the following pages illustrates that at the beginning of the nineteenth century slaves were an essential part of the geopolitical economy and the maintenance of power and influence within strategic locations was more important to Company officials than the total abolition of slavery. Britain's new reforms became policy with the very real potential to jeopardize economic and political relationships between powerful trading partners in the IOW. Warden, like so many of his colleagues stationed in EIC outposts throughout the region, did not "press" the issue of abolition because he understood that doing so would threaten the Company's viability in the region. While the EIC certainly took measures to prohibit the foreign slave trade throughout its diverse eastern territories, the necessity of maintaining key political relationships undergirded a policy of noninterference that gave officials opportunity and motivation to ignore the indigenous, or at least non-European, slave systems they encountered.[5]

---

[5] The following are some of the most interesting examples of colonial officials justifying their lack of aggressive enforcement of antislavery legislation within the three collective volumes of colonial correspondence regarding slavery in the East Indies: *Slavery in India*, pp. 13, 39; Hobhouse, *Returns*, p. 4. A number of the early references to the delicacy of antislavery policy can be found in the first hundred pages of the 1838 report: Evans, *Slave Trade (East India) Slavery in Ceylon*, pp. 20, 28, 32, 37, 56; the latter half of the report examines individual cases more deeply; see p. 240, pp. 407–9.

This perspective is quite different from the dominant narrative within both contemporary and current scholarship that portrays Britain's abolition efforts as a vigorous national campaign to rid the world of a "moral evil."[6] Such interpretations must be tempered with an understanding that the EIC was not a surrogate for the British government; they were a corporation with the intention of expanding into new markets and maximizing profits for its shareholders. After British losses in the Americas at the end of the eighteenth century, the lure of spices, tin, and of course tea drew investors' attentions to ancient trade networks in the east. As Sing Chew explains, "a world system" of trading ports, on both land and sea routes, connected Europe to China via the Mediterranean, the Arabian Peninsula, Indian Ocean World, and Southeast Asia "since the dawn of the current era (first century CE) and even earlier by perhaps 200 B.C.E."[7] Dominated by Chinese, Malay, Indian, and Muslim merchants from the ninth to the seventeenth centuries, Europeans were not significant players in this international marketplace until the Portuguese took Malacca in 1511.

EIC officials who wanted profitable treaties had to foster and maintain good diplomatic relationships with a wealthy elite class who held power and influence over well-established trade networks. As a result, the EIC strictly upheld a "policy of non-interference," which prohibited the Comapny's involvement in matters of "national independence."[8] The foundational role slavery played within these societies meant that antislavery ordinances intervened in the personal lives and households of the powerful and threatened the sovereignty of local governments, which directly contradicted the Company's time-honored policy. Consequently, antislavery policies in Britain's eastern territories became another part of a continuous struggle over power and territory. As we saw with the imam of Muscat, the EIC government calculated their placement of antislavery measures in treaties with local rulers and elites along the eastern coasts of Africa, South Asia, and Southeast Asia to negotiate control of labor flows throughout the Indian and Pacific Ocean worlds.[9]

---

[6] This was a common description of slavery during the period. For a more thorough analysis of the moral perspectives surrounding abolitionism see Elizabeth Chandler, *Essays, Philanthropic and Moral, Principally Relating to the Abolition of Slavery in America* (Philadelphia: T.E. Chapman, 1845); David Brion Davis, *In the Image of God: Religion, Moral Values, and Our Heritage of Slavery* (New Haven: Yale University Press, 2001), pp. 19–45; Ford Risley, *Abolition and the Press: The Moral Struggle against Slavery* (Evanston: Northwestern University Press, 2008), pp. 75–100; Quirk, *The Anti-Slavery Project*, pp. 82–110.

[7] Sing C. Chew, "The Southeast Asian Connection in the First Eurasian World Economy, 200 BCE–CE 500," *Journal of Globalization Studies* 5, no. 1 (May 2014): p. 83.

[8] Evans, *Slave Trade (East India) Slavery in Ceylon*, p. 4.

[9] C. A. Bayly's work, *Imperial Meridian: The British Empire and the World 1780–1830* (London: Longman, 1989), pp. 75–100 offers an important analysis of the European imperial contest and how their territorial expansion into northern Africa and Asia was "central to the emergence and formation of those empires" (p. 75).

The fact that the Company's first antislavery legislation was passed nearly two decades before Parliament's 1807 Slave Trade Act, as Major explains, "is sometimes used to suggest that the EIC was in the vanguard of the antislavery movement."[10] However, as Major's seminal study on the EIC's antislavery efforts, *Slavery, Abolitionism, and Empire in India* demonstrates, early policies may have been initiated by genuine philanthropy on the part of certain individuals but, by the end of the eighteenth century most had more than humanitarian intervention in mind.[11] Indeed, Allen's work on Company slavery in Bencoolen offers evidence of the efforts several directors made to remind local officials that their slaves were humans and instructed them to offer appropriate housing, feed abundantly, and treat them well.[12] Moreover, he rightfully calls our attention to the fact that Company officials asserted the humanity of their slaves at a time when such sentiments were "rarely openly acknowledged" by Europeans.[13] Yet it is also important to note that in the same article, Allen explains Company officials promoted the good treatment of slaves primarily because they believed it to be economically advantageous—keeping them well fed, well clothed, and housed "allowed them to work full time."[14] While it would be unfair to say Company officials were callous business men, indifferent to the suffering of slaves, it is not out of line to say they brought a healthy dose of pragmatism to their humanitarian efforts.

Confronted with an abundance of reports about the kidnapping, enslavement, and transportation of women and children in Bengal, Governor-General Warren Hastings enacted the earliest, although typically unenforced, regulations against slave trading within his jurisdiction in 1774.[15] These ordinances threatened punishments for those who obtained any person through force, fraud, or deceit and then sold them as slaves without a legally authorized deed, as well as for those who sanctioned such sales of illegally acquired slaves. By the 1790s the governors of Bengal, Madras, and Bombay had all implemented measures to prohibit slave trading and the export of slaves within their presidencies, and some had implemented new measures of enforcement.[16] Still, until Parliament's 1807 Slave Trade Act and subsequent Felony Act in 1811, these were sporadic, disparate, and generally the actions of individual administrators in various districts, acting on personal, political, and/or economic aspirations.

---

[10] Major, *Slavery, Abolitionism, and Empire in India*, p. 69.
[11] Ibid., pp. 75–7.
[12] Allen, "Slavery in a Remote but Global Place," p. 160.
[13] Ibid., p. 162.
[14] Ibid., p. 160.
[15] Allen, *European Slave Trading in the Indian Ocean*, p. 182; Major, *Slavery, Abolitionism and Empire in India, 1772–1843*, p. 71.
[16] Allen, *European Slave Trading in the Indian Ocean*, p. 186.

Many saw abolition as a lofty ambition rather than a primary goal—they believed there were other, more important issues to attend to. For example, writing to London's EIC Court of Directors, Secretary to the Indian government T. H. Maddock asserted that the Company

> did not delay to enter upon the subject of slavery after we had been instructed to do so, although it was not without regret that we were compelled to withdraw our attention from several subjects on which we were engaged, and which, in our own opinion, are of still greater importance than slavery.[17]

Disagreement about the value of antislavery legislation in the IOW was evident in the Indian Law Commission's Report; some even questioned whether or not slaves in the East Indies should be emancipated. Political tensions with western planters over sugar markets meant that several of the commissioners felt it was important to clearly differentiate eastern systems from what, at this point, most considered a violent and inhumane system in the west.

Indeed, unlike the European-fabricated trans-Atlantic trade going west, slavery in the IOW had been an entrenched element of African, Arabian, and Asian cultures and economies for as long as they had been trading. Slaves were ubiquitous components within most African and Asian societies, usually a sign of wealth, prestige, and/or power, and lots of people had them. Freeing the slaves of the local elite was the equivalent of emptying the bank accounts of the most wealthy and powerful families of the region. Europeans did not control slave markets in Asia and had only legislative authority within their colonial territories, granted by local leaders in negotiated treaties and contracts. Their position was tenuous at best. During this period, EIC power was limited and their initiatives were regularly circumvented with relative ease. In places like the British Straits Settlements, EIC officials had to be mindful of how far they pushed against existing power structures.

Ironically, Europeans were so heavily involved in both the Indian and Pacific Ocean slave trades during the seventeenth and eighteenth centuries that the abolition of slave trading and subsequent removal of European competition actually boosted profits for indigenous slavers.[18] Initially, EIC officials focused their efforts on eliminating European slaving—most understood that antislavery ordinances had simply pushed existing indigenous slave-trading networks underground. The

---

[17] Hobhouse, *Returns*, p. 5.
[18] Richard Allen's and Anthony Reid's work on eastern slave trades explain the importance of Europeans within these markets. Richard Allen's "Satisfying the 'Want for Labouring People,'" pp. 45–73, explains the ways Europeans utilized indigenous slave systems to aid with imperial expansion. Reid's research on slavery in Southeast Asia is critical for understanding the ways in which British abolitionism boosted the economies of surrounding indigenous slavers. For a more detailed discussion see Reid, "The Decline of Slavery in Nineteenth Century Indonesia," p. 72; Reid and Brewster, *Slavery, Bondage, and Dependency in Southeast Asia*, pp. 17–24.

records are abundantly clear that even after the Felony Act in 1811, the traffic in slaves continued "in secret" throughout the IOW.[19] However, the commission's report also revealed a significant disagreement within the EIC government about the nature of slavery in their eastern territories, as well as how much the Company should involve themselves in the internal affairs of sovereign nations. Not everyone agreed on the boundaries of the Company's policy of noninterference. Some of the commissioners felt that eastern slavery was "stamp[ed] with a character of mildness" and there was, therefore, no need to interfere with eastern slaving at all.[20] Others believed the institution was dying a natural death and that local officials should only concern themselves in matters of abuse and neglect. Many of the commissioners on the board held that slavery in the IOW was essentially "voluntary" and asserted that the Company should not interfere with that decision.[21] In the end, the Law Commission's definitions, descriptions, and perceptions became the dominant narrative about slavery in the East Indies for the next 150 years. EIC officials constructed an image of slavery in the IOW as completely separate from the "dreadful cruelty" of the Atlantic system, were not particularly concerned with its immediate abolition, and approached the enforcement of antislavery measures much differently than they did in the Atlantic. These reports offered Britain's government an image of eastern slavery as a benevolent institution that offered protection and sustenance for the misfortunate, and primarily consisted of happy and loyal servants. Moreover, officials in the Company's eastern settlements clearly understood that they needed to implement ordinances strategically and with caution.[22] As a result, the very real exploitation and violence experienced by Asian slaves was consistently minimized and mitigated.

## Slaveholding and Trading in Southeast Asia

If the subject of slavery in the Indian Ocean has suffered from a "tyranny of the Atlantic," then it is safe to say that the topic of Asian slavery has suffered the same fate from South Asian, more specifically Indian, systems. While foundational and incredibly valuable, research on Indian slavery has dominated the discourse for decades. The work of Indrani Chaterjee has been particularly influential and her book, *Gender, Slavery, and Law in Colonial India* (1999), was

---

[19] Watson-Andaya and Andaya, *A History of Malaysia*, p. 60.
[20] Hobhouse, *Returns*, pp. 192–4.
[21] Ibid., 190.
[22] Ibid., p. 188.

the first full-length examination of the influence that gender and sexuality had on the division of labor and everyday lives of slaves in colonial India. Chatterjee exposed how British officials used antislavery legislation as leverage against indigenous slave-owning elites to enforce policy. Her examination of slaves in the private households of Mughal elites in early nineteenth-century Bengal led her to argue that "in the face of abolitionist agitation, the simple reduction of the complex and different grades of slavery into 'marriage' relations by the Law Commission absolved the Company of any responsibility to legally end slave-concubinage in the English officers and soldiers' households."[23] She demonstrates that the British used language, law, and social constructs of gender to maintain their ability to exploit the ubiquitous domestic and sexual labor of women. Similar to what we will see in the Straits, western misinterpretations (intentional or otherwise) of cultural structures and mores meant that the terms "wife" and "concubine" obscured rather than elucidated the status of women who were clearly slaves. Still, while there are noteworthy connections and similarities with the history and historiography about south Asian slavery, the concentration of this research is the implementation of antislavery legislation in Southeast Asia, a unique region deserving of focused attention.

In Southeast Asia, slavery was an embedded institution within its culture and society, a primary source of labor, and played an essential role in local and regional economies. Imprisonment or capture, debt bondage, and indenture were common methods of enslavement and prevalent among most cultures in Asian, Middle Eastern, and African countries connected to the IOW long before Europeans arrived.[24] This was particularly so in the Straits of Malacca. A pioneer in the field of Southeast Asian History, Anthony Reid is still the most published and among the most cited, within the field. In *Slavery, Bondage, and Dependency in Southeast Asia* (1983), Reid argues that social hierarchies or "vertical bonding" is an "ancient" and elemental component in most all Southeast Asian societies.[25] To illustrate the depths of this structure, Reid explains that "as soon as Southeast Asians speak, they place themselves in a vertical relationship." Indeed, he insists that "the theoretical concept of human equality" does not exist in "the great texts of Southeast Asia high cultures" but that what can be found are celebrations of a "mystical unity between servant

---

[23] Indrani Chatterjee, *Gender, Slavery, and Law in Colonial India* (Oxford: Oxford University Press, 1999), 21.
[24] Anthony Reid, *Charting the Shape of Early Modern Southeast Asia* (Chiang Mai: Silkworm Books, 1999), pp. 181–212; Reid, "The Decline of Slavery in Nineteenth Century Indonesia," pp. 64–80; Andaya, *Other Pasts*, pp. 174–94; Warren, *The Sulu Zone*, pp. 215–51; Tagliacozzo, "Ambiguous Commodities, Unstable Frontiers," pp. 354–77.
[25] Reid and Brewster, *Slavery, Bondage, and Dependency in Southeast Asia*, pp. 6–8.

and master." Reid asserts that Southeast Asians have a characteristic "acceptance of mutual obligation between high and low, or creditor and debtor." Debt and obligation were an established factor of life in this region, regardless of colonial law.

In *Southeast Asia and the Age of Commerce* (1993), Reid tells us that vertical bonding was influenced by three primary factors and that the system had important impacts on the mobilization of labor in the region. He explains that

> [f]irst, the control over manpower was seen as the vital index of power and status, since labour rather than land was identified as a scarce resource. […] Second, human transactions were generally expressed in monetary terms. […] Third, there was a relatively low level of legal and financial security available from the state, so both patrons and clients needed each other's protection and support.[26]

According to Reid, the region had been a center for maritime commerce for so long that people became habituated to the seeing even themselves as "assets having a cash value." Consequently, vertical bonding in Southeast Asia resulted in "a system of bonding based largely on debt, where loyalties were strong and intimate, yet at the same time transferable and even saleable." Most people in Southeast Asia were obligated, often financially, to someone else. Europeans, the British included, found it nearly impossible, certainly cost-prohibitive, to assemble a workforce. With the exception of the occasional unencumbered Chinese worker or traveling foreigners, there was no indigenous "free wage labour" available for hire and slave owners rented their slaves at a rate of up to "ten times a subsistence wage."[27] According to Allen, officials at Bencoolen wrote to London in 1686—a year after founding the establishment—complaining about their "'absolute need' for 50 or 60 slaves because local 'Malay' laborers were expensive to hire, lazy, and difficult to control."[28] They hoped for a group of slaves who, as Allen explains, "could be made to work at all hours and cost little or nothing to maintain since they could be employed in ways that ultimately allowed them to feed themselves." Even as late as 1760, officials made requests to increase their slave population to as many as 1,200, because they argued it was still cheaper to maintain slaves than employ Malays. The economic advantage of importing slaves into the Company's Southeast Asian projects versus hiring local labor remained a common belief until well into the eighteenth century.

Many urban commercial centers in Southeast Asia during the sixteenth and seventeenth centuries such as Malacca, Aceh, Banten, Patani, and Makassar were

---

[26] Anthony Reid, *Southeast Asia in the Age of Commerce 1450–1680, Volume One: The Lands below the Winds* (New Haven: Yale University Press, 1993), p. 129.
[27] Ibid., pp. 129–31.
[28] Allen, "Slavery in a Remote but Global Place," p. 155.

populated with former slaves brought by indigenous elites, affluent immigrants, or as merchandise on a commercial expedition.[29] Some have asserted that the most common service for slaves in Southeast Asia was "domestic," or household servants; however, we should remember that large commercial centers—particularly Malacca and Singapore—often have robust entertainment industries (brothels, taverns, and music halls), which also relied heavily on slave or quasi-slave labor and generated a growing demand for a thriving trade in women and girls that has persisted into the twenty-first century.[30] Slaves were valuable commodities and an important component of many social structures for all the dominant indigenous and immigrating cultures, as well as an important part of the social, political, and economic fabric of Southeast Asian society. Antislavery ordinances directly challenged the sovereignty of several wealthy and powerful groups with whom the Company needed to negotiate.

These groups had been in the Straits since the mid-tenth century, when the lure of international exchange had drawn merchants and travelers from India, China, and the Arabian Peninsula to settle in trading ports all over the region. In addition to trading partners and economic advancements, the cultural exchanges between India and Southeast Asia beginning after the first century CE left behind strong influences of Hinduism and Buddhism that reached beyond the marketplace. The domination of Indian Ocean trade networks by Arab and Persian Muslims from the tenth to the fourteenth century brought a wave of new settlers and traders connecting Southeast Asia to larger global trading networks. This, combined with a concurrently rising class of Chinese merchants who injected currency, capital, and product into emerging ports and urban centers throughout mainland and maritime Southeast Asia, set the foundations for the later "the age of commerce" between the fifteenth and seventeenth centuries described by Reid's work and was certainly part of what made the region so appealing to western empires during the eighteenth and nineteenth centuries.[31] When Europeans arrived in Southeast Asia at the beginning of the sixteenth century, in addition to powerful indigenous trading states like Johor, Java, and Sulu, there were communities of Indian merchants, Muslim trading bases, and Chinese settlements—each of them filled with slaves and indentured servants—throughout the region.[32]

---

[29] Reid, "The Decline of Slavery in Nineteenth Century Indonesia," p. 69.
[30] Suzanne Miers, *Slavery in the Twentieth Century: The Evolution of a Global Problem* (New York: Alta Mira Press, 2003), pp. 415–34; Shawna Herzog, "Selling Sex in Singapore: The Development, Expansion, and Policing of Prostitution in an International Entrepôt," in *Selling Sex in the City: A Global History of Prostitution, 1600s–2000s*, eds. Magaly Rodriguez Garcia, Lex Heerma van Voss, Elise van Nederveen Meerkerk (Leiden: Brill, 2017), pp. 594–620.
[31] Wade, "An Early Age of Commerce in Southeast Asia, 900-1300 CE," pp. 228–31.
[32] Anthony Reid, *Southeast Asia in the Age of Commerce, 1450–1680, Volume Two: Expansion and Crisis* (New Haven: Yale University Press, 1993), pp. 108–14.

EIC officials took note of Chinese successes and hoped to make use of their skills. By 1710, the Company's administration instructed local officials at Bencoolen to do what they could to encourage Chinese settlement, as long as it did not cost the Company money. Once again, turning to Allen's research' we see that by the eighteenth century Chinese labor (indentured and enslaved) had become an attractive alternative to Africans. Recognized for their hard work, agricultural knowledge, and business acumen, Allen explains that Company officials, including future founder of the settlement at Penang Francis Light, "began to take interest in Chinese workers and settlers" after a series of "favorable assessments" and hoped to use Chinese workers to clear the land, build their settlements, then plant and work their fields.[33] He contends that "Company officials looked so favorably on these workers" that it "may have inspired a 1783 proposal to found a small colony of Chinese settlers at Calcutta."[34] In 1786, Light relied on Chinese labor to create the foundations for the Company's settlement at Penang and by 1794 he told the government at Calcutta that the 3,000 Chinese residents living on the island were the "most valuable." According to Light, the Chinese were the only laborers in the east from whom the Company could make a profit "without expence [sic] and Extraordinary Efforts of Government."[35] EIC administrators had such faith in Chinese business and labor that, as Allen explains, the intimation of "Chinese immigration held out the promise of enhancing the value of the company's possessions."

The spread of Indians and their ideas throughout mainland and insular Southeast Asia during the first millennia of the Common Era initiated a period of "Indianization" that made a significant impact on social, economic, and religious structures. From the first to eleventh centuries Hindu-Indian merchants and (after the second century) Buddhist missionaries made their way down the Malay coastline and through the Straits of Melaka, settling in commercial centers along the way. Reid's study of Asian commerce in the fifteenth and sixteenth centuries describes the thriving communities of a "Hindu commercial caste—Gujarati sharafs and South Indian chettiars" that emerged and who were, in addition to being merchants themselves, vital money lenders, as well as "bankers and brokers" for wholesalers and traders throughout the IOW.[36] This merchant class developed a system of credit that extended to a variety of ports commonly visited by Indians, became some of the richest men in trading centers like Melaka, Pegu,

---

[33] Allen, *European Slave Trading in the Indian Ocean*, p. 201.
[34] Ibid., p. 200.
[35] Ibid., p. 201.
[36] Reid, *Southeast Asia in the Age of Commerce, 1450–1680*, p. 112.

Bantan, or Aceh, and would almost certainly have both owned slaves and been connected to the lucrative business of slave trading.

As Indrani Chatterjee has demonstrated, slave-use in India was universal and there were distinct differences between agrestic (agricultural), domestic, and aristocratic slavery.[37] The experience of slaves—like everywhere else in Asia—depended on the position and profession of their masters; some were bought and sold with the land and treated as chattel slaves, while others were kept purely for the status and enjoyment of their masters.[38] While we do not know how many came with them, it is certain these Hindu-Indian merchants, or "Kling" as the Portuguese later called them, brought at least small retinues of personal slaves to help establish trading connections and facilitate business arrangements.[39]

Craig Lockard argues that with the exception of Vietnam, in spite of "longstanding trade connections to China, India exercised more cultural influence on Southeast Asia."[40] Hindu concepts like reincarnation, karma, and hereditary social classes were not surprisingly most influential among the Malay and Javanese upper classes (a slaveholding elite looking to legitimize their power and position). By the middle of the thirteenth century, the "Indianized states on Java" had developed a unique "religious and political blend often termed Hindu-Javanese" and constructed "a complex etiquette" to regulate interactions between those of different social status and maintain rigid hierarchies.[41] Like Hindu caste in India, Hindu-Javanese social hierarchies created a convenient system of "institutionalized inequality" embedded within structures of vertical bonding that played a vital role in maintaining an entire class of exploitable labor.[42] Reid claims that by 1500, the Hindu-Javanese state was the "largest single exporter of slaves" and "supplied much of the urban working class of the Malay cities."[43] Not only was slavery a key component of Hindu social structures and supported by Hindu ideology, the remaining Hindu states were among the most active slave-trading societies in Southeast Asia. The prohibition of slavery and the slave trade had substantial cultural and economic consequences for these communities.

---

[37] Indrani Chatterjee, *Gender, Slavery, and Law in Colonial India* (Oxford: Oxford University Press, 1999), pp. 28–9.
[38] Utsa Patnaik and Manjari Dingwaney, *Chains of Servitude: Bondage and Slavery in India* (India: Sangram Books Ltd., 1985), p. 4.
[39] In the sixteenth century, the Portuguese gave Hindu-Indian merchants trading along the coasts of the Coromandel the name "Kling," and the term was also commonly used by other Europeans; Leonard Andaya, "Interactions with the Outside World and Adaptation in Southeast Asian Society," in *The Cambridge History of Southeast Asia, Volume One Part Two: From c. 1500 to c. 1800*, ed. Nicholas Tarling (Cambridge: Cambridge University Press, 1999), p. 9.
[40] Lockard, *Southeast Asia in World History*, p. 21.
[41] Ibid., p. 45.
[42] Patnaik and Dingwaney, *Chains of Servitude*, p. 3.
[43] Reid, *Southeast Asia in the Age of Commerce, Volume One*, p. 133.

The biggest competitors for Indian traders in the IOW were Arab Muslims. By the fourteenth century, the *Dar al-Islam* ("[t]he House of Islam") linked societies from northern Africa to Indonesia through faith and trade and as William Clarence-Smith explains, slavery in the Islamic world was "on a grand scale."[44] Ironically enough, the egalitarian message found in Islamic teachings spread quickly among peasants and merchants along the coastal regions of the Malay Peninsula and Indonesian islands. The conversions of local leaders brought waves of commercial activity, as they joined what was quickly becoming a global trade network. Lockard argues that "by embracing Islam, some rulers hoped to attract Arab, Persian, and Indian merchants" in hopes of bringing wealth and prosperity to their kingdoms.[45] In addition to converting existing populations, wealthy Muslim merchants immigrated to take advantage of developing opportunities in the Straits and there is no question they brought their slaves, and connections to a thriving slave traffic, with them. When the British arrived in the eighteenth century, there were already several well-established Muslim communities settled within the Straits of Melaka helping to support a flourishing slave trade.[46]

While there were strict regulations and guidelines about slavery within the Islamic World, between the sixteenth and eighteenth centuries, Muslim slavers transported hundreds of thousands of people between Africa, Northern and Central Europe, China, and the IOW.[47] As with most societies within Asia, the institution was embedded within social and cultural systems. Slaves within Islamic societies performed any number of municipal, agricultural, industrial, domestic, or physical labors demanded of them and were an essential part of the Muslim household. "The ownership of concubines was widespread," asserts Clarence-Smith, and eunuchs—if emasculated by an infidel—were regularly in charge of their master's harems and business matters.[48] Additionally, he argues that "servile prostitution" was "explicitly prohibited by the Quran" but "the legal fiction of short-term sales disguised the practice," and it "flourished in the Malay Peninsula."[49]

Colonial antislavery policies inserted the empire into the personal lives of Muslim families and undermined strongly held cultural structures. Perhaps more importantly, these ordinances gave colonial law enforcement officials the

---

[44] Clarence-Smith, *Islam and the Abolition of Slavery*, p. 2.
[45] Lockard, *Southeast Asia in World History*, p. 51.
[46] Lockard, *Southeast Asia in World History*, pp. 44–65; Andaya and Andaya, *A History of Malaysia*, pp. 37–57; Carl A. Trocki, *Singapore: Wealth, Power and the Culture of Control* (London: Routledge, 2006), pp. 15–33.
[47] Clarence-Smith, *Islam and the Abolition of Slavery*, pp. 9–11.
[48] Ibid., pp. 46–8.
[49] Ibid., p. 81.

pretense to question and investigate the private harems of the Muslim elite. To be more specific, it authorized British officials to transgress patriarchal boundaries, as well as the Company's policy of noninterference, and make determinations about how they could accommodate, interact with, and punish their servants and concubines; a measure of caution and compromise was necessary. However, while colonial administrators in the Straits were certainly aware of and made efforts to accommodate some requests from the local Muslim elite, it was the Chinese who garnered a majority of British attention.

As mentioned above, Chinese merchants and settlers began arriving in Southeast Asia during the eleventh century; however, Chinese "companies," or *kongsis*, did not establish themselves until the beginning of the eighteenth century.[50] Despite this late start, they quickly became a dominant and powerful force within economic and political circles within the Malay Peninsula, Sumatra, Java, and surrounding islands. These merchant societies facilitated the flow of labor and goods between China and the *Nanyang* or "land beneath the winds" and initiated what Carl Trocki describes as a "new period of Chinese interaction with Southeast Asia."[51] Some declared the eighteenth century to be "the Chinese century"; however, Trocki asserts that the period from 1720 to 1880 should be known as "the age of the *kongsis*" because of the dramatic increase in the presence of Chinese business, labor, and investment.[52] The *kongsis* maintained a type of "shareholding partnership" between an investor and a group of workers. In this case the investors were generally wealthy businessmen—owners of mines or plantations—and the workers were usually poverty-stricken, famine-driven, and vulnerable exploitive indenture or enslavement. This meant that *kongsis* had access to a seemingly limitless supply of exploitable labor.

In addition to bringing an external boost to the Chinese economy, Trocki asserts that the *kongsis* also facilitated expansion throughout Southeast Asia and this type of organization "characterized most settlements of Chinese labourers" from the beginning of the eighteenth century.[53] In an effort to strengthen their communities, some native rulers even invited *kongsis* to develop businesses in their territory. As they settled, many brought more labor from China and purchased slaves from Bugis and Malay slavers to work in tin and gold mines or on pepper and gambier

---

[50] Wade, "An Early Age of Commerce in Southeast Asia," pp. 228–31; Trocki, "Opium as a Commodity in the Chinese Nanyang Trade," pp. 88–92.
[51] Trocki, *Prince of Pirates*, p. 4.
[52] Craig A. Lockard, "Chinese Migration and Settlement in Southeast Asia before 1850: Making Fields from the Sea," *History Compass* 11, no. 9 (September 2013): p. 767; Trocki, *Prince of Pirates*, pp. 2–4.
[53] Trocki, *Prince of Pirates*, p. 3.

plantations.⁵⁴ By the 1830s, there were close to a million "Baba Chinese," or those born in Malaya, working throughout Southeast Asia.⁵⁵ By the time the British arrived in the Straits, the Chinese were already the largest, most powerful diaspora with control over economic markets and vast amounts of enslaved labor.

The Portuguese conquest of Melaka in 1511 marks the beginning of European trading and settlement in Southeast Asia. They were also the first Europeans to buy and sell slaves in the IOW. According to Allen, they were the "principle suppliers of South Indian, Burmese, Malayan, Javanese, and other Asian slaves to the Philippines," between 1580 and 1640, and by the end of the seventeenth century shipped as many as 40,000–60,000 to Mexico.⁵⁶ The Dutch arrived in Southeast Asia about a century later and dramatically increased the volume of slaves transported throughout the region. Allen's research asserts that between 1678–88, there were an estimated 66,350 slaves within the various Dutch East India Company or *Vereenigde Oost-Indische Compagnie* (VOC) settlements at the Cape of Good Hope, Melaka, Ceylon (Sri Lanka), Jakarta, Indonesia, and the Moluccas. During the seventeenth and eighteenth centuries, the Dutch, Chinese, and indigenous slavers sent almost half a million slaves to these colonial outposts.⁵⁷ By the beginning of the nineteenth century, Nordin Hussin argues that Dutch Burghers in Melaka were among those who owned the most slaves.⁵⁸

British and French slavers jumped into the IOW slave trade in the seventeenth century looking to import, as the Dutch and Portuguese had, cheap labor to build the infrastructure for their emerging colonies. In fact, Allen tells us that the eighteenth century "saw a tripling, if not a fourfold increase, in the volume of European slave trading in the region compared to the seventeenth century."⁵⁹ It is not hard to rationalize the argument that the Company's government had more of an economic, rather than a moral, imperative behind their support of abolitionism. It is also clear that Europeans both participated in and had a significant impact on the slave trade, and the demand for slaves, in Southeast Asia well before the arrival of antislavery ordinances.

There is, indeed, a plethora of evidence that Europeans kept a significant number of slaves in the east. However, as Margot Finn demonstrates, by the end of the seventeenth century the EIC put forth a concerted effort to blame the prevalence and persistence of the institution on native rulers and foreigners

---

⁵⁴ Trocki, *Prince of Pirates*, p. 4; Andaya and Andaya, *A History of Malaysia*, pp. 27–34.
⁵⁵ Trocki, *Prince of Pirates*, p. 4.
⁵⁶ Allen, *European Slave Trading in the Indian Ocean*, p. 9.
⁵⁷ Ibid.
⁵⁸ Nordin Hussin, *Trade and Society in the Straits of Melaka: Dutch Melaka and English Penang, 1780–1830* (Copenhagen: NIAS Press, 2007), p. 182.
⁵⁹ Allen, *European Slave Trading in the Indian Ocean*, p. 19.

(namely the Portuguese and French) and to distance the practice of slaveholding "from Britishness" altogether.[60] Finn's meticulous examination of probate records, private letters, and public documents provide stark evidence of the "substantial sums" Anglo-Indian families "invest[ed] in human property." For our purposes here, the analysis of the Anglo-Indian's "conceptual confusion" surrounding domestic slavery is particularly compelling. Like servants in England, she contends, slaves "inhabited a subject position that lay at the very intersection between family and the market."[61] In addition to frequently manumitting them, the slippery usage of the terms "servant" and "slave" within their personal descriptions and legal documents worked to ideologically separate "persons from possessions" and highlight the familial intimacies and relationships that often developed between Anglo-Indian families and their slaves. British slave masters, she explains, "*could* conceptualize their Indian domestic slaves as mere chattel, most chose not to do so." While some may have seen their domestic slaves as property, to be bought and sold at will, it is clear that most considered them as integral parts of their households and, in some cases, their families. This was likely among the reasons why the EIC government, headed by many of these Anglo-Indian patriarchs, were reluctant to force the universal application of antislavery ordinances and so eager to negotiate a more gradual abolition.

Moreover, when the British began their attempts to abolish the slave trade at the end of the eighteenth century, a significant number of trading networks connected markets in India, the Persian Gulf, and the eastern coast of Africa, including the islands of Madagascar, Réunion, and Mahé.[62] The strategic implementation and political impact of British antislavery ordinances in the Mascarene Islands of Mauritius and Réunion make it abundantly clear that prohibiting slavery was not always about humanitarianism. The prohibition of French slave traffic between India and the Mascarene between 1770 and 1830 helped "undercut the French

[60] Margot Finn, "Slaves out of Context: Domestic Slavery and the Anglo-Indian Family, c. 1780–1830," *Transactions of the Royal Historical Society* 6, no.19 (December 2009): pp. 199, 197.
[61] Ibid., pp. 186–8.
[62] Campbell, *The Structure of Slavery in Indian Ocean Africa and Asia*; Scarr, *Slaving and Slavery in the Indian Ocean*; Richard Allen, "Licentious and Unbridled Proceedings: The Illegal Slave Trade to Mauritius and the Seychelles during the Early Nineteenth Century," *The Journal of African History* 42, no. 1 (2001): pp. 91–116; Richard Allen, "A Traffic Repugnant to Humanity: Children, the Mascarene Slave Trade and British Abolitionism," *Slavery and Abolition* 27, no. 2 (2006): pp. 219–36; Richard Allen, "The Constant Demand of the French: The Mascarene Slave Trade and the Worlds of the Indian Ocean and Atlantic during the Eighteenth and Nineteenth Centuries," *The Journal of African History* 49, no. 1 (2008): pp. 43–72; Allen, "Suppressing a Nefarious Traffic," pp. 873–94; Allen, "Satisfying the 'Want for Labouring People,'" pp. 45–73; David Armitage, *The British Atlantic World, 1500-1800* (New York: Palgrave Macmillan, 2002); Herbert Klein, *The Atlantic Slave Trade* (Cambridge: Cambridge University Press, 1999); David Northrup, *The Atlantic Slave Trade*, 2nd ed. (Boston: Houghton Mifflin Co., 2002); Jan Breman, *Taming the Coolie Beast: Plantation Society and the Colonial Order in Southeast Asia*, 2nd ed. (Delhi: Oxford University Press, 1990).

position in India and the wider Indian Ocean."[63] By forbidding the importation of slaves into French colonial centers like Mauritius and Réunion, the British essentially slashed their supplies of labor and ultimately damaged the settlement's "ability to function."[64] Without slaves to run port facilities, or produce, process, and maintain the necessary food and supplies, the base lost its value as a strategic stronghold. In this instance, Britain used antislavery legislation as a tool to limit France's access to supplies of slave labor, which were the primary component to the success and profitability of these colonies.

In addition to chronicling and attempting to quantifying Europe's involvement in Indian Ocean slave systems, Allen's work is also among the first to demonstrate the interconnectivity of what was by the eighteenth century a global slave-trading network.[65] His essay, "Satisfying the 'Want for Labouring People,'" identifies Africans, Arabs, Indians, and Europeans as the primary slavers in the IOW, although Europeans were not a major force until after the mid-seventeenth century, and asserts that they sold hundreds of thousands of slaves between 1500 and 1850.[66] His work demonstrates that the British, French, and Dutch Empires had each established their own trans-Indian trades between North Africa, the Mascarene Islands, Indonesia, the Straits of Malacca, and India by the eighteenth century. European slavers shipped hundreds of thousands of men, women, and children, from Mozambique, Madagascar, Malagasy, and Angola, to key ports such as Mauritius, Muscat, Sumatra, Goa, Bombay, Penang, Malacca, and Singapore. In Southeast Asia, slaves arriving in these ports were then distributed throughout the commercial centers or sent to mines or plantations to extract and cultivate natural resources like spices, tin, salt, teak, and bullion, while others provided domestic and sexual labor within the settlements.[67]

---

[63] Allen, "Suppressing a Nefarious Traffic," p. 888.
[64] Ibid., p. 889.
[65] Allen, "Satisfying the 'Want for Labouring People,'" p. 47.
[66] Ibid., pp. 54–5.
[67] Ibid., pp. 45–55; Andaya and Andaya, *A History of Malaysia*, pp. 10–15; Takeshi Hamashita, "The Lidai Baoan and the Ryukyu Maritime Tributary Trade Network with China and Southeast Asia, the Fourteenth to Seventeenth Centuries," in *Chinese Circulations: Capital, Commodities, and Networks in Southeast Asia*, eds. Eric Tagliacozzo and Wen-chin Chang (Durham: Duke University Press, 2011), pp. 108–29; Anthony Webster, *Gentleman Capitalists: British Imperialism in Southeast Asia, 1770–1890* (London: I.B. Tauris, 1998), pp. 1–27; Adam McKeown, *Melancholy Order: Asian Migration and the Globalization of Borders* (New York: Columbia University Press, 2008), p. 63; Patrick Manning, *Migration in World History* (New York: Routledge, 2005), pp. 127–40; Reid and Brewster, *Slavery, Bondage, and Dependency in Southeast Asia*, pp. 24–6; Levine, *Prostitution, Race, and Politics*, pp. 251–3; Adele Perry, "Reproducing Colonialism in British Columbia, 1849–1870," in *Bodies in Contact: Rethinking Colonial Encounters in World History*, eds. Tony Ballantyne and Antoinette Burton (Durham: Duke University Press, 2005), pp. 255–6; Durba Ghosh, "Gender and Colonialism: Expansion or Marginalisation," *The Historical Journal* 47, no. 3 (2004): pp. 737–55.

The data from Allen's research is an illustration of Kerry Ward's theory found in *Networks of Empire*; in the IOW, several cities functioned as nodes within a larger web of slave-trading circuits that supplied slave labor to expanding mining and agricultural projects around the world.[68] Colonial trading centers such as Muscat, Bombay, Malacca, or Jakarta were just some of the nodes in a global slave-trading network that, by the sixteenth century, had become embedded within world commodities and labor markets.[69] By the time abolitionist efforts gained traction in Britain at the end of the eighteenth century, Europeans were already successful traders and merchants in ancient slave-trading networks that supplied bodies to labor in colonial centers around the world.[70] Combined, these studies offer evidence that pre-abolition slave trades transported labor to construct and operate developing European settlements around the world. Using Ward's network theory, we see that political, economic, and cultural ties were delicately interwoven to connect trading networks within the Indian, Pacific, and Atlantic worlds. By the seventeenth century, many European colonial cities had become nodes in the slave trade that distributed the working bodies so critical to the expansion of European Empires around the world.[71]

---

[68] Kerry Ward, *Networks of Empire: Forced Migration in the Dutch East India Company* (New York: Cambridge University Press, 2009), 125.

[69] For more on globalization and the intricately connected systems of global trade during this period see Philip Curtin, *Cross-cultural Trade in World History* (Cambridge: Cambridge University Press, 1984); Joseph Stiglitz, *Globalization and Its Discontents*, 1st ed. (New York: W. W. Norton, 2002); Jonathan Reynolds and Erik Gilbert, *Trading Tastes: Commodity and Cultural Exchange to 1750* (Upper Saddle River, NJ: Pearson/Prentice Hall, 2006); Kenneth Pomeranz and Steven Topik, *The World That Trade Created: Society, Culture, and the World Economy, 1400 to the Present*, 2nd ed. (Armonk, NY: M.E. Sharpe, 2006); Jurgen Osterhammel and Niels P. Petersson, *Globalization: A Short History* (Princeton: Princeton University Press, 2009); Ross Dunn, *The Adventures of Ibn Battuta, a Muslim Traveler of the Fourteenth Century* (Berkeley: University of California Press, 1986); Janet Abu-Lughod, *Before European Hegemony: The World System A.D. 1250-1350* (New York: Oxford University Press, 1989).

[70] Andrea Major argues that the abolitionist movement began in 1771 with the trial of James Sommerset, a slave from Virginia, in England. Her study, *Slavery, Abolition and Empire in India*, explains that the antislavery movement erupted after a judge decided to transport Sommerset to Jamaica to work on a plantation as punishment for refusing to return to Virginia with his master (41). While there had certainly been antislavery sentiment before this, Major claims that this was the beginning of the formalized campaign. For more on the Abolitionist movement see Christopher Brown and the Omohundro Institute of Early American History & Culture, *Moral Capital : Foundations of British Abolitionism* (Chapel Hill: University of North Carolina Press, 2006); Blackburn, *Overthrow of Colonial Slavery, 1776-1848*; Thomas Bender, *The Antislavery Debate : Capitalism and Abolitionism as a Problem in Historical Interpretation* (Berkeley: University of California Press, 1992); Drescher, *Abolition*.

[71] Richard S. Dunn, *Sugar and Slaves* (New York: W. W. Norton, 1972), 246–64; Sidney Mintz, *Sweetness and Power: The Place of Sugar in Modern History* (New York: Viking Penguin, 1986), 151–80; Eric Williams, *Capitalism & Slavery* (Chapel Hill: University of North Carolina Press, 1994), 130–42.

Unlike the Atlantic system, Europeans did not create a slave trade in the Indian Ocean. In this ancient network slaves were pervasive commodities who served as personal servants, surplus labor, and anonymous displays of wealth, power, or military strength. Eventually, the high demand for labor in developing colonial settlements incorporated commercial centers linking slave-trades within regional networks to a much larger global system. To that point, access to slave labor had been fundamental to the expansion of European Empires around the world, and in the IOW the British were happy to use antislavery policies to halt competing European expansion in the region. Yet the enforcement of antislavery legislation violated the Company's long-held tradition of noninterference and at times put officials at odds with local leaders. Moreover, there were several indigenous Southeast Asians willing to make up for the growing absence of European slavers in the Asian markets.

The Sulu Sultanate was one of the most dominant slave-trading societies in Southeast Asia and James Warren's research illustrates how, ironically, European abolition increased Sulu profits and expanded indigenous slave traffic in the South China Seas.[72] They controlled a bulk of maritime trade—particularly that of slaves—between China and Indonesia for most of the eighteenth and early nineteenth centuries. In his landmark study, *The Sulu Zone, 1768–1898* (2008), Warren explains that China and the Philippines formed the northern border that extended from southwest Borneo to southeast of the Celebs (modern-day Sulawesi, Indonesia) and the Moluccas. Historic social and economic bonds held these groups of "maritime and nomadic fisherman, and slash and burn agriculturalists of the coastal rim and interior foothills" together, which fostered and supported the success of the Sulu nation.[73] This chain of islands, he explains, functioned as a borderland between the "Muslim maritime world" in Malaysia and the "Christianized" Philippine archipelago in Manila. Sulu slavers brought captured, sold, or indentured Malay, Siamese, and Indonesian slaves, mostly women and children, to trade or sell in colonial centers throughout the region. The islands in the Celebes Sea, Indonesia, and Malaya were all regularly victims of slave raids by the Buginese and the Sulu Sultanate. It is clear from official correspondence and editorials within local newspapers that antislavery ordinances were not effective at deterring indigenous slave trading as some

---

[72] Warren, *The Sulu Zone*, p. 11.
[73] Ibid., p. xliii.

had hoped, local officials Europeans regularly accused Chinese, Bugis, and Malay traders of piracy and illegal slaving in the Straits.[74]

The Buginese, Malay maritime traders who had maintained a love/hate relationship with the Dutch since the first decades of the 1700s, and dominated underground markets in the Straits Settlements before 1850, collaborated with the Sulu and provided slaves to the Philippines, Indonesia, and ports all along the Straits of Malacca.[75] The size and complexity of the Indonesian, Malay, and Philippine archipelagoes that created such formidable challenges to British antislavery laws are apparent in Map 1. Before the 1760s, at least fourteen or fifteen Bugis prahus visited Sulu each year bringing merchants trading the spices and gunpowder they brought with them for Bengal cloth, opium, and slaves. The strength of the Sulu Empire created a lucrative and protected connection between the Pacific and Indian Ocean trading systems outside of European control that afforded them opportunities to exchange on a much larger scale. By the 1770s, Bugis slavers transported several hundred Filipinos from Sulu annually to slave markets on island all over Indonesia and Malaysia where we know Indian and Arab traders had been since at least the first millennium.[76] As we can see from Map 2, Southeast Asia and the Straits of Malacca in particular are a connecting thoroughfare between Indian and Pacific Oceans trades, which between the 15th and 19th centuries, slaves were, like any other valuable commodity and could be found in most any major trading emporium. Reid tells us that slaves traded in this region were commonly incorporated into the "dominant Muslim society" as servants and concubines, or as wives presented to itinerates as "retainers."[77] Additionally, the Sulu regularly sold slaves to established Dutch and Chinese families as "servants, boatmen, labourers, and concubines."[78] The reduction of competition and subsequent increase in demand meant that slave trading had become a windfall to Bugis and Sulu economies; each thrived as a result of antislavery efforts.[79]

---

[74] This is seen with only a preliminary glance at contemporary popular discourse; the following newspapers and correspondence offer some interesting examples: *The Singapore Chronicle*, March 15, 1827; *The Singapore Chronicle*, April 26, 1827; *The Singapore Chronicle*, January 15, 1829; *The Singapore Chronicle*, February 26, 1829; *The Singapore Chronicle*, November 5, 1829; *The Singapore Chronicle*, June 2, 1831; *The Singapore Chronicle*, August 25, 1831; *The Singapore Chronicle*, October 13, 1831; *The Singapore Chronicle*, November 15, 1832. The same sentiment was also found in the following official correspondence about efforts to abolish slavery; see CO273/1/45-136, 179–85; CO273/2/3-5, 66–8, 439–40. CO273/3/908-915.

[75] Dianne Lewis, *Jan Compagnie in the Straits of Malacca, 1641-1795* (Athens: Ohio University Press, 1995), pp. 51–4; Warren, *The Sulu Zone*, p. 11.

[76] Warren, *The Sulu Zone*, pp. 12–13; Andaya and Andaya, *A History of Malaysia*, p. 10.

[77] Reid and Brewster, *Slavery, Bondage, and Dependency in Southeast Asia*, p. 170.

[78] Ibid.

[79] Warren, *The Sulu Zone*, p. 15, pp. 156–7; Reid, "The Decline of Slavery in Nineteenth Century Indonesia," p. 67.

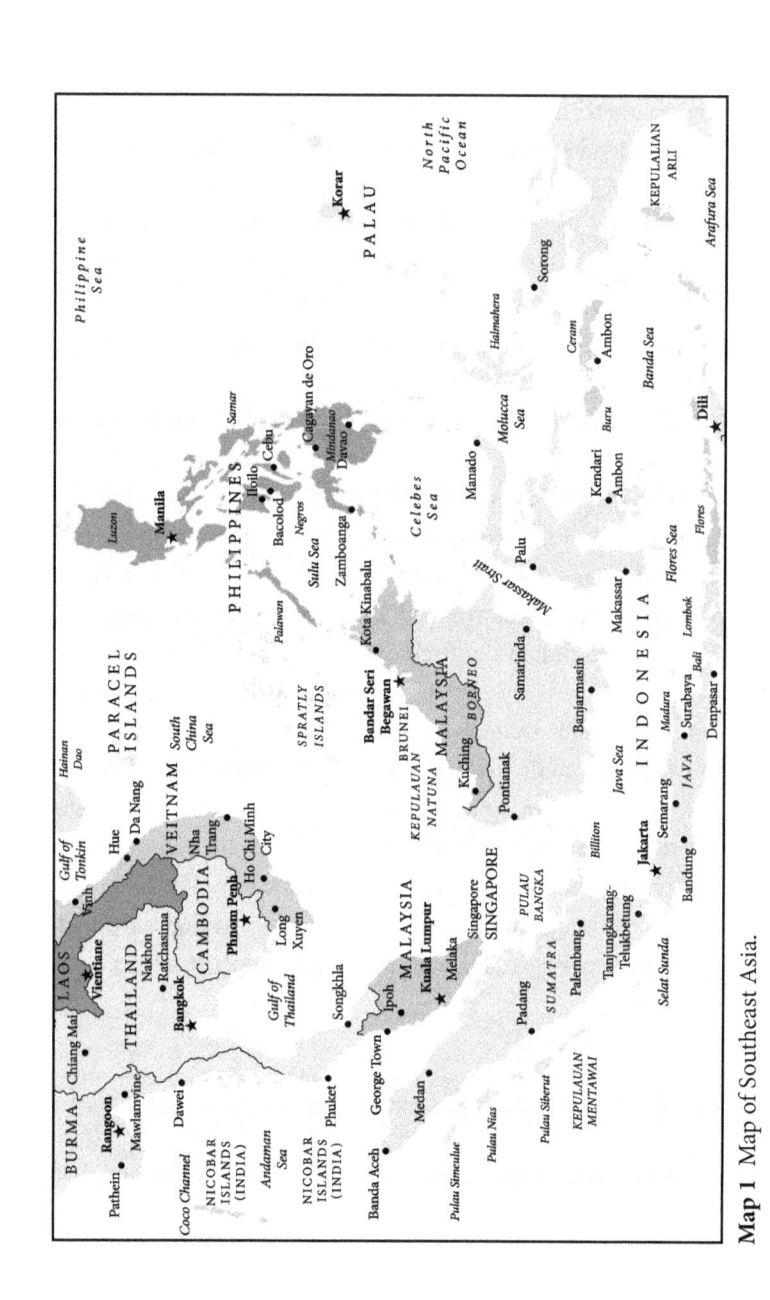

**Map 1** Map of Southeast Asia.

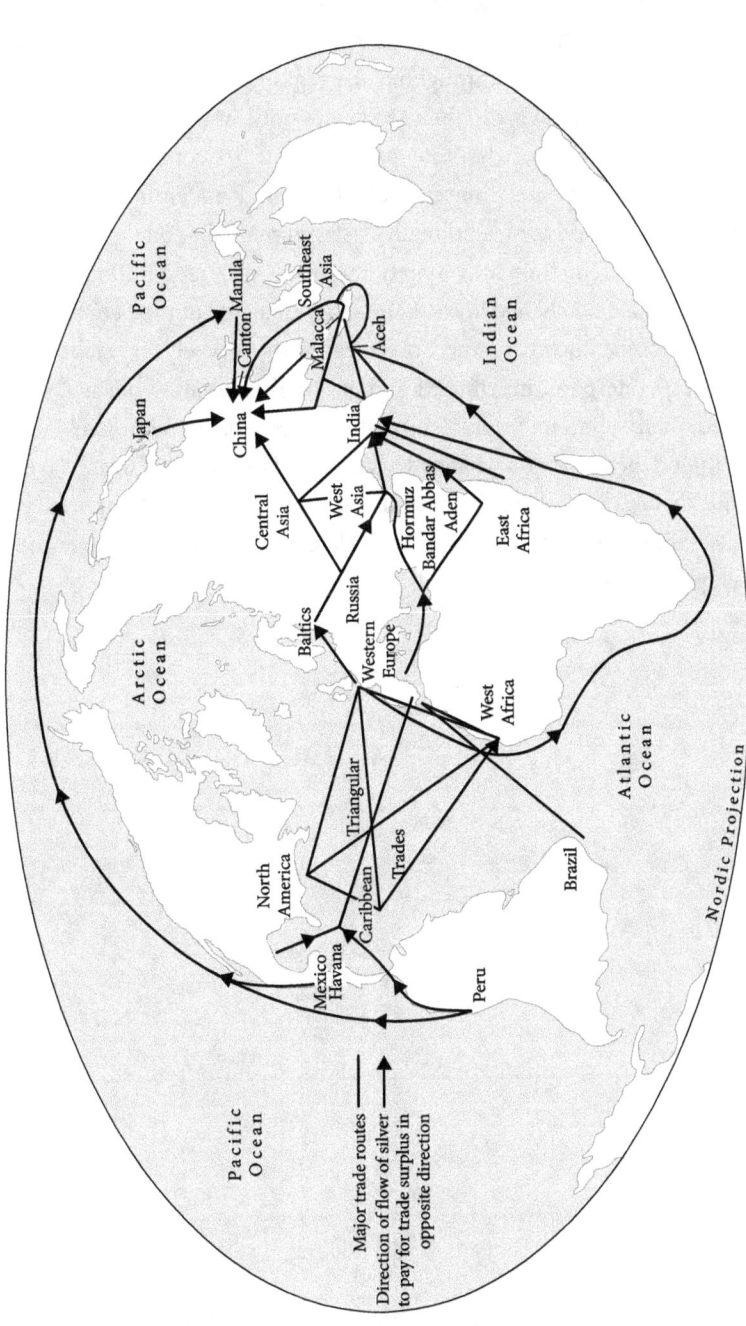

Map 2 Map of Global Trade/Slave Routes.

Before Abolition, most slaves traveled as ubiquitous commodities along established trade routes (as seen in Map 2) and found in most any global market. The underground traffic, or sub-circuits, connected with the main thoroughfares of trade at colonial centers throughout the region.[80] Most local leaders had no interest in abolishing slavery in their territories until, at the end of the eighteenth century, when a flood of destitute poor—willing to contract themselves for minimal wages—increased amount of "free" and indentured laborers and decreased the demand for traditionally enslaved men. Of course, it is important to note that this reduction was merely the result of a redefinition of the term rather than an actual change in social mobility or status of the people working.[81] What will become known as "the Coolie trade," these newly "free laborers" were still the desperate poor, indentured and enslaved to wealthy businessmen who imported their labor to colonial projects as needed. So, although Europeans ceased their dependency on what had historically been referred to as "slave" labor, they quickly began to rely on the steadily increasing supplies of imported coolies, convicts, sailors, soldiers, and debtors, who had become the "new slaves," building their empires around the world.

---

[80] The above is a map of "Major Circum-Global Trade Routes, 1400–1800," taken from the webpage for Reed College's Anthropology 365 course, taught by Professor Charlene Makley, Spring 2012, accessed March 26, 2013, http://academic.reed.edu/anthro/395/schedule.html.
[81] Reid, "The Decline of Slavery in Nineteenth Century Indonesia," p. 68.

2

# Negotiating Abolition in the Indian Ocean World

Although most of Britain's abolitionist fervor was focused on the notorious Atlantic Slave Trade, by 1811 Parliament's Felony Act and the Company's Regulation X had legally abolished slave trading within all of Britain's territories. Developed independently of each other, Parliament's Felony Act, passed in May, focused primarily on curtailing the enslavement of Africans meant for the Atlantic trade but it directly conflicted with existing EIC policy. As a result, by August, the EIC government had enacted Regulation X, which they claimed was more suited to the complexities of eastern slavery.[1] Government officials in London had not considered the vastly different circumstances their new law might encounter in the IOW where slaves had been an entrenched part of society and regional trade networks for millennia and Europeans had only limited control. In fact, EIC officials in India were so concerned about the implications of the government's new law that they chose to minimize its publication—they did not want to create discord and uncertainty among indigenous leaders and elites. But this also meant there was very little uniformity in the understanding or application of Parliament's new legislation in the east. The British intended to overlooked non-European slave networks and it was the inconsistency of enforcement and misunderstandings over the parameters of the ordinances that undermined the enforcement of antislavery legislation and fostered the development of an underground illicit trade that, in the Straits Settlements, primarily consisted of women and girls.

The nature of the EIC's expansion and its role in the formation of Britain's Empire in Asia make it easy to forget that the Company was first and foremost a business venture, and while its objectives were generally in alignment with government, its ultimate goal was to maintain profitable relationships with local

---

[1] Major, *Slavery, Abolitionism and Empire in India*, p. 171.

leaders.² Consequently, local officials cautiously drafted ordinances that upheld the Company's policy not to interfere in matters of "national independence."³ Regulation X interfered too deeply into the personal lives of the wealthy and powerful in Asia and directly conflicted with Company precedent. This was particularly problematic Straits of Malacca, a political and economic choke point between China and Indian Ocean trade, as well as an important pawn in the European imperial chess match playing out in Southeast Asia during this period. In spite of vigorous early antislavery efforts by individual EIC officials to prohibit or curb slavery in the Straits, Europeans were not in charge of slave networks in Southeast Asia and the British had little authority to interfere with the non-European trade.⁴

Most colonial officials understood the expanse of the slave trade in their regions and the suffering of those forced into it; however, the majority serving before the 1780s stood behind a practice of noninterference that officials were sworn to uphold it.⁵ At the same time, it is important to remember that regardless of their intentions, the British had limited power and authority in these regions before the encroaching effects of economic exploitation and "gunboat diplomacy." In spite of the enormous gains from their victories in the Opium Wars during the 1840s and 1850s, the British were not able to fully enforce their political or economic policies on indigenous polities in either Africa or Asia until the latter half of the nineteenth century, when a "technology gap" inhibited native populations' abilities to resist.⁶ Although advancements in weapons technology began in the 1840s, it was not until the 1870 that the British had the

---

2   These works all discuss the complex relationship between the EIC and the British government throughout the Company's tenure as both a global trading giant and representative of Britain's crown: Tirthankar Roy, *The East India Company: The World's Most Powerful Corporation* (New York: Penguin Books India, 2012), pp. 1–4; Anthony Webster, *The Twilight of the East India Company: The Evolution of Anglo-Asian Commerce and Politics, 1790–1860* (Rochester: Boydell Press, 2009); Huw Bowen, Margarette Lincoln, and Nigel Rigby, *The Worlds of the East India Company* (Rochester, NY: D.S. Brewer Lincoln, 2002), pp. 19–32, 169–81, 201–21; Hoh-cheung Mui, *The Management of Monopoly: A Study of the English East India Company's Conduct of Its Tea Trade, 1784–1833* (Vancouver: University of British Columbia Press, 1984), pp. 23–43; C. H. Philips, *The East India Company, 1784–1834* (Manchester: Manchester University Press, 1961), pp. 1–60; Marguerite Wilbur, *The East India Company and the British Empire in the Far East* (New York: R.R. Smith, 1945), pp. 118–68.
3   Evans, *Slave Trade (East India) Slavery in Ceylon*, p. 4; a number of the early references to the delicacy of antislavery policy can be found in the first hundred pages of the 1838 report: pp. 20, 28, 32, 37, 56; the latter half of the report examines individual cases more deeply and these issues are still present; see pp. 240, 407–9.
4   The following offers an interesting discussion about the process the Company took to develop Regulation X: Nancy Gardner Cassels, *Social Legislation of the East India Company: Public Justice versus Public Instruction* (New Delhi: Sage Publications India, 2010), pp. 174–80.
5   Evans, *Slave Trade (East India) Slavery in Ceylon*, p. 56.
6   Daniel R. Headrick, *Power over Peoples: Technology, Environments, and Western Imperialism, 1400 to the Present* (Princeton: Princeton University Press, 2010), pp. 257–91; Daniel R. Headrick, *Tools of Empire: Technology and European Imperialism in the Nineteenth Century* (Oxford: Oxford University Press, 1981), pp. 83–95.

technical superiority to force indigenous rulers to relinquish their sovereignty over previously unattainable territory.[7] Indeed, one of the biggest impediments to antislavery efforts in the East Indies after the implementation of Regulation X was official's inconsistent ability to enforce ordinances, which resulted in an uncoordinated response from local authorities who had undefined political and legal authority. The EIC's erratic and unpredictable enforcement of policy did not have a chance at stopping entrenched indigenous slaving networks, now working underground and enjoying unprecedented profits.

So, although some EIC officials may have lamented the existence of indigenous slave systems—many actively worked to abolish them—however in the east most believed acceptance of local slave trades was a tolerable sacrifice for peace, profits, and colonial stability. At the same time, regardless of their feelings, in most cases the Company had neither the political will nor the practical authority to do much to stop it until after the 1840s. In 1832, after receiving a request from local authorities for assistance with the enforcement of antislavery ordinances, secretary to the Governor W. H. MacNaughton wrote to Governor Lockett in the Rajpoontana district to explain that their hands were tied. The governor-general lamented that while he understood the slave traffic in India was disassociated from "all the cruel features, which characterized the African slave trade," he believed that there were certainly reasons that would "justify every practical effort" made for its suppression.[8] He knew there was a substantial trade in women and girls and sincerely regretted the existence of slavery within his jurisdiction. However, he explained he was bound by treaty "to refrain from interfering with the internal economy of our allies" and that he could not authorize any action that would appear as an official order on their part.[9] Regardless of whether the governor-general agreed with the abolition of slavery or not, there was little he could do without violating Company policy or international treaty. Antislavery

---

[7] This is a common term used in both military and imperial history referring to generally unequal diplomatic negotiations enforced by superior weapons technology, Trevor R. Getz and Heather Streets-Salter, *Modern Imperialism and Colonialism: A Global Perspective* (Boston: Prentice Hall, 2011), pp. 161-5. Headrick's *Power over Peoples* explains that a "technology gap" inhibited native populations' abilities to resist, and during this brief period, western European powers—primarily Britain—were eventually able to assume sovereignty over most of the known world (p. 291). For Headrick, the West's "increased power over nature through advancements in technology" and "access to the products of modern industrial technology" gave them an advantage and "determined the relations" between colonized and colonizer (p. 291). In fact, Kenneth Pomeranz's *The Great Divergence: China, Europe, and the Making of the Modern World Economy* (Princeton: Princeton University Press, 2000) argued that it was European countries' early industrialization—steamships, telegraphs, and modern weaponry—that gave them an advantage in negotiations with nonindustrial nations in the first place (p. 10).

[8] Evans, *Slave Trade (East India) Slavery in Ceylon*, p. 56.

[9] Ibid.

ordinances were in direct opposition to established EIC policy and it was difficult, and would take some time, to change the culture of the community.

The correspondence between MacNaughton and Lockett highlights the quandary that frequently presented itself to EIC officers throughout their eastern settlements during this liminal period. In the first decades of abolition, most officials in the British East Indies saw slavery as a domestic issue in which they had been sworn by Company oath and bound by political treaty not to intervene. Most focused their efforts on inhibiting European slavery where they could find it. Within this context, the enforcement of such an invasive piece of legislation depended on the assistance and support from indigenous rulers and had to take into consideration the Company's specific economic or political circumstances.[10] To maintain the flow of trade, EIC officials strategically enforced these new, often controversial ordinances and, when it was prudent or convenient, overlooked the transgressions they encountered. Prohibiting slavery in the east interfered with historic flows of labor throughout the Indian and Pacific Ocean worlds and subsequently initiated a redistribution of power marked by a new relationship between European capitalists and Asian "free laborers." Inciting local leaders and offending the population at large would have been counterproductive to EIC objectives.

Correspondence about an encounter in 1831 with the "Arab Chief of Wadi" in northern Africa illustrates how British officials negotiated around slave laws to maintain economic and political peace.[11] British commanders on routine patrol in the Red Sea detained several ships and emancipated "upwards of 70 slaves" belonging to the Chief of Wadi in northern Africa. While it was highly unlikely that this chief was truly unaware of the prohibitions against slave-trading, Officials in London decided that in order to appease his vehement protests "some degree of forbearance and consideration should be drawn," particularly since he was already "made to forfeit the fruits of proceedings which he did not know to be a crime." In fact, Britain's Political Department in London elected to compensate the chief for his lost property and ordered the return of his vessels. Nonetheless, because the EIC government was concerned that their generosity might set a precedent, they encouraged local officials to give a "strong and explicit warning throughout the eastern seas, that no indulgence is to be expected by slave traders in the future."[12] It is difficult not to see the admonition to future traffickers as an idle threat. In these indirectly governed territories, local EIC

---

[10] The years of informal imperialism were a period where western powers utilized "coercion, market dominance, and preferential concessions" to garner influence and power "over other states without resorting to formal conquest." Getz and Streets-Salter, *Modern Imperialism and Colonialism*, p. 163.
[11] Evans, *Slave Trade (East India) Slavery in Ceylon*, p. 19.
[12] Ibid., p. 18.

residents and officials would have understood implicitly that to proceed without any "indulgence" of local groups who, at that time, had far more influence and power, would have been logistically and politically impossible.

## The Proposal for Gradual Abolition

In between lengthy historical summaries and a voluminous appendix containing supporting documentation, the EIC's 1841 submission to the House of Commons on the subject of slavery in the East Indies included a 134-page "Observation" from the Indian Law Commissioners about what they believed, "generally, to be the distinguishing features of slavery in this country and point out the evils that belong to it."[13] The commission, established in 1833, was the highest colonial governing body in the East Indies and responsible for overseeing the legal interests of the Company in India and its subordinate colonies, which included the Straits Settlements.[14] So, while the report focused on cases in India, the perceptions represented in this account are indicative of EIC authorities all over their eastern outposts, and these recommendations reflect the attitudes and actions of Company officials throughout the IOW during this period. This report from January 15, 1841—the final of three very large volumes—offers an important lens through which to view EIC and India's government officials' perceptions about slavery in their territories; it contains both a synopsis of previous antislavery reports submitted by local authorities, and a list of "recommendations" for the way the council believed these matters should be handled from that point forward.[15]

It is significant that the commissioners themselves could not agree about their "sentiments" on the subject.[16] The "Minority" consisted of two commissioners assigned the initial chore of writing the brief. However, the "Majority" felt compelled to include an accounting of the division among the Commission Report.[17] Rather than take the time to redraft, and concerned that they had "spent so much time

---

[13] Hobhouse, *Returns*, p. 188. The first commission was established in 1834 under the Charter Act of 1833 when Lord Macaulay recommended codification of Criminal Procedure and the Penal Code. Subsequent Law Commissions were constituted in 1853, 1861 and 1879 and, over fifty years, helped to structure modern Indian Statutes. Naturally, much of the legislations was patterned after English Laws but adapted to Indian conditions. Found on "Early Beginnings," Government of India Law Commission of India: Ministry of Law and Justice, accessed May 15, 2013, http://lawcommissionofindia.nic.in.

[14] George Roukis, "The British East India Company 1600–1858: A Model of Transition Management for the Modern Global Corporation," *Journal of Management Development* 23, no. 10 (December 2004): pp. 938–48, 943.

[15] Hobhouse, *Returns*, pp. 215–22.

[16] Ibid., p. 188.

[17] Ibid., pp. 217, 222.

in the vein endeavor to reconcile their differences," the Majority decided to add an addendum to the original report to avoid any further delay. The variances in their opinions highlight important differences in contemporary perceptions and understandings about slavery and influenced the recommendations each side put forth to suppress it. Ultimately, the entire commission believed that slavery was an important part of intermingled social, economic, and political structures and they all advised against an "abrupt abolition."[18] All of the commissioners agreed that slavery in the east was a different institution than in the west and that abolition, if necessary at all, should only come "gradually."

Most concurred with the Minority's assertions about eastern slavery's fundamental differences from its counterpart in the Caribbean and Americas. The commissioner's insisted that slavery in the east "should be compared with, and distinguished from, those conditions of the human race which in other countries have been called by the same name."[19] Right away, the commissioners wanted to remove the circumstance in the east from the vitriolic contemporary debate that was transpiring in London. They asserted that the East Indian slave trade was not predicated on the violence and "cruelty" found in western systems, that "pecuniary profit" was the motivation for slavery in the west, that and "hired agents" managed most plantations and mines. In the Americas, both colonizers and laborers were foreigners to the land and motivated only by the lure of fortune. The report explained that "the agent comes from his own country to make a fortune, and return with it; the owner is a country gentlemen living on his estate." As a result, neither of them were invested or interested in the success or well-being of their laborers.

The commissioners report assured its readers that in the east, slavery was not an institution based solely on profit, but that it reflected cultural values and helped to maintain the economic welfare of indigenous societies. According to the report, most slaves worked as domestic servants and were important symbols of status for their masters, and explained that the institution also served as a social safety net for the poor.[20] Underscoring the value Asian slave holders placed on their charges, the commissioners contended that "a large retinue of slaves is part of the pomp with which the great men of the country delight to surround themselves."[21] Selling slaves, they declared, gave wealthy men in the East Indies the "same sort of reluctance which a man has selling his family estate." They recognized the existence

---

[18] Ibid., p. 218.
[19] Ibid., p. 188.
[20] Ibid., p. 189; subsequent secondary literature has confirmed this assessment; see Tagliacozzo, *Secret Trades, Porous Borders*, pp. 31–3; Reid and Brewster, *Slavery, Bondage, and Dependency in Southeast Asia*, pp. 17–26; Warren, *The Sulu Zone*, pp. 164–8.
[21] Hobhouse, *Returns*, p. 189.

of agricultural slavery in places such as Malabar and Tamil but claimed "the object of the proprietor is, in the present state of society, to maintain himself, his family, and his slaves by the produce of the land, not to accumulate a fortune out of the surplus." The commissioners claimed slaves in the East Indies were often treated like family members and that masters rarely emancipated them. Instead, they cared for them until "after their maintenance ha[d] become a burthen [sic]." The officials believed there was no "general desire for freedom" among the slaves and argued that "there is nothing, indeed, in the *status* called slavery in this country more remarkable or more characteristic than the fact that it is so frequently a voluntary origin." These commissioners associated the status of eastern slaves with "the institution of pauperism" in England and explained that a master could not refuse to care for one of his slaves any more than a priest in a local parish could refuse the poor.[22] This dimension of social welfare is what, according to the commissioners, "stamp[ed] a character of mildness upon the institution."

The commissioners went on to explain that being a slave in the east was "not an object of aversion" and that most came primarily from indigenous populations, not taken from their native lands and sold as stock, as the Africans were in the west.[23] People regularly bonded themselves to secure care in their old age, to make enough money to get married and have families themselves, or to marry another slave.[24] There were a number of reasons, as the report explained, that native populations "volunteered" to be enslaved, which entitled them to food, shelter, and medical care, as well as offered a community for many who might otherwise be alone.[25] The report maintained that eastern slaves worked as hard as free persons in the knowledge that their fortune was linked to the success of their masters. Slaves understood that their "master's income" was dependent upon their industry and could "be expected to labour, and it is said really does labour, like one interested in the result."[26] Consequently, the

[22] Ibid., p. 191; this became a common theme within contemporary discourse about slavery.
[23] Ibid., p. 188; "Slave Trade," IOR/F4/1130/30195/20-23.
[24] Hobhouse, *Returns*, p. 191.
[25] This narrative sounds suspiciously like those of American slave owners of the south. As part of the debates, which eventually led to the Compromise of 1850 and established boundaries between slave-holding states and non-slave states, John C. Calhoun claimed that "slaves in the South led a more happy, secure, and carefree life than the free laborers" in the North. An American plantation owner from South Carolina, Calhoun was one of slavery's most vehement supporters in the United States. For more see John Caldwell Calhoun and Robert Mercer Taliaferro Hunter, *Life of John C. Calhoun: Presenting a Condensed History of Political Events from 1811 to 1843. Together with a Selection from His Speeches, Reports, and Other Writings Subsequent to His Election as Vice-President of the United States, Including His Leading Speech on the Late War Delivered in 1811* (New York: Harper & Brothers, 1843), p. 388; Mary Bates, *The Private Life of John C. Calhoun: A Letter Originally Addressed to a Brother at the North, Communicated to the "International Magazine," and Now Reprinted at the Request of Many Personal Friends* (Charleston: Walker, Richards & Co., 1852), p. 18.
[26] Hobhouse, *Returns*, p. 191.

commissioners argued that "the moderate demand" the master "makes upon the sweat of his slave's brow, and the interest which the slave feels in complying with that moderate demand, exclude the necessity of the cart-whip." According to this perspective, people worked—both slaves and debtors—without need of physical violence to remind them "why it is worth their while to work." So when considering the enforcement of antislavery legislation during first decades of the nineteenth century, we can see that not only were the circumstances incredibly precarious, but most officials did not even see slavery in the eastern settlements as an oppressive, violent system in need of eradication. Instead, the commission constructed the institution of slavery in Asia as a backward, but relatively benevolent, "native" habit.

It is noteworthy that the commission also argued that the benign environment, "quasi-voluntary" origins, and lack of violence eliminated the threat of racially driven revolutions as seen in the west.[27] Citing de Tocqueville's *Democracy in America* (1835) as evidence, the commission's original report asserted that the subjugated position of African slaves in the Americas and the Caribbean was motivation for their slave revolts.[28] Commissioners used Tocqueville's assertion that "there is a natural prejudice which induces a man to despise one who has been inferior for a long time even after he has become his equal," to contend there would always be a fundamental, "imaginary" difference between the two, regardless of the "real inequality produced by fortune or law." Since, they argued, "no African has come freely to the shores of the New World; whence it follows that all who are now there are either slaves or freedmen." By this logic, the commissioners claimed that the whites in the west had a natural propensity to "despise" Negroes, which induced a racially motivated spirit of resistance and provided whites with a justification for extreme violence.[29]

This was an important detail for the commission because they argued that the stark, visual element of racial categorization was not present in the eastern system. Conjuring images of rampaging murderous slaves, the Minority wrote, "[N]o Indian

---

[27] Ibid.; here the authors are referring to both the Hatian and the American Revolutions, which shook the imperial structures in the west and initiated the abolition movement in the west; for more see Davis, *The Problem of Slavery in the Age of Revolution, 1770–1823*, pp. 72–83.

[28] Hobhouse, *Returns*, p. 191; John Bigelow and Alexis de Tocqueville, *Democracy in America: Volume I* (New York: D. Appleton, 1899), pp. 381–2; Alexis De Tocqueville, *Democracy in America, Vol. 1*, trans. Henry Reeves (Cambridge: Sever and Francis,1863), pp. 476–7.

[29] Hobhouse, *Returns*, p. 191; this is also a common theory put forward by modern scholars explaining the "Age of Revolutions" in Latin America at the end of the eighteenth century. For a more thorough discussion see David Armitage and Sanjay Subrahmanyam, *The Age of Revolutions in Global Context, c. 1760–1840* (New York: Palgrave Macmillan, 2010); Eric Hobsbawm, *Age of Revolution 1789–1848* (London: Orion, 2010); Charles Breunig, *The Age of Revolution and Reaction, 1789–1850* (New York: W. W. Norton, 1977).

master ever harboured a fear that his slaves would assert their liberty by force."[30] They insisted that if slaves were emancipated, they would not "form a hostile community in the midst of their former masters" and then "contest with them the possession of the country."[31] It is hard to miss this reference to the Haitian revolution, and most would have acutely understood this reference to the Caribbean and Latin American slave revolts at the end of the eighteenth century. By 1823, popular discourse began to focus on an essentialized racial element as the root of slave uprisings.[32] With so much invested in its colonial holdings in the east, the government would have been keenly interested in preventing the possibility of a revolution. According to the commissioners, there was little fear of this chaotic scenario within the East Indies—yet another reason the British need not rush into an immediate abolition.[33]

The initial report also put forth several recommendations about how the Commission believed the Company should address the problem of slavery in the future. Although suggestions were not listed numerically, the first proposal (with which all commissioners agreed) was that Europeans should be prohibited from owning slaves in any British territory.[34] The authors emphasized that India was much different from England and gave a lengthy legal explanation about the authority of colonial officials to prohibit a freeman from owning slaves in the British territories; they believed this would model good practice for indigenous peoples. They claimed, "short of the entire abolition of slavery," no measure could "so strongly mark to its native subjects" Britain's disdain for slavery, "as one which prevents the whole European race from taking any part in it."[35] Whether the Company and its government were motivated by humanitarian ideals brought on by Enlightenment thinkers, or by a desire to curtail the historic profits of their competitors being generated by slave-labor is up for debate. What does seem abundantly clear, however, is that Abolitionism in the IOW was less about preventing "natives" from buying or possessing slaves than it was about preventing other Europeans from profiting from the institution.

Although the next recommendation from the commissioners was that all masters be prohibited from hitting their slaves, the main report was clear to establish the board felt the EIC should not "interfere with the substantive legal

---

[30] Hobhouse, *Returns*, p. 192.
[31] Ibid.
[32] Davis, *The Problem of Slavery in the Age of Revolution*, pp. 11–12.
[33] It is a little ironic that the rebellion in 1857, which included slaves and indentured classes, resulted in the dissolution of the EIC's charter. For more on "The Great Rebellion" see Mrinalini Sinha, *Colonial Masculinity: The "Manly Englishman" and the "Effeminate Bengali" in the Late Nineteenth Century* (Manchester: Manchester University Press, 1995); Richard Collier, *The Great Indian Mutiny: A Dramatic Account of the Sepoy Rebellion*, 1st ed. (New York: Dutton, 1964); Christopher Hibbert, *The Great Mutiny: India, 1857* (New York: Viking Press, 1978); Clare Anderson, *The Indian Uprising of 1857-8: Prisons, Prisoners, and Rebellion* (London: Anthem Press, 2007).
[34] Hobhouse, *Returns*, pp. 194, 221.
[35] Ibid., p. 199.

rights of the master" and that local magistrates should not be placed in the role of arbitrator between master and slave. A master, states the report, would have "in law the same dominion over the slave, and everything that is earned by the slave's labour, as he did before"; the only difference was, "he will not have the power of enforcing that right with his own hand." The commission suggested that local authorities could help a master enforce obedience, but that magistrates should not involve themselves in the litigation of petty disagreements or the punishment of slaves. Local authorities should not return runaway slaves to their owners, because it was unfair and invoked the "efficiency of the state" on the side of the masters. If slaves were neglected or abused, the Minority recommended they be emancipated.

However, as mentioned above, there was considerable disagreement among the commission, and the punishment of slaves was one of the first points the Majority addressed in their addendum. Apparently, they did not believe the government should prohibit a slave owner's right to use reasonable force on their slaves and questioned the Minority's assertion that all slaves really worked so diligently for their masters without coercion.[36] The addendum announced that a Majority of the commission did not believe that slaves would work as hard "without a power of moderate correction for neglect of duty lodged somewhere." They challenged the notion that slaves labored for their master's success and were adamant that "hired labourers, whose bread depended" on their industry, were more valuable.[37] Like those in the original report, the addendum echoed common contemporary categorizations and likened slaves to London paupers who were also under immense public scrutiny at this time. The Majority believed, as did many during this period, removing a master's right to correct his slave created a protected circumstance that would make the "status" of slaves desirable, just as "the status of pauperism had become to the laboring classes in parts of England before the new poor law."[38] Passed in 1834, the New Poor Law stemmed from a

---

[36] Ibid., p. 218.
[37] Ibid., p. 219.
[38] Ibid., p. 218. As a result of industrialization, urbanization and an increase in the landless poor social perceptions of poverty also changed. By the end of the eighteenth century, a person's class and economic status were considered reflections of character and the British government revised sixteenth-century poor laws, created to ease the suffering of the most destitute, to include requirements to serve in workhouses. Moreover, there became an increasing stigma on poverty and, as Seth Koven's work *Slumming: Sexual and Social Politics in Victorian London* (Princeton: Princeton University Press, 2004) shows, by the end of the nineteenth century, some middle- and upper-class Britons went "slumming" to look at the poor as though they were animals in a zoo. For more on the British Poor Laws, see Linda Colley, *Britons: Forging the Nation 1707-1837* (Yale: Yale University Press, 1992), pp. 32-3; Judith Walkowitz, *Prostitution and Victorian Society: Women, Class, and the State* (Cambridge: Cambridge University Press, 1980), pp. 35-9; Anna Clark, *The Struggle for the Breeches: Gender and the Making of the British Working Class* (Berkeley: University of California Press, 1995), pp. 187-95; Stephan Collini, Richard Whatmore, and Brian Young, *History, Religion, and Culture: British Intellectual History, 1750-1950* (Cambridge: Cambridge University Press, 2000), pp. 124-30.

growing sentiment among a segment of wealthy British elite who believed only the harshest conditions would make the indigent exert the effort needed to work and support themselves.[39] This meant significantly harsher, in some instances abusive and neglectful, conditions for the impoverished until protest and social pressure brought about small reforms in the 1840s.[40] According to this argument, slaves, like paupers, would not be motivated to work to exertion unless coerced because they knew that their masters (or parish in London) were obliged to care for them regardless of the work they did.

The Minority's position was that taking away the right of masters to physically punish their slaves was the same as giving "the power of parental correction" to the colonial state, which would have been—to them—counterproductive.[41] The Majority contended that if the state intervened with the master's authority, they risked "making the slave dissatisfied with his condition and disposing him to desert."[42] They thought this measure interfered too deeply in the domestic affairs of the masters and were concerned about the potential strain these cases would create on the courts.[43] Reminding their readers that the violence of western systems was still not found in these situations, and as long as the master did not abuse or neglect his slaves, for which there were already established prohibitions, the Majority believed a master should have the authority to punish his slaves as he saw fit.

Of course, context is everything and we must also consider the fact that this entire discourse was embedded within a battle over sugar profits that began at the end of the eighteenth century. Although Caribbean and Indian sugar producers initially worked together to assuage Britain's increasing habit, by the late eighteenth-century boycotts of West-Indian sugar resulting from abolitionist agitation had already motivated some to offer "free grown" East-Indian sugar as a moral alternative.[44] For example, on December 11, 1822, the United Company of Merchants of England Trading to the East Indies presented the EIC Court of Directors with a collection of papers reporting on "the circumstances attending the culture and manufacture of sugar in the East-Indies."[45] The analysis given,

---

[39] Clark, *The Struggle for the Breeches*, pp. 187–8.
[40] Ibid., pp. 220–1.
[41] Hobhouse, *Returns*, p. 203.
[42] Ibid., p. 218.
[43] Ibid., pp. 218–19.
[44] Drescher, *Abolition*, pp. 268–9; Major, *Slavery, Abolitionism and Empire in India*, pp. 296–8; C. A. Bayly, *The Birth of the Modern World, 1780–1914: Global Connections and Comparisons* (Hoboken: Wiley, 2004), p. 5.
[45] *East-India Sugar: Papers Respecting the Culture and Manufacture of Sugar in British India: Also Notices of the Cultivation of Sugar in Other Parts of Asia: With Miscellaneous Information Respecting Sugar. Printed by Order of the Court of Proprietors of the East-India Company* (London: E. Cox and son, 1822), p. 6.

which began as an effort to combat a proposed increase to duties and taxes on eastern sugar production, that was largely fostered and fueled by western planters, provided a "short comparison on the condition of cultivators" to demonstrate the financial benefits of sugar from Bengal.

Echoing the descriptions of the Commissioners, the papers asserted that "none of the West-India labourers are aborigines" and that "the cultivator is either the immediate proprietor of the ground, or he hires it, as in Europe."[46] "The West-India slave," it explains, "has no interest in the success of his labour," whereas the Indian "husbandman is nourished and cloathed [sic] from his own ground." The "Bengal peasant" they claimed was motivated by the "ordinary wants and desires of mankind." It is impossible not to notice the language used to differentiate these two modes of production: western sugar comes from slaves, while eastern sugar is cultivated by a family of "peasants" working together to ensure their survival. An example of expert mercantilist rebranding, the EIC and eastern growers asserted that, rather than funding the exploitation of slaves, the purchase of East Indian sugar, in essence, perpetuated the growth of civilized commerce.

Of course, there were certainly slaves working on at least some sugar plantations in the East Indies during this period; however, most were indebted or indentured labor and this, according to EIC officials in 1822, was not true slavery.[47] This scenario conveniently overlooked the very real oppression, exploitation, violence experienced by those whose circumstances were different from slaves in title only. This was certainly the case in a place where, as has been previously discussed, the socioeconomic obligation such as debt and indenture were so often at the core of enslavement in Asia. While most were not captured, bound, or shipped across seas to their plantation society, slave owners in Southeast Asia and the IOW did not differentiate between debtor and slave—both were subordinate and compelled to work for their masters. Whether or not a person was owned outright, or if their freedom was contingent upon the repayment of an ever-increasing, unpayable loan did not change their unfree status. Essentially, this transition to a reliance on an indentured workforce gave planters a legal way to use slaves. Nonetheless, as far as the British were concerned, indebted laborers who had an opportunity for freedom, no matter how unlikely, were not truly slaves. This is why a little more than a decade later the commissioner saw slavery in the East Indies as essentially "voluntary."[48] Disassociations and misperceptions such as these help

---

[46] Ibid., p. 53.
[47] Hobhouse, *Returns*, pp. 189–91.
[48] Ibid., p. 189.

us understand the perspective of EIC officials and more thoroughly appreciate the challenges antislavery efforts faced in the Straits Settlements during the first three decades of the nineteenth century.

The next point of contention for the commissioners regarding the nature of slavery and the motivations of slaves came in reference to the Minority's assertions that the absence of a racial element in eastern slavery eliminated the violence and oppression of their situation. In response, the Majority pointed to the rigid class distinctions that prevailed "on the east and west coasts of the southern peninsula of India, and it would seem more or less elsewhere, whole tribes have been regarded as impure outcasts." These groups were equally excluded, enslaved, and subjected, "from remote antiquity to the cultivation of the soil," and these commissioners stressed that "the distinction between these outcaste tribes and the pure classes" were just as pronounced, they asserted, "as any that can arise from color."[49]

This exchange highlights a fundamental difference between eastern and western slavery: in the west, "color" or race eventually became a primary indicator of servitude. While we know Africans were neither the first, nor the only group enslaved in the Americas, as Seymour Drescher explains, by the nineteenth century, western slavery had become synonymous with intensely racialized societies in the Americas and, by the 1830s, violent revolutions.[50] In the east, hereditary notions of class determined servile status. People among the lower classes moved in and out of enslavement, debt, and servitude regularly. While some were considered and treated as chattel slaves—war captives, kidnapped villagers, or sentenced prisoners—there was no physical, visible difference between the master and their slaves. In both systems, gender was the most significant identifier of status and experience, but this was true for both the enslaved and free. All of this is to say that, while western slavers used the rhetoric of racial difference, slave masters in the east used religious caste and hereditary class structures to the same end. Both capitalized on notions of otherness and difference to justify the maintenance of a consistently replenished and permanently subjugated population of laborers.

The Commission's Minority also disagreed that the Company should offer compensation to slave owners for the loss of their slaves due to abuse, neglect, or criminal behavior. Since there was no way to quantify the monetary value of a person, any loss on the part of slave owners was of a personal matter. British

---

[49] Ibid., p. 218.
[50] Seymour Drescher, "The Shocking Birth of British Abolitionism," *Slavery & Abolition* 33, no. 4 (December 2012): pp. 588–9.

law provided for compensation in the event of a legal injury, however, since the loss of a slave due to the master's own erroneous behavior was not the same as a "legal injury," slave owners would generally not be eligible for reparations.[51] Those who could demonstrate a legal injury could present their cases to the courts for reimbursement, otherwise, the loss was their's to bare. In sum, the Minority believed that if a slave owner lost his property rights over a slave (or many) due to abuse, neglect, or any other illegal activity, it should not be the responsibility of the colonial government to reimburse him for it.

Conversely, the Majority asserted that the rights and authority slave owners legally exercised could not "justly or prudently be taken away by law without providing compensation."[52] Not only did restricting a master's right to punish his slave go against existing precedent, but it also complicated local politics. They argued that antislavery measures would cause considerable conflict and asserted that there was "reason to fear that it would occasion among them a degree of discontent," which would "not be prudent to provoke." These officials contended that a compensatory measure might appease a potentially volatile situation and protect political and economic ties, while initiating the transition away from a dependence on slavery. Rather than immediate abolition, the Majority of the EIC Law Commission believed that a slow and gradual approach to abolition was in their best interests.

There was very little disagreement about the remaining three points of the commission's report and the final recommendation speaks volumes to the EIC's attention to the maintenance of power structures. The fourth recommendation forbade a master from selling a slave without his consent and the fifth suggested officials include a ban on the importation of slaves by land as a part of the general prohibition on the trade. The sixth and last recommendation, however, made sure to clarify the hierarchy of patriarchal power by proclaiming that, should a female slave marry the male slave of another master, the rights of the woman's master over her must be transferred to the master of her new husband. If her new husband were a free man, she would belong to him; but, being a slave, all his property belonged to his master, including his wife. Officials were willing to intervene and regulate servile relationships, but were careful to preserve patriarchal hierarchies. The Minority conceded that there were abuses of selling women and children for prostitution, but they reminded their readers that there were already laws in place that prohibited this sort of behavior and claimed they trusted the problem would be resolved by the implementation of registration

---

[51] Hobhouse, *Returns*, p. 203.
[52] Ibid., p. 219.

systems. In the end, they were confident that the above recommendations would establish laws and regulations "under which slavery must fall."

Additionally, the Majority's addendum offered an "alternate proposal" to what was initially put forth in the main report. As mentioned above, while all agreed that Europeans should be prohibited from owning slaves, they disagreed with the recommendations to prohibit masters from hitting their slaves and to deny monetary compensation for the loss of slaves. However, the Majority felt strongly that the government should leave the "lawful *status* of slavery," and the master's right to "punish and restrain" them, "untouched" in the East Indies. From their perspective, provisions for emancipation should only be made for cases of abuse and neglect, and every slave should have the right to "purchase his own freedom, the freedom of his wife, and that of his children" from his master. Without a clear directive from the EIC government, both sides believed there was legal footing for their position. The Company had not been clear about the stance its officials should take toward local slavery and even its highest authority was divided about what course the Empire should take. So, pragmatically, rather than directly interfering with indigenous slave systems and effectively initiating an unenforceable "abrupt abolition," the Majority of the commission proposed to negotiate a compromise, focus on the "foreign trade," and recommended that the government implement policies they believed would initiate the gradual dissolution of the institution.[53]

## Conclusion

When the EIC first started down the road to abolition at the end of the eighteenth century, slavery was a highly profitable, culturally and systemically embedded institution in Southeast Asia and the Indian Ocean World and the Company's government did not agree on how to proceed. Few believed that dealing with slavery was the most important of their tasks and, in most cases, local authorities saw indigenous slave trades as internal systems they need not interfere with; magistrates regularly enforced local laws and assisted masters with the return of their runaway or abducted slaves.[54] Not only do the EIC reports expose the absence of a clearly expressed policy or objective to guide the implementation of

---

[53] Ibid., pp. 203–21.
[54] There were several places throughout the submissions, in which EIC officials both punished slaves and returned runaways to their masters. For examples, see Evans, *Slave Trade (East India) Slavery in Ceylon*, pp. 12–15, 41–7, 243, 257, 262, 371, 302, 347, 352.

antislavery measures in the East Indies, they also make it clear that the Company was not willing to sacrifice its hard-won advantages to enforce an unpopular and undefined antislavery policy.

As we have seen, local officials in all of the EIC's territories adapted policy as they went along, and the report from the Indian Law Commission conveniently summarized the experiences found in the correspondence between resident governors, councils, and local magistrates from across the Indian Ocean. More importantly, the commission's report is glaring evidence that Company officials, even the highest levels of government, did not agree on how to proceed with the implementation of antislavery laws in their eastern settlements. The stark brutality and inhumanity of the Atlantic slave trade made it an easier target for abolitionists, and a convenient distraction for slave owners in the east. Eastern planters and EIC representatives had constructed the image of eastern slavery in opposition to the western image of a degraded society.[55] The commissioners all described slavery in the east as a mild and relatively benevolent institution that the British did not initiate and should not put much effort into prohibiting. As the conflict between Police Superintendent W. T. Lewis and Resident in Council Samuel Garling illustrates in Chapter 6, the complications occurred when one British official became a little too zealous in his efforts to eradicate slavery in Malacca. In that case, not only did the British not want to damage important relationships with powerful people, they also did not want to threaten potential profits or entangle themselves in complicated diplomatic disagreements. At the beginning of the nineteenth century, it was still profit first, civilizing mission second.

The EIC was content to focus on the "foreign," or European, trade that offered them opportunities to affect flows of labor to the colonies of competing empires. They were grateful to the imam of Muscat and the chief of Wadi for their help in preventing European slave trading in their regions and elected to leave local systems relatively intact. As we will see, the same was true in Southeast Asia. Abolitionism was just another point of contention within the imperial contest simultaneously occurring within Africa Asia, and the Americas during this period and, in this instance, Britain used its influence to negotiate antislavery legislation focused on its European foes.

The Law Commission's frank discussion of patriarchal authority within colonial legislation, as well as its analysis of race and class are important to our understanding of slavery in the East Indies because they illustrate the reasons why British antislavery measures generally only succeeded in moving the trade

[55] Major, *Slavery, Abolitionism and Empire in India*, pp. 69–74.

into a black market, and the prejudices that excluded Asian slaves from legislative and academic discourse until the end of the twentieth century. Class and cultural lineage were elemental to servitude in Asia and, in this system, more important than conceptions of race. The commissioners worried that prohibiting a master's right to punish his slaves was tantamount to taking the "power of parental correction" from the slave masters, which was a level of interference the Company had thus far avoided. Not only did this new approach present additional struggles for local officials, it signaled emergence of new directions for imperial policy. To this point, the EIC had not interfered in the sovereignty of local governments, particularly in matters of cultural and social significance. Antislavery policies made local authorities the ultimate patriarch responsible for the welfare and discipline of an enormous slave population that belonged to the same indigenous elite and wealthy merchant families they relied on to maintain prosperous political and trading relationships. They were also incredibly hesitant to meddle in the households of other men; this was a step that would almost assuredly spark hostile incredulity and resistance. Antislavery policies forced officials to engage in and micromanage the domestic affairs of indigenous elites, which had been antithetical to the EIC's stated intentions.[56]

The Law Commission's understanding that class was just as divisive a construct in the east as race was in the west, presents an important opportunity for us to see how contemporary officials conceptualized the connections between race, class, and oppression during this period. The commissioners all equated the condition of the slaves in the east with the pauper classes in Britain and, as David Cannadine's *Ornamentalism* (2001) argues, "there were at least two visions of empire that were essentially (and elaborately) hierarchical: one centered on color, the other on class."[57] But it is clear that these were not separate visions of empire. Britain's worldview was hierarchical to be certain, but the categories of race, class, and gender were inextricably intertwined and played alternatively dominant roles in colonial decision-making. The ideas presented by the commission were the foundational elements to the way EIC officials perceived slavery, contingent upon circumstance, which in turn shaped

---

[56] Pateman, *The Sexual Contract*; according to Pateman, this implicit, sometimes explicit, contract is about women, but between men, and secures the transformation of man's "natural right over women into the security of civil and patriarchal right" (p. 6).

[57] David Cannadine, *Ornamentalism: How the British Saw Their Empire* (London: Penguin Books, 2001), p. 8.

the actions of Company representatives.[58] With the impression that this ancient and expansive trade was somehow benign and devoid of racial oppression, and believing that slaves in the east were—in some ways—an indigenous pauper class, EIC officials did not feel compelled to rescue and emancipate them.

While some officers believed they should do everything in their power to put an end to slavery around the world as soon as possible, all too often they were forced to acquiesce to the fact that the British had very little, or at least greatly circumscribed, power with which to enforce antislavery legislation. There is clear evidence that EIC officials did indeed attempt to implement antislavery measures in the East Indies; in fact, they did so at every *convenient* opportunity. However, in the first half of the nineteenth century, the days just before Britain's ascent to global dominance, EIC officials had to negotiate their policies with local leaders and their priority was profit and imperial expansion, not to interfere with "native" habits. The above examples of the EIC's political and economic negotiations of anti-slavery measures with powerful local elites did not concentrate on South or Southeast Asia specifically, they were chosen to illustrate continuities in perceptions and ideologies found throughout the East Indies. The remaining chapters narrow our focus significantly and look more closely at the details of the Company's efforts in Southeast Asia and more specifically the British Straits Settlements.

---

[58] There is a significant historiography about the importance of race, class, and gender within British perceptions of its Empire. For the most interesting works see Stoler, *Carnal Knowledge and Imperial Power*; Ann Laura Stoler, *Race and the Education of Desire: Foucault's History of Sexuality and the Colonial Order of Things* (Durham: Duke University Press, 1995), pp. 97–136; Ann Laura Stoler, "Making Empire Respectable: The Politics of Race and Sexual Morality in 20th-Century Colonial Cultures," *American Ethnologist* 16, no. 4 (November 1989): pp. 634–60; Nupur Chaudhuri and Margaret Strobel, eds., *Western Women and Imperialism* (Bloomington: Indian University Press, 1992), pp. 1–34; Claire Midgley, ed., *Gender and Imperialism* (Manchester: Manchester University Press, 1998), pp. 1–20; Gelman-Taylor, *The Social World of Batavia*, pp. 78–114; Catherine Hall, *Civilising Subjects: Colony and Metropole in the English Imagination, 1830–1867* (Chicago: University of Chicago Press, 2002), pp. 84–170; Heather Streets, *Martial Races: The Military, Race and Masculinity in British Imperial Culture, 1857–1914* (Manchester: Manchester University Press, 2004); Andaya, *Other Pasts*, pp. 147–230; Shirley Foster, "Colonialism and Gender in the East: Representations of the Harem in the Writings of Women Travellers," *The Yearbook of English Studies* 34 (2004): pp. 6–17; Ghosh, "Gender and Colonialism," pp. 735–55; Philippa Levine, "What's British about Gender and Empire? The Problem of Exceptionalism," *Comparative Studies of South Asia, Africa and the Middle East* 27, no. 2 (2007): pp. 273–82; Philippa Levine, "Orientalist Sociology and the Creation of Colonial Sexualities," *Feminist Review, Reconstructing Femininities: Colonial Intersections of Gender, Race, Religion and Class* 65, no. 1 (2000): pp. 5–21.

3

# Redefining Slavery and Servitude in the Straits

In 1841, a pamphlet published by Thomas Ward and Company, titled *Slavery and the Slave Trade in British India*, exposed the remaining elements of a thriving system of human traffic in the British East Indies in spite of colonial authorities' professed efforts toward its abolition. The pamphlet was the extension of a protracted and controversial public debate over the fate of the institution of slavery in the Empire, parts of which were found in the pages of both the *Morning Chronicle* in London and the *Singapore Chronicle*, which was a popular source of news for Europeans living in these remote outposts. In this case, the ostensibly anonymous author from the Straits, very likely the former editor of the *Malacca Observer*, dismissed as a result of scathing expositions on slavery in the Straits Settlements, claimed he hoped this work "might excite public attention to a subject deeply affecting the national honour, and the best interests of the human race."[1] Among its many accusations of blatant violations of Britain's antislavery laws, the pamphlet utilized official documents and correspondence to reveal frequent instances of EIC officers' tolerance for slave-trading systems, which regularly supplied captured, enslaved, or indentured women to work in British settlements.

For the price of one schilling, London's public read about the relative impotence of British authorities to abolish piracy and underground slave trading, parliamentary testimony acknowledging the persistence of female slaves in British colonies throughout the entire East Indies, and official correspondence offered justification for a loose interpretation and application of imperial antislavery laws in frontier garrison towns that lacked women. Moreover, these scandalous allegations contradicted existing perceptions of a "free" labor force created by EIC officers and local colonial officials who had regularly worked to remove the Straits Settlements from the scrutiny of London's abolitionist

[1] British Foreign and Anti-Slavery society, *Slavery and the Slave Trade in British India: With Notices of the Existence of These Evils in the Islands of Ceylon, Malacca, and Penang* (London: Thomas Ward and Co., 1841), p. iii.

campaign. Governed by the authority granted in their imperial charter, profit-focused EIC administrators were more concerned that a gender imbalance threatened the peace and stability of the colony than with the moral debate over slavery. Not only had the publication demonstrated that the Empire's antislavery measures had been less than successful in its eastern territories, the author had accused colonial officials of being complicit with the exploitation of young and vulnerable women and girls within British territories. Antislavery measures had not disrupted classical systems of slave trading in Southeast Asia during the first decades of the nineteenth century and local ordinances focused on European slaving had inadvertently given a boost to the economies of non European slaving states. With significantly less competition, these groups readily accommodated an escalating demand for women and girls who performed a variety of labors, including that of domestic and sexual servitude, for the swelling populations of laboring men in expanding colonial territories on Britain's eastern frontier.

Although London's public may have been shocked to learn about the traffic and enslavement of women to the British East Indies, it was no surprise to those living half a world away in the colonial ports of the Straits. There, slavery and slave-trading networks existed long before European colonialism, and for decades local residents had consistently debated over what the local government should do about the persistence of the institution. Like those in the West, slave owners in the East Indies regularly expressed their concerns about the ways antislavery legislation imposed upon their autonomy and complained about its diminutive effects on their wealth and property. When abolitionists began calls for the immediate emancipation of all slaves after the Felony Act in 1811, officials throughout the Company's territories began to look in earnest for alternative sources of labor.[2] Conveniently enough, as previously discussed, the EIC government had already begun to make use of the available Chinese labor. In the Straits, the first task for Company officials was to identify not only who the slaves were, but also what purpose they served. This process of quantification and identification was key to the classification of the region's workforce and instrumental to the perseverance of many types of servitude and "slave-like" circumstances within Britain's eastern territories.

Indeed, abolitionism and antislavery rhetoric shaped the development of local labor policies and facilitated the success of black-market trafficking networks

---

[2] William Mathieson, *British Slavery and Its Abolition, 1823–1838* (London: Longmans, Green, and Co., 1926), pp. 183–242; Major, *Slavery, Abolitionism and Empire and India*, pp. 3–26.

within the British Straits Settlements until well into the twentieth century. The following chapter examines the cultural and political stage upon which officials attempted to understand indigenous slave systems, maintain colonial authority, and enforce legislation. At the same time, it exposes the tenuous nature of British authority in the Straits, the public discord over the persistence of slavery within the Settlements, and the inconsistent application of ordinances that created such immense challenges for antislavery efforts throughout Britain's eastern territories during this period.

## Slavery in the Straits

Between the 1770s and 1820s, the British and American public experienced "profound social changes" as a result of rising social and economic classes, which initiated a shift in conceptions of slavery.[3] As David Brion Davis explains, for the west this period was piece of "a larger transformation in attitudes toward labor, property, and individual responsibility" that gave unprecedented value to the concept of personal freedom.[4] Slavery was nothing unusual for Europeans, but there was a dramatic shift in the British public's perceptions about the institution after the 1760s that gave motivation for a change in imperial policy. Some have argued that the blow to British psyche caused by the loss of the American Revolution, combined with massive losses of slaves and capitol in their former colonies, created a moment of national crisis that made abolitionism a rallying cry for British citizens and, consequently, far more appealing than it had been a decade earlier. However, according to Seymour Drescher, abolitionism was less appealing to the British during moments of international or cultural crisis but gained its most poignant "victories" during "moments of relative calm, before

---

[3] Some important works covering slavery in world history are: Blackburn, *Overthrow of Colonial Slavery, 1776–1848*; Davis, *The Problem of Slavery in the Age of Revolution, 1770–1823*; Davis, *Inhuman Bondage*; Drescher, *Abolition*; Drescher, *Econocide*; Engerman, Drescher, and Paquette, *Slavery*; Quirk, *The Anti-Slavery Project*; Turley, *Slavery*; Paul E. Lovejoy, *Transformations in Slavery: A History of Slavery in Africa* (Cambridge: Cambridge University Press, 1983); Paul E. Lovejoy, *The Ideology of Slavery in Africa* (Beverly Hills: Sage Publications, 1981); Manning, *Slavery and African Life*; John Thornton, *Africa and Africans in the Making of the Atlantic World, 1400–1680* (Cambridge: Cambridge University Press, 1992); Philip D. Morgan and Sean Hawkins, *The Black Experience and the Empire* (Oxford: Oxford University Press, 2004); Moses Nwulia, *Britain and Slavery in East Africa*, 1st ed. (Washington: Three Continents Press, 1975); Orlando Patterson, *Slavery and Social Death: A Comparative Study* (Harvard: Harvard University Press, 1982); Davis, *The Problem of Slavery in the Age of Revolution, 1770–1823*, p. 82.

[4] Davis, *The Problem of Slavery in the Age of Revolution, 1770–1823*, p. 82.

or after Britain had successfully weathered severe threats."[5] By the beginning of the nineteenth century, many in Britain and their colonial spaces began to see slavery—particularly like that in the Americas—as antithetical to British identity.[6]

Contributing to that shift was a wave of popular sentiment and print culture between 1765 and 1800, which pushed against the idea that certain people could be "animalized."[7] Stories about the horrific and dehumanizing experiences of slaves in the Americas gained popularity throughout Europe, became the foundation for abolitionist's campaigns, and made Atlantic slavery synonymous with violence, cruelty, and sexual depravity. American slavery became the yardstick by which all other systems of servitude were measured. As we saw in the previous chapter, EIC administrators regularly framed slavery in the east in opposition to the western example and, as we saw in the report from the Indian Law Commission in 1841, insisted eastern systems were more "mild" and "quasi-voluntary."[8] These perceptions both ideologically separated Atlantic from Indian Ocean slavery and shielded slaveholders in Britain's Asian territories from the scrutiny of abolitionists in Europe until well into the 1830s.

As mentioned above, there is a long and complex history of slavery, bondage, debt, and obligation within Southeast Asian culture and politics.[9] Low population densities within the insular states meant that the control of people took precedence over the control of land, and slaves were an illustration of power and authority. They could be either "outsiders" or "insiders"—those brought from other places, or people from within the community.[10] Lucrative profits attracted warring tribes and slave raiders who kidnapped and sold captives from neighboring islands. Some bought children from procurers and those saddled with debt could sell themselves into an indenture system that was, more often than not, essentially slavery.[11] By the end of the eighteenth century, a variety of slave raiding and trading groups operated throughout the archipelago making significant profits transporting indentured laborers, purchased slaves, and other commodities

---

[5] Drescher, "The Shocking Birth of British Abolitionism," p. 588.
[6] Davis, *The Problem of Slavery in the Age of Revolution*, p. 41.
[7] Davis, *Inhuman Bondage*, p. 156.
[8] Hobhouse, *Returns*, p. 189.
[9] Andaya and Andaya, *A History of Malaysia*, pp. 160–3; Reid, "The Decline of Slavery in Nineteenth Century Indonesia," pp. 64–82; Reid and Brewster, eds., *Slavery, Bondage, and Dependency in Southeast Asia*; Reid, *Charting the Shape of Early Modern Southeast Asia*, pp. 181–215; Madhavi Kale, *Fragments of Empire* (Philadelphia: University of Pennsylvania Press, 1998); P. C. Emmer, *The Dutch Slave Trade, 1500–1850* (New York: Berghahn Books, 2006); and Major, *Slavery, Abolitionism and Empire in India*.
[10] Reid and Brewster, *Slavery, Bondage, and Dependency in Southeast Asia*, pp. 2–17; Warren, *The Sulu Zone*, pp. 215–51; Tagliacozzo, *Secret Trades, Porous Borders*, pp. 230–50.
[11] Reid and Brewster, *Slavery, Bondage, and Dependency in Southeast Asia*, pp. 9–10.

from one burgeoning colonial port to the next.[12] As one might imagine, British antislavery ordinances conflicted with long-standing slave-owning traditions of local Arab, Chinese, and indigenous elites. During this pre-gunboat period, the Company's strict prohibitions on interfering too deeply in the lives of the locals was critical to the expansion, maintenance, and preservation of profitable trade relationships in this incredibly cosmopolitan space.

While some indigenous societies distinguished between debtors and captured slaves, most did not, which created significant challenges for anyone trying to quantify or tax this particular commodity. In their quest to understand Asian societies, and clearly identify publicly acceptable forms of bondage, it was European colonial administrations that defined and then emphasized these distinctions.[13] However, for Southeast Asians, a *slave* could have been either someone violently torn from their home and living a life of depraved captivity or a person living under the roof of a kind, compassionate merchant or distant family member, simply working off a personal commitment or financial debt they or their family owed.[14] In the pre-abolition era, indigenous customs of slave raiding combined with cultural systems of bondage and personal indenture helped to provide expanding imperial economies and developing colonies in Southeast Asia with steady supplies of laboring bodies to perform any number of undefined tasks.[15]

Slaves were endemic to Southeast Asian societies and, despite Raffles's optimistic and bold assurances to Kadir that HM Government would soon put an end to the despicable institution of slavery, Britain simply did not have the presence, authority, or political will to eradicate slavery or slave trading in the Straits during the first half of the nineteenth century. Raffles's acquisition of Singapore for the EIC in 1819 initiated the demise of the Malay state, seated Britain's imperial dominance in the Straits, and deposed the Dutch of power in the region.[16] This, however, still did not give them hegemonic control of either local politics or regional commerce. Although the British had effectively stifled Dutch expansionism in Malaya with the Anglo-Dutch Treaty of 1824, the entrenchment of Chinese, Arab, and Indian merchants within the trading

---

[12] Warren, *The Sulu Zone*, p. 208.
[13] Reid, "The Decline of Slavery in Nineteenth Century Indonesia," p. 67.
[14] Reid and Brewster, *Slavery, Bondage, and Dependency in Southeast Asia*, pp. 2–17, 156–60.
[15] Warren, *The Sulu Zone*, pp. 230–51.
[16] The following scholars give a much more detailed account of Singapore's importance to British expansionism in the region: Andaya and Andaya, *A History of Malaysia*, pp. 114–23; Trocki, *Singapore*, pp. 7–33; Trocki, *Prince of Pirates*, pp. 21–95; Reid, *Charting the Shape of Early Modern Southeast Asia*, pp. 34–68; Levine, *Prostitution, Race, and Politics*, pp. 23–7; Tagliacozzo, *Secret Trades, Porous Borders*, pp. 29–69.

emporia meant that there were constant reminders of a long history of cross-cultural exchange that had not included them.[17]

China, according to Singapore Resident Councilor John Crawfurd (1823–6), was "the most extensive, intimate, and probably most ancient, of the foreign commercial relations of Indian islands."[18] In fact we know from Sino-Southeast Asian scholar, Geoff Wade, that the Chinese brought a form of "protocapitalism" to the region almost a half century prior to the Portuguese conquest of Malacca in 1511.[19] The British understood that Chinese networks dominated the South China Seas and these two merchant empires had an uneasy and continually changing relationship over the course of the nineteenth century.[20] Coincidentally, the extraordinary growth of Chinese influence in Southeast Asia roughly coincided with Britain's "imperial meridian," when British imperialists shifted their gaze from lost colonial possessions in the Americas toward more promising profits in the east.[21] This meant that between the 1780s and 1830s, EIC traders were in direct competition with Chinese merchants already thoroughly rooted within Southeast Asian communities via investment and kinship ties. Since at least the eleventh century, large sums of Chinese money had boosted local economies and supported the growth of infrastructure throughout the region.[22] Although not endorsed by the Chinese government, the economic and cultural influences of the *kongsis* were vital to the region's development and a direct threat to the EIC's efforts at colonial expansion.[23] Vilified and labeled "Secret Societies" by the colonial government, *kongsis* controlled a majority of the available labor arriving from China along with a range of goods and products traded throughout the region. At the same time, having established communities along the Straits of Malacca since the tenth century, they held a type of "home field" advantage and were Britain's most significant trade rival. The *kongsis*' primary advantages were their long-standing network connections and access to the large amounts of cheap labor these relationships provided. This was particularly valuable after the implementation

---

[17] Andaya and Andaya, *A History of Malaysia*, pp. 114–35; Trocki, *Prince of Pirates*, pp. 62–7; Abdullah Munshi, *The Hikayat Abdullah*, trans. by A.H. Hill (London: Oxford University Press, 1970), pp. 150–1; Lockard, *Southeast Asia in World History*, pp. 44–65; Andaya and Andaya, *A History of Malaysia*, pp. 37–57; Trocki, *Singapore*, pp. 15–33.

[18] John Crawfurd, *History of the Indian Archipelago: Containing an Account of the Manners, Arts, Languages, Religions, Institutions, and Commerce of Its Inhabitants Volume I* (London: A. Constable and Co., 1820), p. 155; Andaya and Andaya, *A History of Malaysia*, pp. 122–4.

[19] Wade, "An Early Age of Commerce in Southeast Asia, 900–1300 CE," pp. 221–65.

[20] Ulrike Hillemann, *Asian Empire and British Knowledge: China and the Networks of British Imperial Expansion* (New York: Palgrave Macmillan, 2009); Nicholas Tarling, *British Policy in the Malay Peninsula and Archipelago, 1824–1871* (Oxford: Oxford University Press, 1957); Wilfred Blythe and Royal Institute of International Affairs, *The Impact of Chinese Secret Societies in Malaya: A Historical Study* (London: Oxford University Press, 1969).

[21] Reid, *Charting the Shape of Early Modern Southeast Asia*, pp. 240–5.

[22] Wade, "An Early Age of Commerce in Southeast Asia," pp. 229–31.

[23] Ibid., p. 243; Trocki, *Prince of Pirates*, pp. 3–4, 148–52.

of antislavery ordinances. When colonial governments could no longer import slaves to build their infrastructure, *kongsis* made sure there were plenty of "free" and indentured Chinese available for hire, while Company officials were limited to imported Indian "coolies" and convicts. We also know from Allen's research describing the Company's affinity for Chinese workers that the EIC was eager to negotiate.[24] Although the British regularly looked for ways to check Chinese power and expansion in the region, local entrepreneurs and colonial officials were not keen on creating tensions that might disrupt their trade and tax income. So a pragmatic need for labor, lack of procedural or economic structures to support the enforcement of legislation, and a necessity to accommodate existing wealthy and powerful slave owners were all key factors here, as they were elsewhere, behind local agents' measured application of antislavery ordinances.

Still, even if every British subject in Malaysia was fervently opposed to slavery and dedicated to its eradication from the globe, which we know was certainly not the case, Company officials were often more interested in the establishment, growth, and financial success of their factories (trading ports) rather than the enforcement of complicated and often unpopular legislation. Until their military expansion in the 1830s to secure China's opium markets, and the industrial weapons revolution in the 1860s, the British were not in a position to effectively enforce antislavery measures in the Straits.[25] Colonial authorities were often little more than a nuisance to Southeast Asian slave traders and, as we will see below, succeeded only in rebranding what was clearly the same product. Nevertheless, Britain's implementation of antislavery ordinances in the early nineteenth century marked the beginning of efforts to prohibit slavery and slave trading in the Straits, which by this period primarily consisted of women and children (girls and boys) for the purpose of domestic and sexual servitude—including prostitution—that has persisted in various forms into the twenty-first century.

## Redefining Slavery in Southeast Asia

As part of a larger imperial project of knowledge gathering, which facilitated British expansion and colonial rule around the world, several serving or retired

---

[24] Clare Anderson, "Convicts and Coolies: Rethinking Indentured Labour in the Nineteenth Century," *Slavery and Abolition* 30, no. 1 (March 2009): pp. 94–7; Ashutosh Kumar, *Coolies of the Empire; Indentured Indians in the Sugar Colonies, 1830–1920* (Cambridge: Cambridge University Press, 2017), 155–6.

[25] Andaya and Andaya, *A History of Malaysia*, pp. 116–23; Trocki, *Prince of Pirates*, pp. 56–97; Warren, *The Sulu Zone*, pp. 149–81; Carl Trocki, *Opium, Empire, and the Global Political Economy: A Study of the Asian Opium Trade, 1750–1950* (London: Routledge, 1999), pp. 85–96.

EIC representatives published histories about the indigenous societies they observed during their appointments.[26] By the 1820s, there were a variety of publications written by former Company officers that introduced the exotic East Indies to English readers. Former residents like William Marsden at Fort Marlborough (Bencoolen), Stamford Raffles in Java and Singapore, and John Crawfurd in Java, Singapore, Siam (Thailand) and Burma were just a few of those who offered thoroughly detailed studies about the commerce, culture, and societies of indigenous and foreign communities in Southeast Asia and the IOW.[27] In addition to highlighting fundamental differences in colonial officers' perceptions about indigenous societies, as well as conflicting opinions about colonial expansion, these works created detailed taxonomies for their eastern territories that identified, quantified, and classified everything they saw—including the people.

Scottish physician, diplomat, and orientalist historian John Crawfurd began his tenure at the EIC as a doctor and, in 1811, was promoted to Resident in Council at Java, and as his biographer, Gareth Knapman has demonstrated, his experienced research, ideological structures, and personal perceptions shaped both EIC strategy and British foreign policy in Southeast Asia until the 1850s.[28] His 1820 publication, *History of the Indian Archipelago*, offered three volumes of descriptions and analysis that included "maps and engravings" about the

---

[26] For more on the imperial project of information accumulation and its impact see Edward Said, *Culture and Imperialism* (New York: Random House, 1993), 3–43; Stoler, *Carnal Knowledge*, 22–41; Frederick Cooper and Ann Laura Stoler, *Tensions of Empire* (Berkeley: University of California Press, 1993), 7–18; Bernard S. Cohn, *Colonialism and Its Forms of Knowledge: The British in India* (Princeton, NJ: Princeton University Press, 1996); Jennifer Morgan, "Male Travelers, Female Bodies, and the Gendering of Racial Ideology, 1500–1770," in *Bodies in Contact: Rethinking Colonial Encounters in World History*, ed. Tony Ballantyne and Antoinette Burton (Durham: Duke University Press, 2005), pp. 57–60. However, all of these scholars were influenced by the theoretical contributions made by Michael Foucault's *The Archaeology of Knowledge* (New York: Tavistock Publications, 1972). Eric Hobsbawn is credited with defining the "long nineteenth century" as the period between 1789 and 1914 in his trilogy, *The Age of Revolution 1789–1848* (Mentor Book, 1962); *Age of Capital 1848–1875* (New York: Pantheon Books, 1979); *Age of Empire 1875–1914* (New York: Pantheon Books, 1987).

[27] William Marsden, *The History of Sumatra Containing an Account of the Government Laws, Customs, and Manners, of the Native Inhabitants with a Description of the Natural Productions, a Relation of the Ancient Political State of That Island* (London, UK: Thomas Payne & Son, 1784); Stamford Raffles, *The History of Java: In Two Volumes* (London: Black, Parbury, and Allen and John Murray, 1817); Crawfurd, *History of the Indian Archipelago, Vol. I & Vol. II*; Anderson, *Mission to the East Coast of Sumatra: in M.DCCC.XXIII, under the Direction of the Government of Prince of Wales Island: Including Historical and Descriptive Sketches of the Country, an Account of the Commerce, Population, and Customs of the Inhabitants, and a Visit to the Batta Cannibal States in the Interior*; George Windsor Earl, *The Eastern Seas: Or, Voyages and Adventures in the Indian Archipelago, in 1832-33-34, Comprising a Tour of the Island of Java—Visits to Borneo, the Malay Peninsula, Siam ...* (London: W. H. Allen, 1837).

[28] Gareth Knapman, *Race and British Colonialism in Southeast Asia, 1770-1870: John Crawfurd and the Politics of Equality* (New York: Routledge, 2017), pp. 7, 35.

"Mariners, Arts, Languages, Religions, institutions and Commerce" in what is now insular Southeast Asia.[29] Unlike his contemporaries focusing on a specific place like Java or Sumatra, Crawfurd's study encapsulated the entire archipelago and drew upon his linguistic and cultural knowledge developed over nine years of EIC service throughout Southeast Asia. It is important to note that the taxonomies these officials created should be read through a critical lens—they were foreigners, there "for commercial purposes," and interpreted what they saw from a turn-of-the-century white male European perspective.[30] The EIC was not in the habit of hiring either women or native men into the Company's upper ranks. Nonetheless, studies like Crawfurd's and Raffels's volumes offer readers a glimpse into the everyday lives of people from places most Europeans considered exotic and mysterious lands. More to our point, their works provide a clearer understanding of the prevailing perceptions and attitudes of EIC officials working closest with native populations during this period.

Although there are descriptions of specific behaviors or expectations for slaves from a variety of societies throughout the region in all three volumes, Crawfurd's third book offers more thorough definitions for general categories of the enslaved and more clearly explains the role of the institution within native society. There, he distinguished the cultures within the "Indian Archipelago" from India and asserted that "there exists no factitious and hereditary distribution of the people in to various employments—no institution of casts."[31] There was, he claimed, a "natural order" that existed among these societies within which there were distinct categories: "the Royal Family—the nobles—the priests—the cultivators, or freemen—debtors—slaves."[32] According to Crawfurd, Southeast Asian slaves were primarily *"prisoners of war; debtors* who cannot redeem themselves; *criminals,* condemned to slavery by sentence of courts or law, and *persons kidnapped."*[33] The existing undefined and transitory nature of slavery and servitude in Southeast Asia made it important for these commercially minded Britons to identify who the available laboring bodies were and how they could recruit them. So, as previously discussed, while most indigenous cultures did not designate between types of servitude it was important for the British colonial administrators trying to make sense of their new territory to categorize and define them—particularly when their objective was ostensibly to make free laborers of them.

---

[29] Crawfurd, *History of the Indian Archipelago, Volumes I–III.*
[30] Crawfurd, *History of the Indian Archipelago, Vol. I,* p. vi.
[31] Crawfurd, *History of the Indian Archipelago, Vol. III,* p. iii.
[32] Ibid., p. 29.
[33] Ibid., p. 40.

By the 1790s abolitionist's public criticism of the Atlantic trade and moral outrage over the abuse of Africans in the West Indies had grown to a fever pitch and had begun to motivate the EIC Board of Directors and those in the India Office to look for ways to differentiate eastern slaves from the "oppressive and inhumane" systems of plantation slavery in the west.[34] As we have seen, regardless of the real violence, abhorrent living conditions, and regional displacement persistent within the Asian systems, colonial officials in London's India Office and Bengal branded slavery in the East Indies as Andrea Major describes "connected to status, 'unproductive' domestic labor and agricultural subsistence, rather than with capitalist production."[35] By the 1820s, EIC officers and colonial officials in India had successfully reconstructed the image of indigenous slavery as "mild" or "benign."[36] Slave owners and eastern sugar planters worked diligently to convince both the government in London and the British public that slavery in the east bore no resemblance to the horrors in the Americas.

More importantly, there was very little plantation slavery in Southeast Asia and direct comparisons were difficult to make. While slaves were a part of every industry, they were predominantly reported, as Reid explains, in "domestic functions, construction and manual labor, and as traders in the market."[37] Their experiences appeared to be nothing like the Africans taken to the west, and many worked to maintain the conceptual separation between eastern societies with slaves and western slave societies. For instance, Crawfurd's study spent considerable time detailing the situation and circumstance of slaves in Southeast Asia and tells us that slavery was a kind of "personal luxury" for wealthy islanders.[38] He claimed that slaves were more for "pomp and display" than for financial gain and that the complete control a master maintained over the "life and fortune" of their slaves gratified the master's "vanity" and induced "supple and flexible manners" that could not be attained by a hired servant. Ironically, in spite of his description of the constant threat of mortal danger, Crawfurd's 1820 publication assured his readers that slaves in the Indian archipelago were treated with gentle "kindness and tenderness" and that they were "considered rather in the light of a child, or favoured domestic, than even a dependent."[39] Of course, such

[34] Ibid., *Vol. III*, p. 41; Major suggests that the case of an escaped slave named James Somerset, brought before a British court in 1771, initiated the abolitionist movement in Britain.
[35] Major, *Slavery, Abolitionism and Empire in India*, p. 13, 149.
[36] Quirk, *The Anti-Slavery Project*, pp. 5–12; Major, *Slavery, Abolitionism and Empire in India*, pp. 131–3.
[37] Reid and Brewster, *Slavery, Bondage, and Dependency in Southeast Asia*, p. 171.
[38] Crawfurd, *History of the Indian Archipelago, Vol. III*, pp. 26–42.
[39] Ibid., p. 42.

descriptions disregarded the violence, suffering, and degradation we know many experienced throughout their lives.

## A Liminal Phase

A key element in this cataloguing process was the implementation of a classification system in the form of slave registries that simultaneously rigidified what was previously a more fluid social structure, and changed the nature of servitude in the region. At first, slave registries in places such as Penang and Malacca made strict distinctions between slaves and *slave-debtors* (those bonded as a result of debt). However, it did not take long for them to recognize abuses and in 1823, Raffles passed new legislation in Singapore that attempted to shield rising populations of debtors from exploitation. Still, progressive laws focused on debtors and excluded registered slaves from any of the same legal protections. These provisions may have made it a felony to import new slaves into the colonies, and officials established guidelines to regulate debtor contracts, but registered slaves still had no rights or protections and were still considered legal property in the eyes of the state. This meant that the first phase of the Anti-Slavery Project in the Straits Settlements was left to the personal judgment of local officials.

The king of Queda ceded Prince of Wales Island (Penang) to the EIC in 1786 and the Company began importing slaves the following year.[40] However, as previously mentioned, officers in the Straits like William Farquhar (resident at Malacca and first superintendent of Singapore) and Superintendent Francis Light in Penang had proactively implemented antislavery legislation in the early stages of colonial development.[41] Light made slave trading illegal in Penang in 1795 and, responding the passage of Regulation X, Farquhar made it a felony in Malacca after 1813, at which time laws forbade "the importation of slaves as presents from chiefs of native states."[42] In 1818, Farquhar began a registry of slaves with the intention of facilitating the eventual eradication, or "gradual abolition," of slavery in Prince of Wales Island and Malacca. By 1820, both Penang and Malacca had implemented slave registries, emancipated all children born of slaves after 1819, and begun imposing regulations on slave-debtor contracts.[43]

---

[40] *Slavery in India*, p. 421.
[41] Trocki, *Prince of Pirates*, pp. 45–6; for relationship between Raffles and Farquhar, see Note 5.
[42] Hobhouse, *Returns: Slavery (East Indies)*, p. 255.
[43] In their report to the House of Commons, the EIC included copies of slavery registrations, birth and death registries, and the designation and definition of labor; Evans, *Slave Trade (East India) Slavery in Ceylon*, pp. 233–306.

Singapore, established and settled well after the passage of Regulation X, had far more latitude with their antislavery ordinances and, according to the 1841 EIC report to the HoC, "no slaves could be introduced there legally."[44] Nonetheless, by 1823 the continued importation of slaves and exploitation of debt-slaves were bad enough that Raffles included Regulation V, "A regulation for the prevention of the slave trade at Singapore," as part of that settlement's foundational legal code.[45] Regularly known as "Raffles Regulations," these ordinances formed the core of Singapore's judicial structure until it was incorporated with Penang and Malacca into the Straits Settlements in 1826. In these six codes, Raffles clearly saw slavery, along with the regulation of ports; establishment of local magistrates, land registries, and police; and the prohibition of gambling houses and "Cockpits," among the principle institutions in need of regulation. In the introductory paragraph for Regulation V, Raffles explains that despite the fact that slavery had been illegal in Singapore—for everyone—"since the establishment of British authority," individuals, either slaves or slave-debtors had been imported into the settlement and "sold for a price."

According to the law, which repeatedly asserts that it applies to *all* permanent residents of Singapore (those who held a continuous residence for twelve months or more), the condition of slavery, "under any denomination," was not recognized in the settlement and that anyone who may have been "imported, transferred, or sold as slaves or slave debtors, since the 26th day of February 1819, [was] entitled to their freedom." Moreover, no individual with "fixed residence under the protection of the British authorities at Singapore, can *hereafter* be considered, or treated as a slave, under any denomination, condition, color, or pretense whatever."[46] EIC records indicate that Raffles and Farquhar established Singapore after the passage of Regulation X in 1811 and, therefore, allegedly set the foundations for a slave-free settlement.[47] Cleary, this was not the case. While some insisted that the system of debt-slavery had not "grown up" in Singapore and generally prevailed in Penang and Malacca, their suppositions could not be more wrong. Singapore had indeed developed long after antislavery laws, and debt-slavery had not "grown up" in Singapore, but both institution nonetheless thrived. Singapore had come of age in a rapidly changing environment in which debtors became a cheap and viable option to slavery and offered the appearance of free labor. The new colony's free trade policies quickly redirected maritime

---

[44] Hobhouse, *Returns: Slavery (East Indies)*, p. 112.
[45] Stamford Raffles, *Singapore Local Laws and Institutions, 1823* (London: Cox and Baylis, 1824), p. 12.
[46] Ibid.
[47] Hobhouse, *Returns: Slavery (East Indies)*, p. 112.

traffic within the Straits, which fueled demands for workers since slavery was illegal, debt-bondage became a convenient alternative for those importing labor.

Governor Raffles attempted to regulate the "bond-debtors" as the only option to hired labor in the colony.[48] Raffles insisted that all debtor agreements must be registered with the local magistrate, that the sum charged for "passage money" not be more than $20, that terms lasted for no more than two years, and that "no creditor shall transfer the services of a party to another."[49] By forcing the registration of debtor contracts, and limiting the amount and duration of the obligation, Raffles hoped to prevent the abuses that most commonly lead to perpetual enslavement. Nevertheless, while Raffles's rules set parameters for slave-debtors in Singapore, and the EIC government had "delegalized" the trade in slaves within their territories, there were still those who were already bound as slaves to settlers—European, indigenous, and Chinese—living in the colonies who, after the passage of antislavery laws, remained slaves. Until 1841, British authorities in the Straits Settlements regularly returned runaways to their owners in order to honor existing treaties and protect the property rights of local slaveholders.[50]

While similarities in governance and ideology between India and Southeast Asia regarding slavery and abolitionism existed, and residents and officials may have taken cues from the British in India, there were still real differences in regional dynamics, politics, and economics between the two that made the British Straits Settlements distinct from colonial India. Still, like administrators in most EIC territories, to accommodate political realities EIC officials in the Straits Settlements chose a "gradual system" of abolition in which they identified existing slaves, prohibited the addition of anyone else to the new registries, and believed the institution would perish as those on the lists died. Some also took advantage of prevailing systems of debt-bondage to help further along the transition from enslaved to free labor.

With neither unified spirit, nor the geopolitical power to unilaterally abolish slavery outright some Company officials initially saw debt-slavery as a viable and attractive alternative to emancipation. There were already any number of people whose servitude was obligated to another as a result of gambling debt or a personal loan, and according to some this system offered the "least pecuniary injury or domestic inconvenience to the proprietor."[51] Ostensibly, once the

[48] *Singapore Local Laws and Institutions, 1823*, p. 14.
[49] Ibid., pp. 14–15.
[50] Evans, *Slave Trade (East India) Slavery in Ceylon*, pp. 245, 575.
[51] *Slavery in India* (1828), pp. 437, 442.

person had repaid their master for his cost, they were free. However, with little or no oversight, augmented years of servitude and other indiscriminate abuses of contracts demonstrated that the transition had been a change in name only. By simply referring to their cargo as "debtors," slave traders could bring in as much enslaved labor as they liked.

These misnomers also helped remove the eastern settlements from the scrutiny of early antislavery discourse focused on the violence and cruelty of the African Trade going west and gave EIC officials time to find alternatives such as convicted, indebted, or indentured labor to fulfill their needs. The enactment of the Slave Trade Act in 1807 created a liminal period for Company officials and eastern slave holders to engage in a process of linguistic gymnastics that obfuscated the use of what was, by the passage of Act V in 1843, still in large part the same labor force. This period allowed for a concretization of the connection between the term *slave* and the trade in Africans across the Atlantic. Using labels like debtor, concubine, and indentured servant excluded Asians who were purchased as slaves, laboring in private households and on plantations, living and working in deplorable conditions, from protections afforded by emerging antislavery ordinances, and shielded slave owners from criminal charges and fines. By the 1830s the Company had begun to rely more heavily on contracted and convicted labor, and according to Clare Anderson the Straits Settlements together received "on an average 200 arrivals per year," from each of the Indian presidencies and estimates they received more than 16,000 convicts by the end of the 1850s.[52] At the same time, entrepreneurs and EIC officials organized systems to recruit and transport contracted and indentured labor, which targeted these same vulnerable populations and was, as several historians have demonstrated, merely "a new system of slavery."[53]

Still, unlike settlements in the West, for the first three decades of the nineteenth century the EIC continued relatively unhindered, which meant that the speed and tenor with which officials implemented antislavery legislation was left to local discretion. At the same time, distance from the imperial center constrained British legal authority, which severely inhibited their enforcement. Regardless of how strongly, or not, a particular official felt about abolition, without immediate reinforcement authorities had to accommodate local power structures. This separation also afforded EIC officers and local colonial officials a great deal of

---

[52] Clare Anderson, "'The Ferringees Are Flying—The Ship Is Ours!': The Convict Middle Passage in Colonial South and Southeast Asia, 1790–1860," *The Indian Economic and Social History Review* 42, no. 2 (2005): pp. 144–5.

[53] Hugh Tinker, *A New System of Slavery: The Export of Indian Labour Overseas, 1830–1920*, 2nd ed. (London: Hansib, 1993); Anderson, "Convicts and Coolies" pp. 93–109.

latitude in their interpretation and application of the progressively restrictive categories of acceptable and unacceptable labor resulting from legal reforms between 1790 and 1843—when the institution of slavery was no longer officially recognized in Britain's East Indian Territories. In less than half a century, the British had initiated a complete transformation of indigenous systems of labor and servitude throughout its eastern territories, but still had neither the will nor a way to eliminate slavery from Southeast Asian society.

Antislavery legislation certainly disrupted classical systems of slavery and servitude, but it also boosted illicit markets controlled by indigenous "pirates" and Chinese Secret Societies.[54] Warren argues that "the patterns of their [indigenous maritime populations] lives altered with the extinction of slavery" as a legitimate system of labor.[55] He argues that slave markets, escape routes, and the strategies of pirates and slave traders within the Sulu archipelago maintained a web of embedded trading networks that operated independently of colonial authority and ultimately profited from European Abolition. It is clear that in Southeast Asia, the enforcement of antislavery laws promised to be a significant challenge. Even at the height of British power between 1865 and 1915 they were never able to completely control the movement of commodities or people within the region.[56]

---

[54] This was both the reality and romantic construction of British colonial authority in the region. As Southeast Asian scholar Eric Tagliacozzo asserts, these groups do continually cross British boundaries and are, in fact, able to smuggle products and humans over Anglo/Dutch borders; Tagliacozzo, *Secret Trades, Porous Borders*, pp. 128–84. However, EIC officers and colonial officials also use piracy and Chinese Secret Societies as scapegoats for their lackadaisical enforcement of imperial legislation in the Straits.

[55] Warren, *The Sulu Zone*, p. xix.

[56] Tagliacozzo, *Secret Trades, Porous Borders*, pp. 362–73.

4

# The Politics of Abolition in the Straits

As has already been mentioned, antislavery policies came early to most British settlements in the East Indies. Company officers like Captain Francis Light prohibited the slave trade to Penang as early as 1795. Focused on preventing any new additions to existing slave populations, Light also enacted registration systems that, theoretically, allowed administrators to oversee the progressive diminishment of slavery on the Island. He did not emancipate those already living as slaves. In fact, despite the rising vehemence of abolitionism in London during the 1790s, EIC negotiations with the King of Queda for the island of Penang specifically stipulated for the immediate return of any runaway slaves.[1] Around this same time, EIC officials also granted a group of "Malays of Arabian extraction" and "considerable property" hoping to immigrate to the island the authority to "govern their own families, slaves, and dependents with an independent power," effectively excluding them from the enforcement of local antislavery laws.[2] In April of 1808, Governor Phillips of Prince of Wales Island (Penang) wrote the Company's Court of Directors in Bengal to request that before they decide to "declare all slaves free after a certain period, a committee should be appointed" to more fully investigate the matter.[3] He wrote that while he wholeheartedly agreed there should be "no further delay" in taking "active measures" to abolish slavery on the island, the "heads of the different casts here, who are the principle holders of slaves," strongly objected. Phillips explained that these "higher classes of natives" settled on the island with "an assurance that their domestic arrangements would never be interfered with." He claimed that no action, "short of absolute coercion, would induce them to set free" their slaves—particularly women in their zinanas.[4] The governor's letter appealed both to the

---

[1] *Slavery in India*, p. 420.
[2] Ibid., p. 435.
[3] Ibid., p. 437.
[4] Ibid.; the "zinanas," like a harem, were the internal part of the home excluded from men who are not family members.

directors' sense of class propriety and their penchant for pragmatism. These influential, wealthy families had already been given assurances that they could continue their habits and customs unmolested, and nothing short of "coercion" would compel them to free their slaves. Antislavery was fine, but many felt the Company's zeal should be tempered by clear boundaries of nonintervention.

Officials also made allowances for wealthy Chinese merchants who frequently had several personal domestic servants and concubines and were among the primary importers of debtors who worked off "the cost of their passage" on tin mines, spice farms, and as manual labor in ports throughout the region.[5] Much the same was true for the powerful Malay and Dutch residents, whose households were generally run by slaves.[6] Local administrators believed, rightly so, that sweeping legislation would impede their efforts at the exclusion of the Dutch and expansion of British power in the Straits. In the spirit of abolition, the colonial government did order these groups to report their slaves to local registries, declared that no new slaves would be recognized, and emancipated the children of their slaves.[7] Nonetheless, those measures were for future generations; slaves entered on the registries were still seen as "property" of the slave owner and British authorities were obliged to respect the rights of residents and return escaped or stolen slaves to their masters.[8] So although Company officials were verbally and legislatively proactive, the action plan as a whole left much to be desired. In the end, those who owned the most slaves were effectively excluded from antislavery ordinances. Antislavery in the east during this period depended on the intention and zeal of individual administrators. As Andrea Major explains, "[T]he EIC was sensitive, from the start, to anti-slavery sentiment," but it "did not translate into early or effective legislation."[9] Although legislation had come early to Southeast Asia, slavery continued in the Straits well after the 1834 Emancipation Act.

For officers in both India and the Straits Settlements, antislavery and emancipation were so intertwined with local social, political, and economic

---

[5] Hobhouse, *Returns*, pp. 108–9, 113.
[6] Reid and Brewster, *Slavery, Bondage, and Dependency in Southeast Asia*, pp. 17–26; Andaya, "From Temporary Wife to Prostitute," pp. 20–5.
[7] Evans, *Slave Trade (East India) Slavery in Ceylon*, pp. 245–55.
[8] Hobhouse, *Returns*, pp. 107–25; this is seen in the contentious debate in the EIC report to the India House, between the superintendent of police and acting assistant resident in council, Mr. W. T. Lewis, and Mr. Garling, the resident of Malacca over the release of a slave. Differing interpretations in antislavery legislation initiated a full investigation from the East India Office in 1829. Mr. Lewis complained because he blamed Mr. Garling for ordering the release of slaves. Mr. Lewis believed that, while a laudable idea, there had been no official legislation "declaring slaves free" and that "excepting in the cases of breeches of the peace," as the sitting magistrate he "refused to hear either the master or the slave." As the sitting magistrate, he followed precedent and generally honored a master's authority over their slaves; Evans, *Slave Trade (East India) Slavery in Ceylon*, p. 253.
[9] Major, *Slavery, Abolitionism, and Empire in India*, p. 43.

systems that the enormity of the task was overwhelming. However, for officials in Bengal, the convenient assumptions about the mildness and temperate nature of Asian slavery did not accurately portray the complexities of bondage and obligation they saw around them.[10] Descriptions regularly overlooked the very real violence and desperation many slaves experienced and afforded officials an enormous amount of flexibility in the interpretations of status and enforcement of statutes. To be fair, it was nearly impossible to determine—just from looking—the difference between a "free" laborer, a debtor, and a slave (that remains true even today). Most believed there was a great deal of conversation and negotiation to be had before EIC officials could completely "free" slaves in the east. In the case of the Straits Settlements, these complexities forced officials to accommodate the realities of frontier life—they had neither the authority nor the will to completely root out such an entrenched institution. Varying interpretations of antislavery legislation, local ordinances, and the extent of British authority made even the best intentions of abolition difficult to accomplish.

As has already been discussed, there were many Europeans who owned and traded slaves throughout Malaya, Indonesia, and the Sulu Archipelago prior to antislavery laws.[11] In fact, during the seventeenth and eighteenth centuries, the powerful in Southeast Asia including British and other European settlers often measured their wealth by the number of slaves they owned; thus, at the beginning of the nineteenth century, antislavery laws and emancipation represented a significant threat to profit, investment, and lifestyles.[12] Some argued that the abolition of slavery in the East Indies would interfere with local authority, threaten the Empire's economic and political advantages, as well as disrupt entrenched cultural systems of welfare and indenture. Others saw the institution's demise as a beacon of civilization.[13] However, in Asia, the growth of impoverished populations resulting from famine and war had already begun to provide cheaper sources of labor throughout Asia.[14] By the beginning of the

---

[10] Ibid., p. 132.
[11] Warren, *The Sulu Zone*, p. xix.
[12] Reid and Brewster, *Slavery, Bondage, and Dependency in Southeast Asia*, pp. 17–26; Andaya, "From Temporary Wife to Prostitute," pp. 14–23.
[13] Major, *Slavery, Abolitionism, and Empire in India*, pp. 42–6, 131–2; Munshi, *The Hikayat Abdullah*, pp. 6–7, 182–4; this is an autobiography of a "Malay scholar," Abdullah Bin Abdul Kadir, who rose to a "position of importance as a member of the harbormaster's department under the Dutch." (pp. 6–7). Then, eventually, he became "the youngest of a number of scribes and copyists whom Raffles employed in his office" and wrote extensively about the negotiations and events surrounding the birth of British Malaya (p. 9). Hill's annotated translation makes note of several factual inconsistencies, but the book is nevertheless valuable as an historical lens.
[14] Mike Davis, *Late Victorian Holocausts: El Nino Famines and the Making of the Third World* (London: Verso, 2001), pp. 80, 122; Kathryn Edgerton-Tarpley, *Tears from Iron: Cultural Responses to Famine in Nineteenth-Century China* (Berkeley, CA: University of California Press, 2008), pp. 26–8.

nineteenth century, the expense of acquiring and maintaining slaves had become financially burdensome for some; in a "free" trade settlement, run by "free" labor, slaves were an ostentatious, irrelevant display of wealth rather than an efficient source of cheap labor.[15] This scenario is likely what inspired the initial plan to convert slaves into debtors a little more palatable.

In an attempt to protect the profits and property of slave owners, some proposed a system of emancipation that converted slave populations into indentured laborers. This plan assigned slaves a monetary value and then gave them the opportunity to buy back their freedom with cash or labor. But similar to slaveholders in the West Indies and the United States, eastern slave owners felt they were being "robbed" of vital members of their households and argued that "good servants could not be hired."[16] As part of an ongoing public debate within the settlements, an editorial in the *Singapore Chronicle* about the recently passed registries and antislavery ordinances rebuked this plan and complained that free laborers were too costly and unreliable.[17] This slave owner believed "free" laborers were too expensive and difficult to obtain and, if the government continued its rigid enforcement of these ordinances, he would have no choice but to move away and leave the "property to its fate."[18] Perhaps a thinly veiled threat, this person clearly understood that the EIC government valued both their agricultural contributions and tax money. Still, recognizing the end of an era, there were those who planned for the complete transition of British colonial slave labor to a quasi-free system of apprenticeship and indenture, which attempted to compensate slave owners for their losses and offer remaining slaves opportunities for freedom.[19]

The following editorial in the *Singapore Chronicle*, published on July 7, 1831, offers readers examples for potential avenues to convert existing slave labor in the Straits Settlements; the author analyzes the recent emancipation of slaves in the Cape of Good Hope and supposes its effects in the East Indies. Painting the happy picture of emancipation, and to quell suspicions that slave populations would either revolt or refuse to work if freed, this colonist explained that "such is the demand for free labour, servants found masters, masters hired servants, all gained homes, and at night scarce an idler was to be seen."[20] The author

---

[15] Reid, "The Decline of Slavery in Nineteenth Century Indonesia," pp. 70–2.
[16] This was a common complaint of slaveholders and, while the example might be regionally specific, the sentiment is the same. For more see Drescher, *Abolition*, pp. 245–66.
[17] "Need for Slavery in Sumatra," *Singapore Chronicle*, January 15, 1829.
[18] Ibid.
[19] Seymour Drescher writes a detailed description about the contentious negotiation of compensation for the emancipation of West Indian slaves; see Drescher, *Abolition*, pp. 262–4.
[20] "Slavery," *Singapore Chronicle*, July 7, 1831. There were many revolts during the antislavery movement in the west, and fears of revolution and violence as a result of abolition were common within British popular and political rhetoric. For more see Drescher, *Abolition*, pp. 205–93.

asserted that the proposed sum of "£1,300,000, or SIXTEEN MILLIONS OF RIX DOLLARS," to be paid to slave owners in the Cape by the British government was quite reasonable. Indeed, he proclaimed that such a plan, extended to all his Majesty's colonies, would add "no more than about four million to the Capital of the National Debt, and only about two millions to the annual expenditure."[21] The optimistic colonist believed that the British government "could relieve herself from the whole in forty years." Furthermore, the author calculated that the interest of this sum, if paid over time, was still a "smaller sum than she now expends to support the System in the West Indies." More importantly, they contended that "the guilty spot of Slavery will be washed out forever and all the claims of Justice and Humanity finally satisfied." This is not the direction Company officials took in the Straits, but for some, compensation programs like these, or the apprenticeship programs in the Caribbean and India, allowed everyone—British Parliament, slaveholders, and slaves—to participate in the Empire's shift in dependence from slave to free labor around the globe.[22]

Although the Dutch brought rigidity to the concept of slavery in Southeast Asia during the eighteenth century, by the nineteenth century the British had fine-tuned a system of categorization and classification they later used to gain legal authority over the flows of laboring bodies in the region.[23] Penang's and Malacca's pre-abolition registry made slavery easier to monitor and tax and helped officials plan for a slave-free future. Singapore's history with slave-debtors also marked an important period in Southeast Asia's Anti-Slavery Project. By establishing regulations for slave-debtors, they temporarily legitimized debt-slavery as an alternative between slave and free labor and initiated a transitional period in which slave, slave-debtor, and free worker legally coexisted.[24] This period allowed officials to mitigate realities and overlook what they knew to be an established slave traffic. However, as we will see in the next chapter, letter from the Reverend Mr. Boucho, a Portuguese missionary in Penang, set in motion an investigation that led to the prohibition of debt-slavery and the cancellation of the *Malacca Observer*. In the end, it was undeniable that the reading public in the Straits was more than aware of the thriving underground market for female slaves that remained in their settlements.

---

[21] *The Singapore Chronicle*, July 7, 1831.
[22] Drescher describes the apprenticeship system developed for the West Indies, and Major explains its existence in India. For more detail see Drescher, *Abolition*, pp. 263–6; Major, *Slavery, Abolitionism and Empire in India*, p. 69.
[23] Reid, "The Decline of Slavery in Nineteenth Century Indonesia," p. 69.
[24] Evans, *Slave Trade (East India) Slavery in Ceylon*, p. 290.

## Three Junks from Nias

According to colonial correspondence, on June 13, 1828, a Portuguese missionary living in Penang, Reverend Boucho, wrote to Resident Robert Ibbetson regarding three Chinese junks from Sumatra that had "imported to this island not less than 80 captives" who had "been sold to different Chinese" on the island.[25] The reverend complained that "a few young girls have been seen in the houses, entertained by some Chinese, for the purposes of prostitution." An eye-witness statement from the community meant that, whether he agreed or not, the matter had to be looked into. However, he was clearly convinced by Boucho's descriptions of an illegal slave trafficking because Ibbetson immediately ordered Master Attendant Wright to confiscate the aforementioned junks on the pretense that they had been used to commit a felony and asked the police to investigate.

The record indicates that Superintendent of Police Richard Caunter responded to Ibbetson's order of inquiry on June 19 and affirmed Boucho's assertions. He told the resident that "there is a reason to believe the Chinese junks from this port do deal in slaves when trading in the west coast of Sumatra." However, Caunter's position as a law enforcement officer would have made him thoroughly aware of the legal and illegal categories of labor in the Straits. Therefore, when Caunter expressed doubt that "the persons brought here were slaves, or ever intended as such," he meant that he considered the eighty people Mr. Boucho discussed were slave-debtors, rather than actual *slaves*—the former being an entirely acceptable possibility during this period. Caunter believed they had come to the colonies to be domestic servants and explained that "the females, when grown up, become the wives or concubines of their Chinese masters." He posited that, in general, they "benefited by the change" and that if the slave trade were not illegal, "their importation into the British territories must be greatly for the advantage of these poor people, who would otherwise, in all probability, be sold as slaves into native states, without any hope or prospect of redemption." For Caunter, these new slaves, or debtors, were—regardless of their circumstance—in a much better position under the legislative protections within British territory. The gendered presumptions undergirding these perceptions are discussed further in later chapters; for now, it is clear that Caunter felt, regardless of the unlikelihood that any of these women would ever be able to afford to satisfy their debt and gain their freedom, their enslavement within British territory made their situation—wife,

---

[25] "Slave Trade," IOR/F4/1130/5-15.

concubine, servant, or prostitute—more acceptable than those who had gone to serve in the native states.

After hearing about the case against the Chinese junks' alleged slave trading, governor for the Straits Settlements, Robert Fullerton, ordered a full investigation of the matter. On July 8, Secretary John Anderson wrote jointly to the Harbor Master and the superintendent of police ordering a "more vigilant search and inquiry on the arrival of junks and native vessels than there seems to have been observed on this occasion." Moreover, "in the manner least calculated to attract notice," Anderson told them to inquire about the "abominable traffic of slave-dealing, which the laws of the country, as well as every principle of humanity, require this government to suppress." Nonetheless, "in consequence of a defect of evidence," the Chinese junks and their ship's nakhodas, or commanders, who most certainly understood by that point that the slave trade was illegal and that slave-debtors were not, avoided prosecution. Their vessels were returned to them on August 15.[26] Although the owners of the junks had not reported the aforementioned people to the proper authorities when they arrived, per the local ordinance, and several witness testimonies, correspondence from Anderson claimed that the lack of evidence "rendered it hazardous for the prosecutor to proceed to trial" and the case was held in abeyance for future evidence.

Meanwhile, the local magistrate and police office collected records on the numbers of Chinese junks that had arrived from the west coast of Sumatra since May 1 of that year. From this list, officials were able to determine that out of the six junks anchoring at Prince of Wales Island in the previous month, nineteen people—eleven women, four girls, and two boys—were illegally imported into the colony. No longer able to claim ignorance, Ibbetson and Fullerton wrote to Rear Admiral William Hall Gage of the British Navy asking that he help "put an end to this illegal traffic."[27] At the same time, the officials sent their findings to the residents at Malacca and Singapore "in view to check the practice generally in these Straits."[28] Less than ten days later, Gage regretfully responded to their letter and told them that while he had "looked very narrowly into the power with which [he was] invested" his authority was "too circumscribed to be made available in any way." According to Gage's interpretation, he would have to

---

[26] Ibid., pp. 17–18; it is clear by the differences in testimony between the nakhodas and the "debtors" that they believed themselves to be slaves and that the crew had taken precautionary measures in efforts to elude authorities.
[27] Ibid., pp. 35–7. William Hall Gage played an important role in "suppressing piracy in the Straits of Malacca," before he returned home in 1831. William R. O'Byrne, *A Naval Biographical Dictionary: Comprising the Life and Services of Every Living Officer in Her Majesty's Navy, from the Rank of Admiral of the Fleet to That of Lieutenant, Inclusive* (London: The Admiralty, 1849), p. 31.
[28] "Slave Trade," IOR/F4/1130/31-39.

have indisputable evidence that a ship, flying a British flag—or subject to His Majesty's jurisdiction—was in the process of trading slaves before he could intervene. The rear admiral advised officials in the Straits that he was "wholly without authority, during a period of peace," to detain and search the vessels "of any power in amity with his Majesty." Gage's letter reminded the officials of the potential political complications that might incur as a result of an officer of his Majesty's navy detaining and examining ships in the region without a "strict letter of his authority." The admiral explained that "the footing on which the trade within these settlements in placed" does not lend itself to effective enforcement; even if one could "detect any illegality in their proceedings," the political circumstance would likely "relieve him of any such responsibility." He believed his boundaries were clear: slavery, and the trade, was only illegal when Europeans—particularly British—were involved.

## Public Controversy

Not only did the case of the Chinese junks slave trading at Penang initiate an official investigation into the status of slavery and debtors in the Straits Settlements, but the release of the nakhodas and return of their property also came in the middle of a fiery controversy already occurring within the local newspapers. Residents had already read that the predominant number of those trafficked were women and girls and were beginning to wonder out loud why authorities had not done more to stop it. After piecing together clues from colonial correspondence and articles in the *Singapore Chronicle*, it seems that after learning that the owners of the slave-trading junks had gone unpunished, the editor of the *Malacca Observer* began to make accusations against local authorities' lack of enforcement. This led to the authorities' cancellation of the paper in October 1830.[29] Then, on November 5, the *Singapore Chronicle* published a scathing letter signed "The editor of the late Malacca Observer," in which the author complained of censorship within the local papers regarding the "true extent of piracy and slavery" because he "imagined it reflected somewhat too severely on the supiness [sic] of the government to the commercial interests of these settlements."[30] Abolitionist sentiment had made its way to the Straits and, with more British eyes watching, it was becoming more difficult for Company

---

[29] Ibid., p. 234.
[30] "Correspondence—Malacca," *The Singapore Chronicle*, November 5, 1829.

officials to strategically ignore the institution that everyone in the settlements seemed to know about.

On 30 November 1829, the secretary to government for the Straits Settlements, John Patullo, wrote to the "Managing School Committee at Malacca" that the editor of the *Malacca Observer* was "employed as Schoolmaster, under your superintendence, and paid by means of a monthly allowance granted by the government for schools."[31] Therefore, should any further "publication averting to slavery, and emanating from the same person, appear hereafter, the allowance will be immediately withdrawn by government." The EIC and colonial government did not mince words; should the unnamed editor continue to publicly stir controversy about slavery, Malacca's schools would suffer consequences.

Next, to address the scathing letter published in the *Singapore Chronicle*, Secretary Patullo wrote to the resident at Singapore, Kenneth Murchison, and noted that "by the withdrawal of the fixed payment of 60 dollars, it was not intended that the supervision over the press hitherto exercised should cease, which from the insertion of such a letter appears to have supposed." The "partial and offensive styles adopted by the editor," asserted Patullo, "tended to destroy the peace, harmony, and good order of the settlement." He told Murchison that per "the decision of the highest authorities, executive and judicial, it is most desirable that the subsisting irritation should be allowed to subside." However, the secretary was clear that Singapore's government should not only discourage any "observations bearing on the question of slavery" be permitted in the *Singapore Chronicle*, but that his Honourable Murchison should understand that if this scandal was not controlled, it would be a point for "the consideration of those in Europe from whom they draw their principal support." The Company had managed to operate under the radar for decades and Patullo insinuated Murchison's lack of oversight might threaten their neglected luxury.

After delivering his veiled threats, Patullo also told Murchison he had been directed to inform the resident that "although it is expected that you will act on these principles here laid down, it is not advisable that you should either send this letter for publication, or give any reason or ground for your proceeding in the admission or rejection of any paragraph that seems to you to be offensive." Patullo ordered Murchison not to discuss his orders in public; the attention to slavery in the local papers, including the controversy over the three Chinese junks trading slaves from Pulau Nias, had placed so much pressure on officials

---

[31] Evans, *Slave Trade (East India) Slavery in Ceylon*, p. 234.

that the government took steps to stifle the discourse. An increased public interest preceding the incident in Penang combined with public assertions made by colonial officials about the government's inefficient antislavery efforts created a community discourse about the illegal traffic in women and girls and the EIC's inability to prevent it, and the government wanted to stifle it. With the same sentiment Superintendent Caunter expressed earlier, testimony from colonial officials in response to public scrutiny asserted that while their circumstance might be lamentable, these slave women were ultimately in a better situation; more importantly, the trade in female slaves was important to the growth and stability of the settlements.

This ideology was also present in Judge Loch's interpretation of the antislavery ordinance in March of 1830. As acting register for the Court of Judicature for the entire Straits Settlements, Loch's decision set precedent for both interpretation and enforcement of the new legislation and illustrates the disparate perceptions and application of this legislation. In a case against a runaway slave, Sabina, serving a sentence for petty theft, the judge ruled that colonial authority had no jurisdiction to deny any Dutch inhabitant of their "right of property in a slave."[32] Without an Act Parliamentary or change "by his Majesty in Council," he was "bound to adhere to the laws, customs and usages in force regarding them [slaves]." Loch asserted that "the court will protect all slaves from ill-treatment and improper usage on the part of the masters, they must, at the same time, enforce due obedience on the part of the slave." While not as blatant as Caunter, the judge clearly chose the most conservative and politically bland interpretation of the antislavery ordinance and, so long as they were not being mistreated, he was not going to disrupt existing systems.

Another example of this sentiment appeared in a "Minute by the President," recorded from the Singapore Consultations on March 12, 1830, "on the subject of slave-debtors."[33] Here, the president believed that the opportunity for freedom would eventually make itself available for slaves with access to British courts. After reminding council members of the protracted and pervasive nature of domestic slavery—of females in particular—within the Straits Settlements, President Fullerton stated that "the only remaining part of the discussion" was that of slaves who had been brought into the settlements and improperly disposed of.[34] Fullerton asserted that anyone in this circumstance was "*ipso facto* free, and that no one can from such a transaction establish legal claim

---

[32] Ibid., p. 236.
[33] Ibid., pp. 238–9.
[34] Ibid., p. 239.

to their service against their consent." If any persons had found themselves in such a situation, "an application to the magistrates, before whom such cases must regularly come, would insure their discharge." However, Fullerton argued, while some slaves were "detained against their consent, and even ill treated," most were "satisfied with their situation," and they would have objected to the interference of the government. He claimed that forcing an immediate abolition of the current system "might be the means of throwing many out of immediate employ."

Like his colleagues in the Law Commission, Fullerton believed that for many, slavery was the only means of ensuring subsistence for those "who would otherwise be left to starve." He contended that "so long as the servant is well treated by the master and satisfied with his condition, there can be no moral reason or call for interference." Furthermore, he claimed that if people were "ill-used and dissatisfied, there cannot be a doubt that here, as in other places, such will find their way to the proper tribunal." He contended there could be "little doubt that the magistrates would annul a claim to forced service founded on no better title than the sale of an imaginary debt to be due to a nakhoda, without either the knowledge or admission by the party transferred with it." Moreover, the governor believed that such cases brought before the magistrate would inspire "others who felt the desire to be released and had the means of deriving subsistence by their own free labor." For Fullerton, abolition was best won in the courts, although he admitted that there were, indeed, slaves in the Straits brought in against their will, forced to work, and who had little to say about their situation. Still, as he indicated above, Fullerton assumed that these people's situation was better within British territory because a magistrate could nullify their obligation if their master abused their authority. Of course, this ignores the reality that the de jure emancipation of a British magistrate at this time did not negate the de facto debt (monetary or not) that a slave had with their master. Nevertheless, he clearly believed that while it would be nearly impossible to stop the slave trade in the British Straits Settlements, the slaves were better off than if they had been taken somewhere outside of His Majesty's protection.

## Closing Loopholes

The case of the "some 80 persons" imported from Pulau Nias in June of 1828 exposed the government's dirty little secret and forced them to address the problem, at least publicly, of an illicit slave trade in the community.[35] Residents like the Reverend Boucho and editors of the *Malacca Observer* and the *Singapore Chronicle* saw the importation of "slave-debtors" as simply another name for an enduring system and they wanted authorities to stop the traffic and hold the slavers accountable. This is why the colonial government at Prince of Wales Island did not want the reverend or the papers to continue their pursuit to expose and punish those complicit in the illicit slave trade. However, the attention these citizens called to the slave traffic they knew existed in their communities motivated more than threatening correspondence from the secretary of the government; there were also significant changes made to local policies.

On November 30, the same day Secretary Patullo wrote his warning letters to the Malaccan school committee and the resident of Singapore, Governor Fullerton recorded a minute to the Government in Council.[36] Fullerton told the council that due to the recent publicity regarding "the question of slavery," the matter required further investigation. To be clear, he explained that "a slave-debtor is understood to be one who receives a certain sum or acknowledges a certain debt to another, on the understanding that his services are pledged until the repayment of the sum takes place." Fullerton contended that the practice was "desirable" because it facilitated "free and voluntary" contracts that promoted "the cultivation and improvement of the place." However, he warned that he thought the practice was an expedient means to perpetuate "mere slavery under another name."

After his public address, the governor launched an inquiry into the status and efficiency of the slave-debtor system in the Straits then, he ordered the residents at Malacca and Singapore, and the superintendent of police at Prince of Wales Island, to respond to the following questions as soon as was possible.

1st Does the practice generally prevail at the settlement?

2nd Are slave debtors imported? Are the services of natives of the place so sold?

3rd If so, by what description of people, generally?

4th Of what race or nation are the slave debtors generally so imported?

5th In what manner is it supposed the importers obtain the slave debtors?

6th Are agreements generally made between debtor and the employer, or are the arrangements made between the proprietor and the intended employer?

---

[35] This is what John Anderson told the council in his article in *Quarterly Review* that the editor of the *Singapore Chronicle* took such offense to, April 26, 1827.

[36] Evans, *Slave Trade (East India) Slavery in Ceylon*, pp. 234–5.

7th If money is paid, who receives it; the importer or the slave debtor?

8th Does the slave debtor always know or understand the engagements entered into?

9th Does the slave debtor know the terms and conditions, that is the exact relation in which he stands to the employer bargaining for his service?

10th Is it in your opinion advisable to require a registry of all such engagements, and these being made at the police-office before a magistrate, as done at Penang, in order to secure to all parties full understanding of the bargain they are entering into, examining the nature of the case, as to prevent abuses, that is, the practice of importing slaves under the name of slave debtors?[37]

Fullerton wanted a survey that identified, classified, and categorized slave-debtors in the Straits.

The following February, acting Resident Councilor E. Presgrave submitted the extensive report on the subject of slave-debtors the government office needed to identify and classify them. What they found was that the debt-slavery in the Straits was different from classical slavery only in name. To begin his explanation on the differences between native and European understandings and usages of debt-slavery the official writes that two types of people are subject to slavery in Malaya: "[t]hese are the hamba and orang utang or merghering (as they are termed in Sumatra), the former term signifying a slave and, the latter, a debtor standing in a certain relation to his creditor."[38] He dismissed any need to discuss the existence of true *slaves* in the colonies; the institution was not, in those settlements, legal, and "no remarks were necessary, their relative condition in society being universally understood." As far as he was concerned, the only slaves recognized in the Straits Settlements were those entered onto the registries at Penang and Malacca.[39] Then, Presgrave defined, as did Fullerton, "slave-debtors" as "an insolvent debtor who is bound by law or custom to serve his creditor until the debt is satisfied."[40] Presgrave stressed that the debtor differed "little from a slave while in actual servitude, except that he does not part with his rights and privileges as a free man." He explained that "according to the native usage," the person indebted was bound to their debtor, no matter how little or small the debt, regardless of how long they served, "no deduction is made in the amount required from the debtor, his labor being only an equivalent for his food, clothing, and the interest of the debt." However, the only requirement for the

[37] Ibid., p. 235.
[38] Ibid., p. 304.
[39] Ibid., pp. 285–300; there are copies of both the Penang and the Malaccan Registries included in this report.
[40] Ibid., pp. 304–5.

debtor to gain their freedom was that they pay off the original sum owed. The possibility of redemption being the key difference, at least for the British, was what separated the "universally understood" position of a *slave* and the clearly misunderstood experience of a debtor.

Presgrave told the council that in order to avoid prohibitory slave laws established by the British, "powers in the East were restrained in their former dealings, and slaves were not allowed to be bought or sold as formerly." As a result, slaves were sold as slave-debtors and, since there were generally no explicit agreements made between the debtor and "employer," Presgrave surmised that "the debtor might languish in slavery for life, and his progeny after him, if he had any." As we would expect, the resident told the council that Europeans were more vigilant in maintaining the parameters of a "voluntary contract," due to their better understanding of the "penal consequences of dealing in slaves." With Europeans, he claimed, there was more "strictness and regularity" with length of service, wages, and portions of that wage paying toward the original debt. The lengthy report explained how, prior to British legislation, slaves brought a much higher price in the region and that debtors were "seldom or ever brought from a distance, as a removal to a foreign country would infallibly reduce him to the condition of slave by taking him from his relations and friends, who might absolve him from servitude by assisting him to pay his debt."

According to this perception, the people imported from Pulau Nias were more likely slaves than debtors; even though they had not been properly registered with authorities, they had no knowledge of a negotiated contract, and they were too far from home for any of their friends or family to have helped them. In the end, Resident Presgrave provides us with an answer to the questions at hand. He asserted that debtors "first introduced into our settlements are *bôna fide* slaves." The official claimed that the price of these laborers had not fallen "as a result of their new name" and that there was essentially the same demand that had been there before.[41] Presgrave felt that "all the peculiar hardship and cruelty of the slave trade may be said to be perpetuated by sanctioning the free introduction of slave debtors (actual slaves)." The women and children on the three Chinese junks in Penang were, without question, purchased and treated as slaves, regardless of the title Superintendent Caunter wanted to use for them.

On March 12, 1830, seven years after Raffles regulated debt-slavery in Singapore, Governor Fullerton declared that he believed that the status of slave-

---

[41] Ibid., p. 306.

debtor was "a mere cover for slavery."[42] He summarized the information from assessments like Presgrave's and told the council that the practice of importing slave-debtors clandestinely was primarily conducted by native vessels, who gathered slaves from adjacent islands—by purchase, barter, or as "captives taken by the pirates." He explained that they "were procured in exactly the same manner as regular slaves" and that the slaves were treated "to all intents and purposes, as articles of trade." Fullerton argued that many were without a "voice in the transaction, or even knowledge of the terms of transfer, but considers him or herself as a slave." While the governor did not see that he had legal authority to nullify existing circumstances, and cautioned against the government interfering in master-servant disputes unless there were instances of neglect or abuse, as of March 4, Governor Fullerton prohibited the importation of slave-debtors and ordered the abolition of the practice of employing slave-debtors in the Straits.[43]

## Conclusion

While the public forced EIC officers and colonial officials to fine-tune their definitions and categories of servitude, residents in Malacca declared a definitive end to domestic slavery in their colony. On November 30, 1829, now acting Resident W. T. Lewis said that he was particularly honored to announce that in spite of the tremendous sacrifice, particularly on the part of native populations, the "whole of the inhabitants of Malacca" came entirely "voluntarily and unanimously to the determination of emancipating their domestic slaves."[44] As the last lynchpin keeping the remnants of classical systems of slavery intact within the Straits, debt-slavery had been removed; legal slavery, of any type, would no longer have a place among the colony's workforce as of December 31, 1841. This, in combination with the government's tighter definitions and narrowing allowances for debt-slavery, pushed antislavery laws in the Straits Settlements out of their liminal phase when slavery and free laborers coexisted and into a period in which servitude became less susceptible to interpretation and the

---

[42] Ibid., p. 238.
[43] From Singapore, Secretary Patullo issued a government notification to Prince of Wales Island and Malacca that the practice of employing slave-debtors was to be abolished in the Straits; Evans, *Slave Trade (East India) Slavery in Ceylon*, p. 240.
[44] As an addendum to the letter to the government, Lewis included a copy of the declaration signed by "Chooliats," "Malays," and "Chinese." There are no Europeans on this list—in spite of the fact that there are Dutch inhabitants strongly vocalizing their opposition to emancipation; Evans, *Slave Trade (East India) Slavery in Ceylon*, pp. 210–17.

division between "slave" and "free" labor more defined. However, as EIC and colonial officials continued to redefine and categorize workers in the region, the demands for domestic servants did not change. Illegal supplies continued to come through classical networks, which persisted under a different label. For the first few decades of the nineteenth century, embracing the nebulous category of debt-slave provided a transitional period that allowed the British to extend the duration and method of abolition and emancipation. The regulations Raffles established for Singapore in 1823 created the facade of a labor contract, in which brokers (like the nakhodas of the three Chinese junks in Penang) imported *debtors* (actual slaves traded, bought, or kidnapped from surrounding island) to *employers* (who rarely disclosed the amount of the obligation or the duration of indenture). Of course, the Pulau Nias case disabused both the public and officials of that delusion.

After Patullos's threats, there were very few articles about local slavery in *the Singapore Chronicle,* and the paper folded in 1835.[45] This issue had by no means been resolved, but from that point forward, the government had undeniable knowledge that there was an illicit trade in slaves and that the majority of them were women and girls. Reports from EIC officers in the field provided observations as evidence that, while the officially defined slave had been banned, an entrenched and thriving system of underground slave-like traffic sidestepped colonial authority and flowed through the Straits. More importantly, through the testimony from Superintendent Caunter and Rear Admiral Gage they learned that very often it was their legislation that opened the doors for inconsistent interpretation and limited applications. By the end of the 1830s, having legally abolished slavery in the Straits and prohibited the employment of slave-debtors, the colonial government readjusted its priorities and began to look more at why people, mainly women and girls, were being trafficked.

So, by 1841, when our anonymous whistleblower from London was writing to defend "national honor," he was a decade behind the contentious debate that had already played out in the Straits for over two years.[46] The EIC and colonial officials had done a great job shielding the public in Britain from the truth behind East Indian slave trading and many in England believed that slavery did not exist in the east. The reality was that the policies and procedures of the colonial government in the Straits Settlements had not only prolonged the legal status of slavery as an institution, but also inadvertently strengthened a flourishing

---

[45] Francis T. Seow, *The Media Enthralled: Singapore Revisited* (Boulder: Lynne Rienner Publishers, 1998), pp. 4–7.
[46] *Slavery and the Slave Trade in British India,* p. iii.

black-market system that British officials would spend the rest of the century trying to combat. Residents complained of the visible and thriving trade around them, but officials had neither the desire, nor the authority to stop it. Their early enactment of antislavery policies is certainly evidence of good intentions on the part of some local administrations, however, as the Foreign and British Anti-Slavery Society's pamphlet so aptly illustrates, the abolition of slavery had not been a priority for local administrators in the Straits.

5

# Tolerance vs. Emancipation: Abolition in Malacca

In addition to having a vague directive, Company officials in the Straits also argued vehemently among themselves about the enforcement of antislavery. For example, Resident of Malacca, Samuel Garling, believed Governor of the Straits Settlements, Robert Fullerton, had misinterpreted the law and limits to British authority, and consequently held him responsible for the perpetuation of slavery in the region. In the summer of 1829, the two came to a standoff in a legal debate about the existence of slaves in Malacca. On November 26 of that year, both officials wrote to the governors-general at Fort William in Bengal requesting that the EIC Board of Control adjudicate what had become a contentious internal debate over the interpretation and implementation of British antislavery legislation in Malacca.[1] Resident Garling vehemently disagreed with the fact that on several occasions, the Superintendent of Police W. T. Lewis had violated his understanding of the EIC's directive and honored existing slave laws; this included returning absconded slaves to their owners. Frustrated by Garling's accusations, Lewis wrote to Governor Fullerton seeking guidance, which, in turn, prompted Fullerton to publicly criticize Garling's interpretations and resulting actions. In the meantime, Fullerton ordered Lewis to "collect and lay before the Governor in Council every rule, order, or regulation, or decision that may have been passed before on the subject, from the year 1795 to the present day."[2] Then, Fullerton wrote to the board and stressed that the subject was "of considerable importance, and one which excite[d] much interest amongst the community." In fact, Lewis ceased all communication with Resident Garling over his allegations of insubordination.[3] Both Governor Fullerton and Resident Garling wrote to the superior officers

---

[1] Evans, *Slave Trade (East India) Slavery in Ceylon*, pp. 303–4.
[2] Ibid., p. 241.
[3] Ibid., p. 251.

asking for a definitive statement as to "whether slaves registered under the preceding Netherlands Government are to be legally considered in a state of slavery since the transfer of this place to the British authority, and the establishment of an English Court Justice."[4] Malacca's long history as a society essentially built and populated by slaves, the creation of slave registries by the Dutch, and the EIC's undefined antislavery policies are what shaped the path to gradual abolition in this ancient cosmopolitan port. Moreover, the challenges "public functionaries" in Malacca encountered in their efforts to implement antislavery legislation exemplify the obstacles to the enforcement of antislavery laws that many of their colleagues faced throughout the British East Indies in the first four decades of the nineteenth century.[5]

An examination of official correspondence between local officials and the EIC Board provides an enlightening picture of the early stages of Britain's Anti-Slavery Project in the ancient trading entrepôt of Malacca.[6] As we will see, this first phase of in the Straits required a significant amount of compromise and negotiation on the part of local colonial authorities.[7] Because it was one most vibrant and diverse of Southeast Asia's ancient port cities, the beginning of the EIC's attempts to implement and enforce antislavery ordinances in Malacca had to be strategic. This international entrepôt had served as a strategic gateway and vital choke point connecting Indian and Pacific Ocean trade networks for at least a century before the arrival of Europeans. Here, slaves served vital roles in its development, expansion, and function of the port city until Britain's final acquisition of it in 1825. Resident Garling's sudden emancipation of Malacca's slaves threatened to disrupt existing economic, social, and political structures and erode hard-won diplomatic trust between local authorities and influential merchant families. His new and unprecedented interpretations of British law exposed two sides of the abolition argument within the east and illustrate the Company's preference for policies that favored minimal interference and honored the personal property rights of slave owners. More importantly, this argument demonstrates that each of these EIC representatives, from the local superintendent of police to the governors-general in Bengal, was unsure about their legal authority and the Company's official position on the subject of abolition. Inconsistent interpretations and unclear directives created an

---

[4] Ibid., p. 304.
[5] Ibid., p. 21. This was the term the governors-general in Fort William used for the colonial officials stationed within the British Straits Settlements.
[6] Ibid., p. i. The Anti-Slavery Project is what Joel Quirk describes as a process that is working toward abolition. Quirk, *The Anti-Slavery Project*, pp. 4–5.
[7] Quirk, *The Anti-Slavery Project*, p. 5.

immense amount of confusion, animosity (and an impressive amount of paperwork) within settlements throughout the IOW, and contributed to the success of underground networks, which continued to plague the region for the next century and beyond. Without specific instructions to do otherwise, local officials exercised their "own discretion" and plotted a course for the "gradual abolition" of slavery in their jurisdictions, just as the campaign for the total emancipation of slaves in the West Indies had ignited.[8] Malacca provides an important example of why the EIC was unable to effect a complete end to slavery in the East Indies and how inconsistent interpretation and application of antislavery legislation in the 1820s and 1830s only complicated the process even further.

## Melaka and Its Heirs

In their unmatched study about the history of Malaysia, Leonard Andaya and Barbara Watson-Andaya clearly demonstrate that when the British began to establish themselves in the Straits at the end of the eighteenth century, "Melaka," or Malacca, had been a central node in an intricate trading network that spanned from China to Africa since at least 1400.[9] During the first millennium CE, the skills, ideologies, and commodities from sailors, merchants, and travelers were tightly woven into complex business relationships between Africa, the Arabian Peninsula, India, China, and Malaya. The Malay archipelago was at the center of two primary sea routes and contained an abundance of valuable aromatic woods, resins, rattans, gold, cowries, tortoise shells, and had fertile soil. Dense teak forests and tin mines surrounded the city and a freshwater stream ran through its center—a perfect forward port for any long-distance trade missions and international emporium to sell and trade any merchandise on its return. The natural resource wealth of the oceans and jungles in the archipelago brought the outside world to Malaya, where many settled and traded all along the Straits of Malacca.

According to Malay lore, in the 1390s, a Malayan prince named Parameśvara wanted to move away from the Javanese center of power at Palembang and

---

[8] The EIC often counselled its officers to exercise their own discretion and many of the officers reported that they were taking the course of "gradual abolition" because of local circumstances. Evans, *Slave Trade (East India) Slavery in Ceylon*, pp. 9, 40, 180, 150, 235–6, 256, 261–3, 352, 588; Davis's, *Inhuman Bondage*, pp. 236–8, explains the various stages of abolition and describes the motivations behind the movement to emancipate the slaves in the "new world."

[9] Andaya and Andaya, *A History of Malaysia*, pp. 10–12.

established himself on the island of Tumasik (modern Singapore).[10] As Keith Taylor explains, archeologists like John Miksic have used earthenware and glass beads to demonstrate the flow of trade and how "the late fourteenth century was an especially prosperous time" for the island but it was too vulnerable to attack.[11] Eventually, continuous pressure from the powerful Siamese state of Ayutthaya motivated the prince to move further into the Straits where he, as Taylor avers, established the port city of Malacca and "presided over the rebirth of Malay political authority under the protection of the Chinese."[12] While just one among many established communities along the coast of the peninsula, Malacca greatly benefited from China's renewed interest in Southeast Asian trade and quickly became a strategic and lucrative anchorage, located at the mouth of one of the busiest international maritime trade routes in the world. The thriving entrepôt was regularly the prize in a perpetual contest between regional powers vying for trading dominance in the Straits.[13] However, rather than participating in trade themselves, Malay noblemen protected the merchandise of arriving traders from the piracy rampant in the Straits after the fall of the Srivijain Empire in the tenth century.[14] To facilitate the safety and efficiency of trade, they created a governing body and court system and actively policed the sea-lanes around Malacca to deter pirates and encourage traffic into the Straits toward their harbor.[15] Prince Parameśvara and his Chinese allies worked diligently to attract foreign merchants and the passing trade and made this cosmopolitan city one of the most important and strategic international ports of the Malay kingdom until its fall in the nineteenth century.[16]

By the middle of the fifteenth century, China's government lost its zeal for foreign trade and prohibited all private ventures in the South Seas. If they wanted to continue the flow of trade, Malacca's rulers had no choice but to look to India and foster new relationships with the communities of merchants already connected to networks as far as the eastern coast of Africa and the Red Sea. Eventually, Indian merchants primarily from the Gujarat, Malabar, Coromandel, and Bengal regions brought foods like rice, cane sugar, and salted meats, as well

---

[10] Keith W. Taylor, "The Early Kingdoms," in *The Cambridge History of Southeast Asia, Volume One Part One: From Early Times to c. 1500*, ed. Nicholas Tarling (Cambridge: Cambridge University Press, 1999), p. 175.
[11] John N. Miksic, *Archeological Research on the "Forbidden Hill" of Singapore: Excavation at Fort Canning 1984* (Singapore, 1985), pp. 44–60.
[12] Taylor, "The Early Kingdoms," p. 175.
[13] Andaya and Andaya, *A History of Malaysia*, p. 5; Lewis, *Jan Compagnie in the Straits of Malacca, 1641-1795*, p. 5.
[14] Taylor, "The Early Kingdoms," p. 174; Lewis, *Jan Compagnie in the Straits of Malacca*, p. 5.
[15] Lewis, *Jan Compagnie in the Straits of Malacca*, p. 5.
[16] Andaya and Andaya, *A History of Malaysia*, pp. 31–6.

as candied fruits, cotton cloth, pepper, and at times slaves, to Malaccan markets.[17] The conversion of Malacca's third ruler to Islam quickly connected the entrepôt to Muslim trading networks that had previously frequented Sumatran ports, and its economy exploded.[18] Over the course of a century Malacca became one of Southeast Asia's busiest trading centers and had attracted the attention of an increasingly wealthy merchant class looking for new markets in which to settle.

The Portuguese entered the IOW at the end of the fifteenth century, and their establishment of an administrative center in Goa was the final link in a system connecting China to Europe via the Indian Ocean. The Portuguese quickly recognized the incredibly vibrant and profitable system of trade and endeavored to keep discovery of the prize and the accompanying resources to themselves. In fact, according to Leonard Andaya, King Manuel was so impressed with the potential for profit and eager to keep the new route a secret that in 1504 he decreed, "[U]pon pain of death, complete secrecy must be maintained with regard to the new discoveries."[19] This, says Andaya, seemed to have worked because there are no known works published by the Portuguese about the first fifty years of their expansion into Asia.

As part of a grand scheme to create a trading post empire in Asia, Portuguese general and maritime explorer, Afonso de Albuquerque, made plans to conquer and control the major cities along the spice route between their administrative center in Goa and the Moluccas. As the principle market for cloves, pepper, nutmeg, and mace, Malacca was at the top of his list.[20] After Albuquerque's conquest of the city in 1511, the Portuguese apothecary Tomé Pires wrote that Malacca had risen to "such importance and profit that it seems to me it has no equal in the world."[21] However, as Dianne Lewis explains, "[I]nstead of capturing Malacca's trade, the Portuguese had fragmented it."[22] As many future colonizers would quickly learn, Malacca was a popular center, but certainly not the only Malay port. In this region trade was not place-bound; rather, it often followed the most powerful or appealing ruler; without the accompanying social or political capital, taking control of one area simply diverted the trade somewhere else. Lewis contends that Portuguese conquest inspired Malacca's then Malay ruler, Sultan Mahmud, to

---

[17] Andaya, "Interactions with the Outside World and Adaptation in Southeast Asian Society, 1500–1800," p. 8; Lewis, *Jan Compagnie in the Straits of Malacca*, p. 7.
[18] Lewis, *Jan Compagnie in the Straits of Malacca*, p. 6.
[19] Andaya, "Interactions with the Outside World and Adaptation in Southeast Asian Society," p. 10.
[20] Ibid.
[21] Andaya and Andaya, *A History of Malaysia*, p. 32.
[22] Lewis, *Jan Compagnie in the Straits of Malacca*, p. 9.

create a new, competing, "fervently Muslim" Malay port at Banda Aceh, in the north of Sumatra. This, of course, capitalized on religious tensions between Muslims and Christians, gaining him favor with local Muslim merchants. As part of the new state of Johor, Mahmud attacked the Portuguese from Banda Aceh for the next decade; then, the northern Sumatran kingdom in Aceh and the Javanese state in Japara "followed suit" between 1558 and 1574. Not only had the conquest of Malacca driven away much of the lucrative trade that had been their original motivation, they had initiated conflict and increased instability within the Straits, which reduced trade flows and profit margins. Nonetheless, the port remained a lucrative acquisition for the Portuguese, and their presence, in the form of wealthy merchants, religious missionaries, and mestizo families, was more than evident at the turn of the nineteenth century.

The Dutch took this trading mecca from the Portuguese in 1641 and quickly made it their primary outpost on the Peninsula, which was still largely controlled by the Malay kingdom.[23] In spite of the significant efforts made by each new imperial government, Europeans were never able to monopolize trade as efficiently as the Malay rulers in Malacca had during the fifteenth century. Nonetheless, the Dutch East India Company's (VOC) procurement of Malacca entered them into a contest for dominance and control over this strategic waterway, which had existed among rulers along the straits for hundreds of years. The VOC battled for power with Bugis and other Malay leaders who had maintained their hold on the region from Riau, another prestigious and influential Malay trading center, which, as one VOC official described, was "crowded with 'Moors, Armenians, Danes, Portuguese, and other nations.'"[24] Still, for the latter half of the seventeenth and first half of the eighteenth century, the VOC was the dominant European power in Malaysia and Indonesia.[25] But that all changed in the 1750s, when political and economic weaknesses within the VOC made them vulnerable to their long-time adversary, the British EIC.[26]

Motivated by their loss in the American colonies, the British did not begin their eastern expansion in earnest until the second half of the eighteenth

---

[23] Andaya and Andaya, *A History of Malaysia*, pp. 68–75.
[24] This quote was taken from a VOC officer describing the diversity of trade in Riau; Andaya and Andaya, *A History of Malaysia*, p. 79. Riau, like Malacca, was another center of trade along the Straits but was ruled by Malay nobles that were allied with Bugis leaders. The Bugis are whom both the Dutch and British labeled as "pirates," because they did not follow European trade laws; Andaya and Andaya, *A History of Malaysia*, p. 109. For more on the Bugis and piracy in Southeast Asia see Trocki, *Prince of Pirates*, pp. 56–70; Warren, *The Sulu Zone*, pp. 252–5; Tagliacozzo, *Secret Trades, Porous Borders*, pp. 55–66.
[25] Andaya and Andaya, *A History of Malaysia*, pp. 1, 76–113; Reid, *Charting the Shape of Early Modern Southeast Asia*, pp. 92–9; Munshi, *The Hikayat Abdullah*, pp. 33–4.
[26] Andaya and Andaya, *A History of Malaysia*, pp. 99–102.

century.²⁷ With an eye on expansion, by the 1780s English country traders were making a concerted effort to undermine Dutch authority and profits in the region. As the mighty Malay kingdom of Johor began to crumble from internal instability and economic pressures at the end of the century, these two European imperial forces, fueled by a centuries-long rivalry, entered the contest for succession and bitterly fought for control over the Straits.²⁸ The EIC's establishment of a factory in Penang (1786) drastically reduced Dutch profits in Malacca and initiated the VOC's decline of power in the archipelago.²⁹ By the time the Dutch transferred control of Malacca to the British in 1795, as a result of their losses in the Napoleonic Wars in Europe, the EIC had initiated a "relatively nonviolent" occupation of the Straits and were on their way to establishing trading dominance in the region.³⁰ Even though the Dutch resumed control of Malacca for the brief period between 1818 and 1825, they were never able to regain their economic or political strength in Malaya. Interestingly enough in a brief collaborative effort to halt French expansionism in Southeast Asia, the British and Dutch negotiated the Anglo-Dutch Treaty of 1824 and were able to set aside "centuries of history without a qualm" and partitioned the Malay world down the middle of the Straits.³¹ In this case, British and Dutch officials decided it was better to share between each other than to contend with the French.

It is also significant that EIC officials did not forcibly take its settlements in the Straits: Prince of Wales Island (Penang), Singapore, or Malacca. Rather, the EIC acquired them through negotiation and trade agreements.³² Britain's acceptance by indigenous Malay rulers was partly predicated on the fact that they had theoretically negotiated with Malay rulers for these territories and the exchange was surrounded by the pretense of law.³³ Unlike the violent battles between previous Portuguese and Dutch invaders, the British presented themselves as

---

²⁷ For more about the shift in British imperial focus after the American Revolution: Hobsbawm, *Age of Revolution 1789-1848*, pp. 109–30; Bayly, *The Birth of the Modern World, 1780-1914*, pp. 86–99; Bayly, *Imperial Meridian*, pp. 75–99; P. J. Cain and A. G. Hopkins, *British Imperialism: Crisis and Deconstruction, 1914-1990* (London: Longman, 1993), pp. 53–6.
²⁸ Andaya and Andaya, *A History of Malaysia*, pp. 100–1.
²⁹ Donald Freeman, *The Straits of Malacca: Gateway or Gauntlet?* (Montreal: McGill-Queen's University Press, 2003), pp. 132–4.
³⁰ Freeman, *The Straits of Malacca*, p. 133. For more on the Napoleonic Wars and the conflict between European nations see Bayly, *The Birth of the Modern World*, pp. 96–117; Bayly, *Imperial Meridian*, pp. 164–91; Geoffrey Best, *War and Society in Revolutionary Europe* (New York: St. Martin's Press, 1982), pp. 63–184.
³¹ Andaya and Andaya, *A History of Malaysia*, p. 122; Carl A. Trocki, "Borders and the Mapping of the Malay World" (paper presented at the Annual Meeting of the Association for Asian Studies, San Diego, March 9, 2000).
³² Freeman, *The Straits of Malacca*, pp. 125–6. This report from the EIC contains a section that briefly describes the way each of these colonies was brought under British control; Hobhouse, *Returns: Slavery (East Indies)*, pp. 107–12.
³³ Andaya and Andaya, *A History of Malaysia*, p. 114.

business partners rather than colonizers.[34] Consequently, while trade agreements may have given the EIC a place to establish themselves, as we have seen, this did not include unlimited power and many of the treaties specifically defined parameters around colonial authority over indigenous populations.

The EIC's treaty with the king of Queda in 1791 highlights the Company's circumscribed authority when it came to slaves. For example, the king of Queda insisted that existing slave systems were recognized and that "all slaves be returned to their masters, for they are part of their property."[35] Moreover, EIC correspondence explained that in 1791, "for the mutual benefit of both parties," the king inserted an additional article to clarify that "all slaves running from Queda to Pulo [sic] Penang, or from Pulo Penang shall be returned to their owners."[36] Clearly, it was important to the Malay king—long before abolitionism had arrived—that the British authorities honored Malay custom and that the institution of slavery be left alone. This did not prevent Captain Light from prohibiting the import and export of slaves in Penang because those ordinances were, which primarily aimed at disrupting the "foreign" (or European) slave trade in the region, rather than intervening in local systems.[37] As previously discussed, treaties and agreements with local leaders in the western littorals of the Indian Ocean had allowed British antislavery ordinances to disrupt French slaving in the Indian Ocean, and the Treaty of 1824 compelled the Dutch to abide by and enforce Britain's 1823 Slave Trade Act.[38] By 1825, it was illegal for Europeans to trade slaves in Southeast Asia and in some settlements officials had already begun work on the first phase of gradual abolition: the identification and registration of all known slaves within their territories.

## Slaves in Malacca

After regaining possession of Malacca from the Dutch in March of 1825, the complex economic and political dynamics within the Straits created significant challenges for EIC officers and colonial officials enforcing antislavery legislation.

---

[34] Carl A. Trocki, *Singapore: Wealth, Power and the Culture of Control* (New York: Routledge, 2006), p. 9.
[35] Hobhouse, *Returns: Slavery (East Indies)*, pp. 107–12.
[36] Ibid., p. 107.
[37] Trocki, *Prince of Pirates*, pp. 45–6; Major, *Slavery, Abolitionism and Empire in India, 1772–1843*, p. 43; Andaya and Andaya, *A History of Malaysia*, pp. 114–30; Allen, "Suppressing a Nefarious Traffic," pp. 873–94.
[38] Tarling, *British Policy in the Malay Peninsula and Archipelago, 1824–1871*, pp. 176–87; Nicholas Tarling, *The Cambridge History of Southeast Asia, Volume Two Part One: From c.1800 to the 1930s* (Cambridge: Cambridge University Press, 1999), pp. 5–30.

Not only had Malacca been a primary trading entrepôt that connected the Indian and Pacific Oceans since the fifteenth century, slavery and the slave trade were a major portion of that trade. It supplied labor, both domestic and agricultural, to the well-established and wealthy Malaysian, Arab, Chinese, Portuguese, and Dutch residents of the community.[39] A large portion of the city was built and populated by slaves imported from all over the Indian Ocean World.[40] During its most prosperous years, cities like Malacca imported slaves on a considerable scale that were, as Reid describes, "drawn from every nation and race."[41] At the same time, rulers gave itinerates captive women as wives and concubines, who produced children and became part of Malacca's elite. In fact, Chinese settlers and Indian sailors were the only free wage labor available for many centuries.[42]

According to Nordin Hussin, during the Dutch period, "slaves in Melaka could be classified into two categories, namely, those owned by the Company (VOC) and those owned by private individuals."[43] At the end of the eighteenth century, there was a marked reduction in the Company's ownership of slaves from 106 in 1775 to 34 in 1806; however, there seemed to be little change in individual ownership. By 1824, most slaveholders were Europeans—primarily Dutch Burghers—followed by Chinese and Malay.[44] Before the arrival of abolition, slaves were considered an investment and the measure of an individual's wealth and influence in Southeast Asian communities; the Portuguese and Dutch had assimilated the practice and come to rely on the institution as a source of cheap labor.[45] In fact the governor of Malacca, J. S. Timmerman Thyssen, owned thirty-seven slaves of his own.[46] The immediate abolition of slavery and emancipation of slaves would have been the equivalent of liquidating the accounts of the most wealthy and powerful people who would not likely have taken this siphoning of capital lightly.

Consequently, regardless of what any one individual officer may, or may not, have wanted to do, the Anti-Slavery Project in Malacca, like so many other colonial cities, was a process that had to be negotiated step by step. As Major explains, in addition to emotional arguments from abolitionists and concerns from the military over compromised borders, contemporary debates about slave trading

---

[39] Andaya and Andaya, *A History of Malaysia*, pp. 160–1; Reid, "The Decline of Slavery in Nineteenth Century Indonesia," pp. 67–9. Moreover, the 1838 EIC report illustrates that there was a diverse population of wealthy slave owners in Malacca during this period; Evans, *Slave Trade (East India) Slavery in Ceylon*, pp. 249–53.
[40] Reid, "The Decline of Slavery in Nineteenth Century Indonesia," pp. 68–9.
[41] Reid and Brewster, *Slavery, Bondage, and Dependency in Southeast Asia*, 170.
[42] Reid, "The Decline of Slavery in Nineteenth Century Indonesia," p. 67.
[43] Hussin, *Trade and Society in the Straits of Melaka*, p. 177.
[44] Ibid., p. 179.
[45] Reid, "The Decline of Slavery in Nineteenth Century Indonesia," p. 68.
[46] Evans, *Slave Trade (East India) Slavery in Ceylon*, p. 285.

contained political worries about the acceptable parameters of British authority.[47] British officials felt it paramount to preserve positive political relationships in Malacca in order to secure their position of power within the Straits. Initially, a dogmatic adherence to the preservation of private property motivated them to tolerate slavery and look for alternatives to immediate emancipation. After all, their official orders were to abolish the trade as soon as was practical; in Malacca, local authorities felt this was the best they could accomplish.[48]

## The Registries

In his requested report to the British Straits Government in Council in October of 1829, Superintendent W. T. Lewis explained to his superiors that "slavery ha[d] existed at Malacca from time immemorial, and that the first check to it was the Act of 51 Geo.3, c23" (1811 Slave Trade Felony Act).[49] According to Lewis, after the British took possession of Malacca, Resident Farquhar enacted the Slave Trade Act on January 30, 1813, and declared it a felony to trade slaves in the city. Farquhar was so keen to abolish slavery within Britain's territories that, during a trip to Penang in September of 1816, the Raj of Borneo sent him two slaves, a man and woman, as a gift of friendship. Ignoring custom, the resident returned them immediately and told the Raj that "under existing laws against slavery, it is not permitted for any one residing under British Government to receive slaves under any circumstance." Then, he ordered the slaves be either returned at "the first opportunity from whence they came by the person to whom they were consigned" or "emancipated forthwith in the fullest and most public manner, according to the established forms of the settlement." Farquhar wanted to be sure that everyone in the community understood the importation of new slaves was illegal in Malacca, even for the highest officials.

This new law, however, did not affect the status of those already enslaved or imported before the 1813 proclamation. Moreover, the colonial maintained their established right to punish slaves for crimes, and public offenses and disputes were still settled by the police. While it could hardly be called sweeping reform, Farquhar had laid the foundational blocks for future antislavery ordinances and, eventually, the end of state-sanctioned slavery in Malacca. However, very little was done to actually enforce these regulations. Until the enactment

---

[47] Major, *Slavery, Abolitionism and Empire in India*, p. 137.
[48] Ibid., pp. 70–4.
[49] Evans, *Slave Trade (East India) Slavery in Ceylon*, pp. 244–6.

of the registries in 1818, aside from prohibiting the trade, neither British nor Dutch authorities had made any effort to identify those who had been illegally trafficked in the community.

As instructed, Lewis' report provided President Fullerton with all the official communications available concerning slavery in Malacca during Dutch occupation between 1818 and 1825. Not only did the Netherlands have obligations to Britain as a result of treaties, local Dutch administrators were also interested in taking advantage of the potential tax income that could be drawn from slave owners.[50] Within the documents Lewis reviewed, a translated announcement from Governor-General Thyssen that proclaimed "the abolition of the slave trade as of, 30 January 1813." He later ordered the creation of the first slave registry that would become mandatory in 1819.[51] The process began on October 10, 1818, when Governor Thyssen asserted to VOC officials that in order to "prevent the clandestine importation of slaves," the government "should be fully made acquainted with the number of slaves at present in the settlements."[52] As a result, he ordered all slave owners in Malacca and its dependencies, "before the 1st November next, to deliver at the office of the fiscal an account, statement of the names, native country, and age of their slaves; whether they are married or unmarried, how employed, and the number of children, with their age." A fear of losing valuable income motivated inhabitants to more clearly define the relationships with their servants. This is how the Dutch began to rigidify conceptions of slavery and servitude in Southeast Asia, and those entered onto the registry acquired a newly constructed, legally defined status of slave.

The following July, the Dutch governor-general, Godert Alexander Gerard Phillip Baron van der Capellen, informed local inhabitants that "the present rules respecting slaves have become unavoidable under existing circumstances, and much inconvenience is experienced in the absence of a registry of slaves." Framing it as an unavoidable circumstance, Governor van der Capellen deflected

---

[50] Trocki, "Borders and the Mapping of the Malay World." The Dutch did regain control of Malacca on May 4, 1818, as a result of treaties signed with Britain after the Napoleonic Wars; however, as President Fullerton explains in his minutes to the government on November 9, 1829, the Dutch had to stipulate to actively implement antislavery legislation as part of negotiations; Evans, *Slave Trade (East India) Slavery in Ceylon*, p. 255. There is actually very little written in English or Dutch about abolitionism in the Dutch Empire; however, the following are detailed examinations: Gert Oostindie, *Fifty Years Later: Antislavery, Capitalism and Modernity in the Dutch Orbit* (Pittsburgh: University of Pittsburgh Press, 1996); Emmer, *The Dutch Slave Trade, 1500–1850*. These are a few important studies in Dutch on the abolition of slavery in Southeast Asia: Ellen Klinkers, "Op Hoop van Vrijheid: van Slavensamenleving Naar Creoolse Gemeenschap in Suriname, 1830–1880," (PhD diss., University of Utrecht, 1997); Elmer Kolfin, *Van de Slavenzweep En de Muze: Twee Eeuwen Verbeelding van Slavernij in Suriname* (Leiden: KITLV, 1997).

[51] Evans, *Slave Trade (East India) Slavery in Ceylon*, p. 273.

[52] Ibid., p. 216.

resistance by blaming British antislavery measures as a whole and constructed the registries as the most efficient solution to accommodate Britain's demands. Evidence suggests that while the Dutch might not have been enthusiastic about abolition in Malacca, they did recognize an opportunity for profit. In his November 9 minute presented to the Government in Council in 1829, Fullerton suggested that the parameters for the registries seemed "to have been framed, besides the prevention of abuse and misconstruction, with the view of insuring regularity in the collection of the tax on slaves, called 'Head Money.'"[53] This system was clearly more concerned with quantifying and taxing residents for the number of slaves they owned than the eradication of slavery.

According to records, the Dutch governor ordered two registries: one for slaves over the age of eight, another for those under—only slaves over the age of eight were subject to tax.[54] He vowed that the registries would be open within the year on the islands of Java and Madura and insisted that plans for the rest were forthcoming. In Malacca, each slave received a certificate, given to slaveholders, to "convince authorities" of their bondage. The authorities allowed slave owners to register slaves in absentia; so, if slaves ran away, officials simply entered their missing status on the registry next to their name. All transfers of slaves had to be recorded with the registrar, and slave owners had forty-eight hours to report the births of all "slave-born children" and the deaths of any slaves. Finally, if a slaveholder wanted to move from one settlement to another in Dutch territory, the law required they notify the registrars of both settlements, "on pain of the above forfeiture." These registries treated the slaves on the list as expensive luxuries and the government wanted local residents to pay for them. Naturally, many neglected to register all of their slaves, but as long as they were within Dutch territories, officials wanted to be able to track and tax them. However, the registries also provided slaveholders a guarantee of ownership or insurance against future ordinances at a time when the market for slaves appeared to be collapsing. The prohibition of the trade and local antislavery ordinances had done little more than criminalize European slave trading in British and Dutch ports. Ironically, the financial burden from new taxes, insecurities considering incoming legislation, and competition from an expanding force of cheap, "free," laborers had been far more damaging to the institution of slavery in Southeast Asia than any abolitionist sentiment or legislation.

On October 12, 1819, just short of a year after van der Capellen's initial announcement, the first slave registry opened in Malacca. The Dutch colonial

---

[53] Ibid., p. 255.
[54] Ibid., pp. 246–8.

government ordered local officials to read the registry of slaves aloud, in its entirety, "in the different languages at the Government House, and subsequently be published." The order directed local inhabitants to proceed, "as soon as possible before the 15th of next month, to call upon the fiscal as this place, who will make the necessary entry of their slaves." Finally, and perhaps more importantly, the declaration stated that "all slaves which are not registered within the time specified will be considered as having been emancipated and freed from the bonds of slavery." Slave owners had to choose between increased costs from taxation or complete loss of value after emancipation. The VOC government wanted this completed "immediately" and ordered that the fiscal (administrative tax officer), Mr. J. H. Stecher, finish the registry by December 15, 1819, and then send it directly to the governor-general. With an eye on generating tax revenue, this first registry was focused on identifying the population of taxable slaves within the community and creating a way for their masters to protect their right to authority over their "personal property." If slave owners did not want to pay the taxes and did not register a portion of their slaves, theoretically, their slaves were entitled to be released from servitude. Such a loss of property, without compensation, was likely a key motivator for residents to participate in the registry.

Coinciding with the formation of the registries, local owners of registered slaves also signed an agreement on December 6 proclaiming "that no children of their slaves that may be born from and after this date [would] be considered slaves."[55] Moreover, since the children were unable to take care of themselves, the government ordered that they "shall remain with their parents, and be under the immediate care of the master or mistress of their parents until they shall have attained the age of 16 years." A gesture in celebration of "the memorial birthday of their beloved and honored hereditary Prince of the Netherlands," the emancipation of slave-born children after 1819 created a definitive marker in Malacca's transition from a society with an entrenched system of legal slavery to a slave-free settlement. While neither of these actions abolished slavery in Malacca, the registries made the legal possession of slaves much more expensive and gave an unexpected window of opportunity for the children of slaves born after 1819. So, while the British were not directly responsible, their negotiation of antislavery measures within the parameters of treaties ensured that the Dutch colonial government began work toward abolition in Malacca.

The report also tells us that Dutch administrators opened a second registry on September 19, 1822, "in order to prevent any individuals from suffering losses." They offered a period of amnesty for those who may not have taken advantage

[55] Ibid., pp. 248–9.

of the first registration and announced to local slaveholders that "during the period of six months, beginning from the 1st October next to ultimo March 1823, all slaves which have not been registered will be admitted to registry by the fiscal at this place." Yet again, colonial authorities pronounced all slaves not registered after this period would be considered "emancipated from the bonds of slavery." Secretary to the government H. Van San insisted that the declaration be published and read out loud in Netherlands, Portuguese, Chinese, Kling, and Malay languages, "so that no person may plead ignorance of this order." As with the first, once the registry was closed, those not on it would no longer be recognized as slaves.

Then, in January of 1823, Secretary Van San authorized the VOC officer in charge of the slave registry to "adjust at his discretion" the "treatment and punishment of slaves, against whom complaints may be preferred by their masters or mistresses, for misbehavior."[56] Taking an unprecedented and drastic step, the VOC claimed legal authority over slaves in Malacca—within any household—and placed themselves in charge of punishing them. Moreover, rather than fill out a report for each incident and "await for authority to act," Dutch colonial officials gave their local officers, as representatives of the colonial state, the power to interfere between master and slave and adjudicate complaints of "obstinacy, disobedience, drunkenness, and such other like misconduct." So, in the space of a decade, Dutch colonial officials had prohibited the legal import and export of slaves, developed a comprehensive list of slaves within the city and its dependencies, declared the children of slaves born after 1819 free, and assumed the authority to punish disobedient slaves. Still, none of these measures specifically prohibited slave ownership nor did they categorically emancipate slaves. Their policy of taxed tolerance rather than immediate emancipation worked to accommodate existing slave owners in the community but set in motion the process, which eventually led to the gradual abolition of slavery in Malacca.

The VOC began a third registry on January 1, 1824, "for the purpose of entering all the registered slaves who might arrive with certificates from other Netherlands settlements" This third registry was kept open and allowed Dutch inhabitants to immigrate between settlements without the threat of losing their property. Unlike the first two, new slaves could be added to the third list. From

---

[56] Ibid., p. 249.

1819 to 1824, the Dutch fiscal entered a total of 1,482 slaves on the Malaccan registries.[57] The first registry contained 685 men, 581 women, and 165 boys and girls under the age of 8. The second list added thirty-nine men and twenty-eight women, and the third, just twelve more. As Fullerton would explain to the Government in Council in 1829, "all slaves unregistered at the latter date" were concidered "emancipated and free." It is easy to see, at this stage, how the repeated threats of emancipation might have seemed hollow. It is highly likely that there were still many unregistered slaves in the city when the British finally reassumed control in April of 1825.

As we know, Farquhar had already taken the first steps in the antislavery process by prohibiting the import or export of slaves in 1813 and, then in 1816 he forbade British residents from owning slaves. The Dutch continued the process by creating the registries that specifically identified a slave population, and implemented more concrete conceptions of slave status and servitude in Southeast Asia.[58] The colonial government had established itself as the ultimate authority in master-servant disputes and, when they returned, British EIC officials believed that slavery would eventually die out with the "demise" of those listed on the registry. Consequently, they preserved existing Dutch policies, slave regulations, and registries when they reassumed control of the colony in the spring of 1825.[59] Maintainig the status quo and proceeding toward the gradual abolition of slavery allowed EIC officials to preserve the appearance of noninterference, while following the Company's directives to implement antislavery measures when possible.[60] British authorities initially approached the subject as a legal matter; if a slave was registered, EIC officers respected the slave owner's property rights, which—in the eyes of the British—gave them no more authority than "a master over a servant."[61] If the slaves were not registered, the magistrate considered them free and would not hear the case.[62] So while British colonial officials tolerated slavery in Malacca, while attempting to construct policies that they believed ensured its eventual demise. This meant maintaining the status quo as they bided their time waiting for those on the registries to die.

---

[57] Ibid., p. 256.
[58] Reid, "The Decline of Slavery in Nineteenth Century Indonesia," p. 68.
[59] Evans, *Slave Trade (East India) Slavery in Ceylon*, p. 256.
[60] Major, *Slavery, Abolitionism and Empire in India*, pp. 69–72.
[61] Evans, *Slave Trade (East India) Slavery in Ceylon*, p. 257.
[62] Ibid., p. 256.

6

# A Convenient Compromise

Malacca's policy of tolerance did not change when the EIC joined the city with Penang and Singapore to form the British Straits Settlements in 1826. According the British authorities, each of those settlements had already prohibited slavery and did not have the sizable slave populations found in that international entrepôt. The police records Superintendent Lewis provided demonstrated that he, as the British magistrate, had simply been following precedent. In Lewis' defense, Governor Fullerton addressed the Straits' Government in Council and explained that the authorities in Malacca had, until Garling's rash behavior, generally been unified in their approach by "punishing slaves for misconduct or running away; fining masters for ill treatment of slaves; liberating all not proved to be slaves on the registry, and on some occasions liberating the slave on repeated ill-usage of the master."[1] Fullerton told the council that in the summer of 1829, Resident Garling had attempted to circumvent the government's policy of patience and took it "upon himself to subvert the established practice" and declared "slaves to be free." The controversy that followed Garling's declaration not only exposed inconsistencies in the Company's perspective on antislavery ordinances and ideological divisions between officials in the Straits, the matter forced the EIC government to more clearly articulate their expectations for the enforcement of antislavery policy in the region. However, the conflict also highlighted the ways Company culture and bureaucratic tape stifled the actions of abolitionists who ignored previously established habits of temperance and caution to bring about a more abrupt end to the institution. There were few in the east ready or willing to invest the time, energy, or the political and social capital necessary to affect the immediate abolition of slavery in the Straits.

According to a complaint made by the "Inhabitants of Malacca," the problems began when—without provocation or direction from any EIC authority—Resident Garling and a local missionalry, Reverend Smith, began to encourage

[1] Evans, *Slave Trade (East India) Slavery in Ceylon*, p. 257.

slaves to tender their resignations and leave their masters.² The petition claimed that "persons in the employ of the English missionaries" had interfered with existing habits, disturbed the "domestic comforts" of slave-owning residents, and that the settlement was "thrown into confusion" by these reckless and impromptu emancipations. To complicate matters, Garling placed himself in direct opposition with legal precedent and Superintendent Lewis, who had thus far been ordered to follow established custom and enforce existing slave laws. What ensued was a heated legal debate between government officials that resulted in the formalization of the EIC's policy on slavery in the Straits Settlement and a signed declaration by local residents marking December 31, 1841, as the definitive end to the recognition of legal slavery in Malacca.

The standoff between Resident Garling and Superintendent Lewis erupted early in the summer of 1829. According to two signed depositions, on May 11, slave owners Renga Sammee and Abdullah Trunkerrah took their slaves—Mootoo and Salamat—to see Reverend Smith who had given them a note that contained "the resident's order to consider himself free."³ Each of the complainants, both of whom had produced their certificates to prove ownership, immediately applied to Lewis to request an audience "at the next court of justice" to recover damages. Ironically, in this circumstance, both the slave and the slave owner possessed legal documents supporting their positions. Later that month, Resident Garling wrote to Lewis complaining that "some measures adopted in the police department have not had a salutary tendency" toward the abolition of slavery, which meant he did not agree with how Lewis was doing his job.⁴ The resident explained that there had been "several instances in which" many had been "left exposed to the unhappy consequence" of having been designated slaves and, to his understanding, when Malacca was made a British territory, its inhabitants became British subjects. Since slavery was not recognized in England, Garling determined that it should not be recognized in its colonies. Of course, the decision to register and legally designate the status of slaves in Malacca had not been Superintendent Lewis' decision; nevertheless, Garling accused Lewis of "needlessly" creating "obstacles" for those seeking their freedom. He asserted that the superintendent's actions were evidence that he was "opposed the gradual emancipation" of slaves in Malacca. Even though he was following the precedent set by his colleagues and Company officers before him, because Lewis acknowledged the rights of slave owners and enforced the

---

² Ibid., pp. 253–7.
³ Ibid., p. 301.
⁴ Ibid., p. 214.

Dutch slave systems, Garling felt he was working in opposition of the Empire's objective to abolish slavery.

Resident Garling's letter called attention to the experiences of Menah, a slave woman who reported "herself to be kept in Mr. D. Kock's premises as a slave, and habited in a garb corresponding with that description." According to Garling, she "sought refuge on the grounds of a gentleman, who complains that his name has been needlessly and painfully dragged into notice." The official informed Lewis that "two men, as from Mr. Kock, endeavored to seize the woman in the above sanctuary; they were at first prevented," but he claimed "the gentlemen received private information that the woman had been led back to her former master." Garling wanted the superintendent of police to "take such measures as you esteem the case to demand for ascertaining whether or not the woman had been taken back." The official told Lewis that the woman was "so unprotected" that she could not "be expected to have a friend versed in legal forms who can take the proper measures for securing her liberty." At the end of his letter, Garling reasserted that he "hoped" Lewis would "take active measures for personally conferring with the woman referred to." From his words Garling believed that Menah had runaway, sought protection from a local "gentleman," and her master had sent two men to retrieve her. He also clearly thought that his official reassurances of legal authority would compel Lewis to arrive on the scene, investigate the matter, and rescue the poor slave woman if he found any evidence of abuse. Malacca was British territory and Garling wanted Lewis to enforce what he understood to be the law.

Much to Garling's chagrin, Superintendent Lewis' response made clear that he saw things differently. Lewis wrote that he was not aware of any new legislation forbidding the possession of slaves in Malacca, or measures for police response to them, and that his policy on runaway slaves simply followed long-established precedent. The superintendent told Garling that, save for cases of cruelty and violence brought before him as magistrate, he did not consider himself as "the arbiter of right of persons." Lewis assured the resident that he had consulted the Company's visiting court recorder on the matter who, he claimed, "cautioned [him] not to interfere in cases which belong to the higher court."[5] Lewis told Garling that if anyone had returned slaves to their registered owners, it would have been him. He explained that he had been given no guidance other than the "public orders" and registries, and reminded Garling that local slave owners were not going to let him simply free their slaves without some sort of explanation

---

[5] Ibid.

and/or compensation. If Garling possessed a different understanding of EIC precedent and policy, Lewis asked that he be more explicit with his instructions and provide the appropriate supporting legal documentation while he was at it.

Lewis was not concerned with Garling's theoretical argument, nor was he interested in leading an unprecedented crusade against the slave-owning elite in the city. He believed Garling's actions were in direct conflict with the Company's long-held position of noninterference and wanted more clear direction if the government or any official intended on changing things. A few days later, Garling wrote back to Lewis criticizing his job performance, accused him of interfering with the process of abolition, and officially directed him to personally inquire about the absconded slave woman. The resident believed there was no circumstance under which slavery could be tolerated within Britain's territories and it was Lewis' responsibility as a representative of the benevolent patriarchal British Empire to assist these poor souls in attaining their freedom. It was clear to Lewis that he would need to seek direction from a higher level of government. These vastly different interpretations of the situation are emblematic of the Anti-Slavery Project in the East Indies, as a whole. Like Raffles, Garling believed a strong assertion of British values and culture—a civilizing mission—should be a key component of EIC expansion, while pragmatists like Crawfurd and Lewis worked to preserve the Company's traditional policy of noninterference to maintain the peace.

Garling's letters and actions demonstrate he felt Britain's Parliament intended not only to prohibit the trade in slaves, but also to actively assist the enslaved in their efforts for freedom. He blamed Lewis' attitude for the stagnation of antislavery efforts in Malacca and accused Lewis of "a bias unfavorable to the cause of local freedom." Garling claimed that because of the superintendent's attitude, "those who have had slaves feel indisposed to recognize their freedom, and consequently averse to make any compromise."[6] Garling blamed Lewis of agitating "the proprietors" and asserted that he was responsible for the angry altercations that were likely to result when the "menials hear of the right to freedom" and learn that "obstacles oppose themselves to the exercise of this liberty." While he left Lewis to "the full exercise" of his own discretion, Garling invited him to seriously consider whether the magistrate might take his lead and use his authority to usher in a more swift abolition of slavery in Malacca.

It is worth noting that there were only two slaves registered to a Mr. Daniel Kock, a boy named Bitjoe and a girl named Soenting.[7] He registered each as a small child and they would have been around 10 and 12 at the time of this

---

[6] Ibid., p. 216.
[7] Ibid., p. 287.

dispute. There was no record of a slave woman named "Menah" registered to him, or anyone else, on any of the three Malaccan slave registries. Technically, then, she was a free woman because she was not registered. It was more likely, however, that Menah was an unregistered slave woman, perhaps a domestic servant or concubine. It would have been illegal for him to import her as a slave. Was she Bitjoe and Soenting's mother or caregiver? Garling said she was dressed like a slave, so it is doubtful she was living as mistress of that or any household. She filed a complaint against a Jozeph Hock "for beating and ill-treating" on May 23, but the case was dismissed "for non appearance" two days later.[8] According to the letter, Mr. Kock's men lured her back, but there is no evidence or any more record of Menah. Garling's implication was that Lewis was personally responsible for any tragedy that may have befallen this young woman.

Resident Garling trusted that if masters believed colonial authorities were sympathetic to the slaves' cause, they "might be induced to acquiesce in the adoption of more temporizing measures with their menials."[9] Moreover, he hoped if slave owners thought officials were going to help slaves obtain freedom, they might be more inclined to accept British demands and independently negotiate emancipation more quickly. Of course, this solution did not address the real loss of property that concerned Superintendent Lewis, nor did it acknowledge that his interpretations were counter to established practice. Despite being Resident of that settlement, Garling's letter read as though he had no idea slavery had been an entrenched institution within Malaccan history or that any other colonial official had taken steps to address it. As far as he was concerned, the passage of the 1811 Felony Act was a directive to Company officials to bring an end to slavery as expediently as possible and this method sped things up considerably.[10] According to later correspondence with Governor Fullerton, Garling said that Lewis ceased all direct communication with him after that point. Clearly, there was a breakdown in communication across the board; this disconnect between these two EIC servants shines a stark light on how ill-prepared and unorganized the Company's antislavery efforts were in this region as a whole. In the Straits, some officials found the institution of slavery abhorrent and believed they were on a campaign to bring an immediate end to the institution within British territories. Others, less convinced of the need for prohibitions in the first place, chose a more tolerant and pragmatic approach; any acts of unnecessary violence (as determined by local magistrates) brought to their attention were investigated

[8] Ibid., p. 300.
[9] Ibid., p. 215.
[10] Ibid., p. 251.

and prosecuted. However, they were not willing to threaten the settlement's economic viability. Moreover, many saw slaves and bonded people in the Straits as either future household servants or the mistresses and wives of wealthy non-European elites or, perhaps the potential mothers of a future workforce. We should wonder if Garling was not briefed on the Company's long history of tolerance and noninterference, or if he just chose to ignore it.

As expected, Dutch "Burghers and Native [slave holding] Inhabitants of Malacca" protested Garling's unprecedented actions with a signed petition sent to the Government in Council at Prince of Wales Island in the beginning of October requesting assistance from Governor Fullerton. Drawing upon EIC Captain Phillip's 1808 assurances when their families arrived in the community, the document asserted that they "and their fathers before them, were allowed to retain the use of slaves."[11] The petitioners explained that before the British arrived in Malacca, for those in the "Netherland India much of the property of individuals, and more particularly of natives, consisted in the number of slaves in their possession." They questioned the EIC's right to emancipate their slaves and argued that, "this mode adopted of depriving them of their property [was] unexampled in the annals of the English Government." They wondered why, if Fullerton's intention was the total abolition of slavery in the Straits, there was not a notice or proclamation stating such. The slave owners reminded the president that both the Dutch and the British governments had "derived their profits by levying the sum of $7 on each slave imported and sold at this place," that the owners had already agreed to emancipate children born after 1819, and that "slavery in the course of time would have by itself ceased." The petitioners wanted Fullerton to explain why, when all believed the issue had been settled, had Garling begun to indiscriminately setting their slaves free.

Malacca's slaveholders felt Resident Garling had irresponsibly emancipated slaves who did not have "the sense to appreciate the comforts they [were] forfeiting, for what [was] termed their liberty." Moreover, they asserted that those slaves already freed offered a glimpse of what could be expected. The letter complained that the "idol, riotous life" these newly emancipated slaves cultivated left them "without any means of gaining a livelihood, living 10 and 15 in a house, women and men mixing promiscuously together," which he asserted was "a sight not before witnessed by the oldest inhabitants of Malacca." Garling's indiscriminate emancipation of their slaves had upset the social order. They believed such an abrupt abolition would cause chaos in the community and

---

[11] Ibid., pp. 249–50.

wanted to know what English law or authority had given this resident the right to dispossess them of their slaves without any discussion of compensation for their loss of property. They were indignant at the EIC government's indiscretion and asserted that more provisions had been made for the notoriously cruel owners of African slaves in the west and "these people [had] been treated more as children than slaves." They hoped the president would at least give them the opportunity to apply to His Majesty's Government to find redress for their grievances. The inhabitants of this community did not agree with Garling's legal interpretations and were going to take the case to court. Had Malacca been a newly formed colony, as in the case of Penang and Singapore, Garling may have had an easier time initiating his sweeping changes. However, Malaccan petitioners were wealthy, thoroughly established inhabitants familiar with their legal rights—some of them European—deeply enmeshed in the regional trade economy. Fullerton could have ignored or dismissed their complaints, but such actions would have very likely damaged important political and economic relationships. As we will see from both the local and supreme government's response, in this instance politics and economics were more important than the eradication of slavery and Garling had overstepped his authority.

On October 20, 1829, in response to the inhabitants' petition, Governor Fullerton ordered Superintendent Lewis to conduct a full investigation of slavery in Malacca, "from the year 1795 to the present day."[12] Although it had been less than twenty-five years since the agreements were made, even the president of the Straits Settlements did not fully understand the status of slaves, or the rights of their owners. Clearly, the abolition of slavery had not been a pressing issue for any them during their time in the Straits. Eight days after Fullerton began the investigation, Garling wrote the governor complaining about the return of slaves by his local magistrate (Superintendent Lewis) and stated his firm belief that "slavery [had] no legal existence in Malacca." Garling told Fullerton he felt that Lewis had been insubordinate and had neglected his duty. The official wrote that he had personal information that slaves were still being imported and exported into the settlement from "beyond seas." He insisted that he was aware of the "objections against the sudden emancipation of slaves," but he felt his views were "strictly in unison with the verbal suggestions of the Honourable President [Fullerton]"; his goal was that "slavery be put down and the people be relieved, by any convenient compromise, of their present and degrading bonds." Garling proposed that a "compromise should be rendered acceptable

---

[12] Ibid., p. 241.

to the slaves as well as to their proprietors" and asserted that "the real rights of the one party should be as invincible as those of the other." Garling quite naively proclaimed the slaves' right to freedom was just as important as the owner's right to their property and he was betting Fullerton agreed with him. Garling believed that Company officials should legally have supported the efforts of runaway slaves seeking refuge in British territories. Even though his actions had not been in accordance with the EIC's general policy of noninterference, nor had he time-honored agreements between Company officials and the local elites in the Straits. However, Fullerton's actions suggested he was more inclined to follow precedent.

Clearly, not everyone had the same interpretation of the EIC's expectations and—more importantly—were not drawing from, or have access to, the same sections of the legal code. The left hand had no idea what the right hand was planning. Garling's fervency led him to look for ways to use the law to accomplish his goal to end slavery, while local officials tried to accommodate the inconvenience of antislavery legislation within the quest for stability and profits. The EIC had neither explicitly stated their intentions nor developed a comprehensive policy and Garling had been left to his own ideological compass. Did Garling's lack of communication and independent actions ignite the hostilities between him and Lewis, and then later with Fullerton, or was it Garling's unbridled abolitionism make them bristle? While Garling does come off a bit overconfident in his demands, both men seemed taken aback by the resident's vitriolic campaign; Lewis clearly believed he was doing his job and Fullerton was obviously caught off guard. The governor needed to know more about his legal footing, the history of slavery in Malacca—and the Company's reaction to it—before making any concrete decisions.

When Superintendent Lewis' report arrived about a week later, it provided Fullerton with a brief legislative history and copies of everything he had "been enabled to find in the offices respecting slavery," in Malacca.[13] The superintendent informed the government that the British court of justice in Malacca had left him "little to say on the subject of these slaves, and of their treatment." He asserted, as other EIC officials had, that the slaves were rarely ill-treated in the settlement and those that were, had been "recommended" for emancipation. Lewis echoed the sentiment of most of his colleagues in the east explaining that slaves in Malacca were generally for "domestic purposes" and concurred with the inhabitants that "they were treated more as children than as slaves." Lewis echoed what had, by

[13] Ibid., pp. 244–5.

that point, become a common attitude within contemporary slavery discourse: slaves in the east were domestics and treated more like family than the beastly abuse showered on slaves in the west, they were not "true" slaves and did not *need* the same protections, and therefore, there was less of a necessity for an immediate and total abolition of the institution.

Proposing a compromise, Lewis suggested to Fullerton that "the inhabitants be invited to" bring a "termination to slavery" themselves, by offering them a "fair price for the value of their slave." He recommended that slaves "henceforth should be considered as debtors, and a certain sum struck off the debt annually." The magistrate doubted the correctness of the current statistics about the number of slaves actually living in Malacca because he believed there was confusion about the laws concerning the legality of slavery; logically, he believed most slave owners only reported the registered slaves, or those born to them, on the annual census because they believed the declaration of any new slaves would be illegal. Consequently, there were very likely even more slaves in Malacca than officials knew. Lewis surmised that converting a slave's value into a debt would compensate the owners for their financial loss, ease tensions and expedite the process, as well as appease the EIC government's "anxieties" about bringing a swift end to slavery.[14] As we will see from both the governor and the Company's response, it seemed Lewis had a better grasp on EIC objectives regarding the implementation of antislavery ordinances, as well as what was actually transpiring in the community than Garling.

On October 29, Fullerton recorded a less than cordial minute for the Government in Council responding to Resident Garling's public declarations.[15] The official had misread Fullerton's statements; the governor did not agree with Garling's interpretation of British law and believed he had "blended together questions perfectly distinct." As Fullerton saw it, the first issue was whether or not slaves within Malacca, "under the preceding Netherland's Government, at the time of cession, by previous purchase, or by birth, recognized and registered as such," were still recognized under British law. He felt he could not make a decision on such an important case without first seeing translations of all the relevant documents concerning this issue since the addition of the settlement. The governor expressed his doubts about Garling's interpretation that slaves had no legal existence within Malacca and told the resident that he must

---

[14] Ibid., p. 260; Secretary Patullo addressed the inhabitants of Malacca for President Fullerton in reply to their petition and told them, "[H]e need hardly remind [them] of the extreme anxiety evinced by the British Legislature for the total suppression of slavery."

[15] Ibid., p. 242.

"protest against being forced into a premature discussion." Moreover, Fullerton admonished Garling for using "casual expressions used by me in private conversations being made the ground for public minutes." He was not happy that Garling had taken statements made in private conversations out of context to use in a public debate and, without expressly stating it, placed himself on the side of Lewis and maintenance of the status quo. While they had clearly discussed the matter in private, Garling had obviously misunderstood the conversation.

"As to the next point," Fullerton added, he would not make a decision about the specific cases described because he insisted that if Garling had any evidence of slaves being imported and exported into the settlement, he should "lay that information before any one of the magistrates, with the list of witnesses." The governor assured Garling that "no magistrate" would refuse such a case or "summon the accused to take the depositions, and eventually commit the party for trial." Fullerton believed that offering a blanket decision now would create a conflict of interest and circumvent the legal process. He argued he should refrain from intervening, "when an indictment will be prepared for the grand jury, at the next sessions, and all will proceed in regular course, without the previous interposition of the court in a case, which they themselves must try." Fullerton explained that the magistrates would "of course proceed at their own discretion," based on the evidence given, but that Lewis had acted in accordance with "existing practice," which was clearly established from the very first treaty with the king of Quedah in 1786, "servants quitting their masters without notice are returned to them." Fullerton stressed it was not the responsibility of the local magistrate to declare "whether the person so returned is, or is not a slave, and thus prejudging a question on which no legal decision has yet been given." Each of the slave owners had documentation from the slave registry that those were their slaves. Their responsibility was to "the superior courts" and could not be expected to "pay obedience to their executive superior, contrary to their own judgment." The governor was clear: Lewis was performing his duty according to law and precedent and Garling's letters indiscriminately emancipating slaves had not honored political agreements and threatened to upend the legal system. As we might imagine, Fullerton's public rebuke did not assuage the dispute between the two officials. Instead, it motivated Garling to bring the issue to the attention of the Company's government in India; he believed that both Lewis and Fullerton had misinterpreted British law and were inhibiting the progress of abolitionism in the Straits Settlements. Irate with the governor's decision, or lack thereof, he was going to go over both of their heads.

On November 2 Garling responded to the petition from Malacca's inhabitants and Fullerton's reprimand with a refutation of their collective assertion that slaves were treated as children. His letter complained that even if these slaves were free, their children were not converted to Christianity and nonetheless lost.[16] Garling ignored the reality that, according to legal precedent, slave owners had a legitimate right to their property and that they might expect some financial compensation for their loss. He claimed that the superintendent had unjustly made accusations against his and the Reverend Smith's character and asserted that the alleged agreement by local residents "that the children of slaves be born free" after 1819 was not legitimate. Garling made it clear that he did not agree with either the magistrate's interpretation of British law or Fullerton's October 29 minute and requested he be allowed to review any further documents questioning his character, since the proceedings were going to be forwarded to the EIC Board of Control. Although Garling had produced no evidence of anything resembling what authorities considered actual slavery or illegal activity, he was certain he had correctly interpreted the law, as well as the intentions of the governor. He felt justified in his actions, and saw Lewis' resistance to his orders as blatant insubordination.

The situation was exacerbated by the announcement of Fullerton's official legal decision in another public minute on November 9, which he described as "a general review of the slave question and proposing a reference to the Supreme Government." This was the governor's final judgment on the matter for the benefit of officials within the Straits. His intention was that from that point, local magistrates would be able to use his statements to guide their actions until a "higher court" had a chance to review the situation. Of course, Fullerton drafted this minute more for the EIC Board in Bengal than for those in the Straits and began by providing an extensive explanation about both the context and the grounds on which he formed his decision. He knew his decision would be reviewed in the very near future and, as both the presiding legal authority and highest executive official, the governor/president organized this statement to create a foundation for his, and future, legal opinions. He recognized that his decision could have much larger implications for EIC policy throughout its territories and wanted to be sure he had the support of his superiors. Consequently, Fullerton began by carefully defining the relevant legal and political context surrounding the case.

Fullerton offered the chronology and descriptions of the registration system from Superintendent Lewis' October 28 report and, even though he knew it was not the case, assured the council that they "may safely therefore assume the fact that these three registers contain the names of all that can on any construction be viewed as slaves now in this settlement, town, and country."[17] He felt confident

[16] Ibid., pp. 254–5.
[17] Ibid., pp. 256–8.

that "with the demise of these named persons, slavery must entirely cease." Without any acknowledgment that he understood there were likely unregistered slaves in the city, his proclamation demonstrated his desire to keep things the way they were. As he reminded his colleagues about the EIC's long-held policy of noninterference, the governor provided examples of other settlements within the EIC territories in which slavery persisted and then declared that Malacca's magistrate had rightfully followed precedent. He explained that EIC officials in ancient cities throughout the British East Indies had regularly chosen a path of tolerance rather than an abrupt emancipation to accommodate the existing local system. He insisted that Garling had taken it upon himself to "subvert established practice." Then, like so many of his colleagues governing Britain's eastern territories, Fullerton qualified the Company's tolerance and inaction by reducing the experiences of the enslaved to household chores. Yes, there were slaves in the Straits, but in Malacca, they were primarily "domestic, doing the work of house servants" and that "there [were] no slaves here driven to their labor with a whip." He assured council members that their masters exercised "nor more power or authority" over their slaves than any other master to his servant. Fullerton echoed the sentiments of the Indian Law Commission: the slaves were treated well; the masters had no need for violence; therefore, immediate measures toward abolition were unnecessary.

Fullerton articulated common perceptions among his contemporaries who felt slaves in the east were like the pauper classes in London; he agreed with the inhabitants of the settlements that indiscriminate emancipation was problematic for the community.[18] The governor stated that he believed the original Acts had been more focused on prohibiting the trade, import, and export of slaves rather than the abolition of local slavery and that "the manner in which the slaves released or absconded" were living should be used as an "example of what might eventually be expected on a greater scale."[19] Now that the government's attention has been drawn to the matter, he intended his recommendations to become the standard response throughout the settlements. He encouraged the magistrate to continue the established practice of punishing verified slaves for disobedience and returning runaways and recommended fines for owners found guilty of mistreatment or impropriety. The governor ordered that "should persons be brought up who prove not to be slaves," the local magistrate must "explain to the parties their true situation." Colonial officials could not indiscriminately emancipate legal slaves, but they could explain to anyone brought before them

---

[18] Ibid., p. 258.
[19] Ibid., p. 257.

who was not registered that they were, in fact, legally free. Had Menah made it to court, the magistrate would have had to let her go free—she was not on any of the registries.

Nonetheless, Fullerton was not interested in immediately liberating the enslaved and reasoned that "even servants are not allowed to quit their masters without some notice." He felt "a reasonable period should be allowed" before slaves leave and argued, "[T]he servant should be recommended to secure other service before he quits the one he holds," to subdue the lawless and "riotous life" the inhabitants already complained about. The governor advised the magistrate to hold the existing three registers "under lock and key" to prevent any "interpolation" and suggested they "be used when necessary to decide a case of doubt." The slave registries had become legal evidence within this contested terrain of antislavery legislation, and to ensure a smooth execution of their plan for gradual abolition, Fullerton wanted to protect their integrity. Moreover, the official's legal decision codified Lewis' practice and official procedure. As long as they were identified on the registry, slaves still belonged to their masters and the EIC courts were clear about their priority not to "infringe" on anyone's "private rights" over their personal property.

In spite of real evidence to the contrary, the existence of ordinances against physical and/or sexual violence assuaged any concern or guilt about the living conditions or victimization of slaves. At the same time, even after the Age of Enlightenment, the dominant narrative was about the banality of the system and that eastern slave-masters treated their vassals as family members or children—the topic of their humanity and right to self-determination never entered into the conversation. Instead, Fullerton explained that, although they were "bound by the circumstances to acknowledge the existence of slavery for a time," it was "most desirable" that they put an end to it as soon as possible. He recommended that Lewis "take the first favorable opportunity of proposing" to local owners the idea of transferring their "slaves" into "debtors" after evaluating their value. Notice he did not instruct the superintendent to negotiate the emancipation of Malaccan slaves; he did not believe they needed that. The Company official was more concerned with the optics. For Fullerton and most Britons of the period, being a debtor, technically, allowed slaves the "opportunity" to buy their freedom—however unlikely it might be. With this decision, Fullerton created an important precedent; he offered local officials a linguistic loophole through which at least a decade of slave owners happily jumped. All they had to do was call their "slaves," "debtors." Moreover, while Europeans may have seen a difference between debtors and slaves, as we have learned from previous chapters, most living in Southeast Asia did not. Ultimately, the governor's announcement notified local slave owners that they would have to find new terms for the people in their work force.

Fullerton closed his address to the Supreme Government reinforcing his description of the unique circumstances of slavery in the British East Indies. He asserted that "it must be remembered that in so very poor a country as this, the service must generally assume the form of domestic slavery." They are so desperate, he explained, that "the lower classes are happy, in order to obtain subsistence, to attach themselves to families on no other consideration beyond food, clothing, a house room, and the masters generally are too poor to employ servants or any other." Again, mitigating the realities of enslavement, Fullerton reminded the government that rather than the cruel, forced labor systems found in the West Indies, the EIC tolerated slavery in the east because it was an endemic and entrenched system of welfare within the region. He informed his superiors directly that they could not immediately eradicate the institution without straining political relationships and violating established treaties, but also intimated that there would be significant economic and social ramifications for such a decision. In the end, the governor's advice was, "so long as the master is satisfied with his servant, and the servant or slaves is satisfied with his master, it is certainly not advisable for the Government to interfere."

In addition to sending Fullerton further information about the Malaccan registries, on November 13, Superintendent Lewis wrote to the council and impressed on officials how important slavery had been to the ancient city and that British officers in the past had chosen this path as a way to maintain political and economic relationships within the region.[20] Highlighting Garling's brazen behavior, Lewis stressed to the officials that while he was not an "upholder of slavery" and that he would be glad to see the institution abolished, he did not feel that he was qualified to take such drastic measures. He asserted that slavery was a subject that had "engrossed the attention of the brightest members of the British Senate for half a century past" and that if a decision had not yet been made, "after all that has been said in support and against the slave question by such able rhetoricians," then he surely would not presume to "act upon his own opinion." Not only had Superintendent Lewis accused Garling of overstepping his authority, he also cast doubt on the resident's legal interpretations of the situation and made a backhanded jab at Garling's ability to govern. The superintendent wanted to be clear that he disagreed with the institution of slavery—he was a civilized Briton, after all—however, he was not willing to go beyond established

[20] Ibid., pp. 252–3.

legal parameters to abolish it. Moreover, he resented Resident Garling for putting him in the awkward position of being the local magistrate operating at odds with the settlement's resident official. If freeing slaves were as easy as a simple proclamation, HM Government would have already done it. It is hard not to notice the political and professional posturing here; Lewis presented himself as a rational Company man and Garling the impetuous idealist.

Lewis also blamed the "the missionary gentlemen (Mr. Smith)" for "being active in supporting the slaves against their masters" and complained that "a servant belonging to him was continually seen in the town, aiding and abetting the slaves to go to his master for redress." Lewis told the council that he did not "adopt the same opinions as the Resident" and that the resident disagreed with his practice of returning slaves to their masters. The magistrate suggested that, rather than arbitrarily emancipating slaves, he should make an official "proclamation, declaring slaves free." In this way, the magistrate would at least have had an official order to support such a drastic divergence from previous policies. Then, Garling could have taken responsibility. While these were all useful suggestions, they were obviously not meant as solutions and, by the end, Lewis' letter had the tone of a campaign for a promotion.

As we learned above, local law enforcement had thus far honored the registry system, and a scan through the dispositions Lewis provided to the government offers clear evidence that British officials punished slaves and assisted in the return of runaways only after their status had been verified against the register.[21] Garling's rash behavior put the superintendent of police in a precarious situation; from Lewis' perspective, the reverend and the resident were conspirators to a crime. According to practical and legal precedent, slaves on the registries were considered the rightful property of their owners; although he was a high-ranking official, Garling's immediate emancipation of the men was essentially the same as aiding and abetting a theft. Since Lewis' responsibility was to the superior courts, as the magistrate, he could not, as Fullerton argued in his response, be expected to acquiesce to "his executive superior, contrary to" his own interpretations.[22] In the end, the superintendent received the full backing of the governor and was ultimately lauded for the way he handled the situation. Of course, Fullerton prefaced his statements by insisting that the Supreme Government review and confirm, or correct, his analysis, which left the discussion open. After all of this internal disagreement about legal priorities, one thing was certain: neither the

---

[21] Ibid., pp. 292–301.
[22] Ibid., p. 242.

government in India, nor the Board of Control in London, had been clear about how, exactly, they wanted EIC administrators to proceed with the administration of such a controversial law. Fullerton's decision as governor overruled Garling's emancipatory efforts and established that unless a higher court contradicted him, Lewis' method of gradual abolition would be the prescribed course for Malacca.

In response, an agitated Garling complained in a letter to the council that the governor's minute demanded "a very particular reply" and insisted it was vital "the two minutes may be seen together, and together be transmitted to Bengal, and to England."[23] Perhaps, knowing that the reports would be sent to British colonial officials, Garling was more concerned with the perceptions of the zealot abolitionist critics in London than the censure of the EIC Board. Nevertheless, Garling recorded his minute on November 17, which included fourteen enclosures of various correspondence, previously recorded statements, his grievances against the superintendent's conduct, and accusations of Lewis' dereliction of duties.[24] The resident insisted that neither he nor the Reverend Smith had intended to incite anyone, "but that, on the contrary," he had "exerted [his] utmost to avoid bringing it to precipitate issue." He believed that both the magistrate and the president had misinterpreted British law and provided inaccurate data. Moreover, he did not think that his actions had been "dictated by overweening zeal or mistaken notions of humanity," and he resented the "odium and damage with which [his] character and [his] property appear to be threatened." Garling wanted to be sure his superiors knew he did not agree with the presiding legal interpretations within the settlements and that he and his associates had been wrongly slandered. He had done everything in his power to implement His Majesty's wishes and bring about the end of slavery but had been met with nothing but resistance. Garling, like Lewis and Fullerton, anxiously awaited a response from the Supreme Government.

## As They Waited

Just after the governor's announcement on November 9, secretary to the government J. Patullo wrote a letter in reply "to the inhabitants who had petitioned the Government respecting slavery."[25] Patullo affirmed the petitioner's

[23] Ibid., p. 259.
[24] Ibid., pp. 260–72.
[25] Ibid., pp. 259–60.

assertion that slavery had, indeed, been an historic fixture within Malaccan society and that he understood that they had already compromised and signed a petition declaring the children of their slaves free after 1819. He assured them the governor ordered that EIC officers take "every possible regard to the right and property of the inhabitants of Malacca," as well as "the general prosperity of the place." However, he could not impress upon them enough how important the abolition of slavery was to His Majesty's Government and hoped for their "readiness to enter into some arrangement for the more speedy termination of the state of slavery, in name and substance, than can be expected from the gradual demise of the persons on the list." Finally, he told the inhabitants that the "Governor, acting under the belief that Mr. Lewis, the present Superintendent of Police, possesses your full confidence, has authorized him to receive and submit any proposition that may occur to you." Considering the previously discussed minutes, this was the official letter that gave Lewis the authority to negotiate with local slave owners in Malacca, and it is safe to assume that the EIC government expected Lewis to broach the idea of converting local slaves into debtors, theoretically, achieving their goal of abolition more swiftly.

On November 30, Lewis proudly wrote to Secretary Patullo to inform the Government in Council that the inhabitants of Malacca had met and agreed to a specific date for the end of slavery in Malacca.[26] He told the council that he felt extremely honored at "having been called upon" to report to the governor "these meritorious proceedings, which reflect the highest honor and credit on the inhabitants of Malacca." Lewis pronounced that, in honor of the governor's request to find a more expedient end to slavery than the demise of those on the registry, five representatives on behalf of the Portuguese, Chinese, Malay, and "Chooliats" signed an agreement, which declared "slavery shall not be recognized in the town and territory of Malacca after the 31st of December, 1841." Lewis relayed the appreciation of local inhabitants who acknowledged the governor's "regard for their interests," shown by his consideration of the grievances found in their petition.

The inhabitants recognized that Fullerton's ruling had temporarily given them legal permission to own slaves, although they understood that the decision was dependent upon the approval of a higher authority. Lewis claimed that in spite of the favorable ruling, "in general" the inhabitant's "motives have been guided by a sense of humanity." So, in the end, Lewis came out smelling like a

---

[26] Ibid., pp. 235–6.

rose. He had both protected the property rights of slave owners against Garling's sudden emancipation efforts and negotiated a quicker end to the institution all together. Naturally, most everyone in Fullerton's local government, except perhaps Samuel Garling, approved of Lewis' communication and recorded "its entire approval thereof, pending reference to a higher authority." Furthermore, the council ordered that copies of the letter and the record of proceedings be sent as an enclosure with the other documents that were then "under preparation," for the Honourable Court of Directors. While it was not the immediate end Garling sought, EIC officials were pleased they had been able to negotiate a peaceful and expedient end to slavery in Malacca. Unfortunately, none of them were really sure if they had the authority to make such negotiations and everything still depended upon the approval of the Company's Court of Directors.[27]

## The Official Decision

The EIC's first official response to the issue of slavery in Malacca came from Fort William in Bengal on May 5, 1830.[28] The Advocate General John Pearson delivered an opinion on the legal and political implications of slavery in Malacca and, essentially, affirmed Fullerton's analysis. The judge said that "where no express enactment exists, the laws of the Government state are only so far introduced into a settlement as are suitable to the position in which it is placed." He refuted Garling's claim that since Malacca was now British territory, and slavery was no longer recognized in Britain, the state of slavery was thus no longer recognized in any of its colonies. He reasoned that "the Legislature has often interfered to extend or limit or regulate slavery in the colonies belonging to England" and that the facts presented by Garling absolutely did not automatically emancipate slaves serving within British territories. He asserted that the laws of England "are extended to its eastern possessions as are applicable to their respective situations." Pearson affirmed established parameters that "the master had no right of his person any more than over an ordinary servant." Nevertheless, he claimed that according to his understanding, there were statutes within British law that both "acknowledge, and even to guarantee the possession of slaves, and their transfer from one part of the colony to another." He decided that "since

---

[27] For more on the structure and operations of the East India Company, see Bowen, *The Worlds of the East India Company*; Mui, *The Management of Monopoly*; Philips, *The East India Company, 1784-1834*; Roy, *The East India Company*; Webster, *The Twilight of the East India Company*; Wilbur, *The East India Company and the British Empire in the Far East*.

[28] Evans, *Slave Trade (East India) Slavery in Ceylon*, pp. 237-8.

slavery had existed for so long in Malacca, and not having been abolished by any express law, the relation continues at present day." Then, to be explicitly clear, the judge summarized his thoughts and plainly stated, "In other words, I think that those persons who were slaves, and entered as such in the register under the government of the Netherlands, are legally to be considered in a state of slavery." Clearly, it was Garling who had misinterpreted antislavery laws or at least the authority of the EIC's government to enforce them. According to the Company's legal representative, they had very little legal authority to impose antislavery legislation, and local authorities should implement ordinances that were applicable to their circumstances. Pearson's ruling clearly demonstrates that the EIC had not intended to implement an immediate abolition of slavery in the East Indies and that the policy of gradual abolition found in the Straits had become the Company's approach throughout their eastern territories.

A second letter from Bengal came on May 11, 1830, from the Governors-General Bentinck, Bayley, and Metcalfe. The correspondence declared that having reviewed the materials sent to them by officials in the Straits, and taken the opinion of the advocate general into consideration, Company's government affirmed both Pearson and Fullerton's decisions. The governors-general ordered that "the government and local authorities at Malacca must be guided until a different construction be put on the law by higher authority." Ironically, even at this level, officials were willing to offer their interpretation of the EIC's legal and political boundaries, but not to make a definitive statement on the matter of total criminalization. In fact, on June 16, 1830, the governors-general sent copies of the correspondence and all the enclosures up the next rung on the ladder of command, the board of directors in London, for their review of the decision and to affirm their ruling.[29] Nevertheless, in light of the agreement made by the inhabitants of Malacca, and the legal argument set forth by Advocate General Pearson, Governor and President Fullerton, and Superintendent Lewis, the Court of Directors upheld the decision of its lower courts. A later report on slavery, submitted in 1841, confirmed that the EIC Board had upheld all the rulings and this was, indeed, how EIC officials negotiated the end of legal slavery in Malacca.[30]

---

[29] Ibid., p. 21.
[30] Hobhouse, *Returns*, pp. 111–12; Dr. Lushington, *Return to an Order: A Continuation to the Present Time of the Papers Respecting Slavery in the East Indies, Which Were Printed by the Order of This House on the 31st Day of July 1838* (London: Great Britain Foreign Office, 1841), pp. 117–18.

## Conclusion

Antislavery measures in the ancient trading entrepôt of Malacca in the first decades of the nineteenth century needed to be introduced incrementally. In this ancient city, slaves were an important part of the local population and economy, and not everyone agreed about how to enforce the laws or how long it should take. However, it was clear to most that antislavery legislation required careful negotiation. The fact that the EIC had not conquered its territories in the Straits of Malacca turned out to be a double-edged sword; while it lent them an air of legal legitimacy, it meant that they had to accommodate local wealthy and powerful groups to maintain their influence and this meant tolerating their slaves. Meanwhile, the Dutch, acting under force of treaty, were the one that created the slave registries that laid the foundations for the emancipation of Malacca's slaves. While some were zealously invested in the enforcement of antislavery measures throughout Britain's Empire—regardless of circumstance—the preservation of personal property and very real limitations to the Company's legal authority were the primary obstacles to the Anti-Slavery Project in the Straits.

However, while this has focused on the administrative arguments and legal parameters EIC's officials established to identify slaves and enforce antislavery ordinances, it is crucial not to forget that this discourse did not address the illegal traffic in slaves, which, both Southeast Asian scholars Warren and Reid tell us, gained momentum during this period as a result of British antislavery measures.[31] Local newspapers such as the *Singapore Chronicle* or the *Singapore Free Press* were riddled with articles in the 1820s and 1830s about pirates smuggling commodities, including slaves, and kidnapping victims for the slave trade.[32] While Europeans struggled with morality and began to develop increasingly prohibitive laws, Bugis, Malay, and Chinese traders profited from an increased demand for slaves and reduced competition.[33] Although the registries

---

[31] Reid, "The Decline of Slavery in Nineteenth Century Indonesia," p. 71; Warren, *The Sulu Zone*, pp. xv–xxi.

[32] Although this is far from being a comprehensive list, the following are examples of the frequency that these stories appeared. For articles in *The Singapore Chronicle and Commercial Register*, see *The Singapore Chronicle*, March 15, 1827; *The Singapore Chronicle*, April 26, 1827; *The Singapore Chronicle*, January 15, 1829; *The Singapore Chronicle*, February 26, 1829; *The Singapore Chronicle*, November 5, 1829; *The Singapore Chronicle*, June 2, 1831; *The Singapore Chronicle*, August 25, 1831; *The Singapore Chronicle*, October 13, 1831; *The Singapore Chronicle*, November 15, 1832. For articles in *The Singapore Free Press and Advertiser*, see *The Singapore Free Press*, October 22, 1835: p. 1; *The Singapore Free Press*, December 24, 1835: p. 2; *The Singapore Free Press*, January 14, 1836: p. 6; *The Singapore Free Press*, April 28, 1836: p. 2; *The Singapore Free Press*, September 1, 1836: p. 2; *The Singapore Free Press*, December 8, 1836: p. 3.

[33] Reid, "The Decline of Slavery in Nineteenth Century Indonesia," pp. 71–3.

attempted to form an efficient means of accurately identifying existing slaves, it is not likely that the inhabitants, all of them, followed the ordinance to the letter. As Lewis explained, legal misunderstandings and attempts to circumvent taxes mean that it was more likely owners did not report all of, or any new slaves they acquired after the close of the registries in 1824. Again, Menah insisted she was Mr. Kock's slave and was dressed to indicate she was telling the truth, but she was not on the registry. Technically, Garling was right; according to the law, the colonial government should not have recognized her slave status and immediately offered her protection. Since she identified herself as a slave and was applying to the magistrate according to the slave ordinance for relief from abuse, we can only assume Mr. Kock had neglected to tell her that she was, technically, free.

The Anti-Slavery Project in Malacca began with Farquhar's prohibition of the slave trade in 1813 and continued with the Dutch slave registries, and then the inhabitants declared they would free the children born of slaves after 1819. Those three elements were what initiated the definitive end to legal slavery in Malacca. Although the EIC government had ordered its officials to bring about an end to slavery as soon as possible, they had neglected to tell them how. Lewis did not exaggerate when he told Garling that he "had nothing to guide" him but "public orders"; the EIC did not have an organized or plainly stated plan regarding the implementation of antislavery and, as we see in the story above, officials often established law through precedent as they went along. Moreover, to continue with their overall objective for profit and expansion, those laws had to accommodate the wealthy and influential Dutch, Chinese, Arab, and Malay inhabitants who had been living in Malacca, with their slaves, for generations. Tolerating slavery meant the preservation of political and economic growth, while emancipation meant legal action and political controversy. Together, the EIC's unclear directives, internal disagreements, and undefined legal authority is what inhibited the implementation of antislavery ordinances in Malacca during the first thirty years of the nineteenth century.

# 7

# An Illicit Trade to Penang and Singapore

On January 19, 1837, four years after Britain's Parliament passed its Abolition Act and seven years after Fullerton's declaration of the Company's policy in the Straits, the *Singapore Free Press* published two articles that called its readers' attention to the persistence of the "horrible traffic in human beings," which incorporated Singapore and targeted the people of the island of Nias.¹ The first article, a letter to the editor and signed "Humanitas," read much like Abdullah Bin Abdul Kadir's account of Singapore's slave markets.² This letter, however written almost fifteen years later, claimed that indigenous groups still conducted an expansive slave trade in the region; they asserted that all along the western coast of Sumatra, one could find "unhappy victims exposed for sale in their shops like any other merchandise."³ Like Kadir's story of the girls on the dock dehumanized by their owner, the author remembered four young women in particular whom he had seen. He described them as "companions in misery" and wrote that they "huddled themselves into the back part of the shop; and from native modesty, or absorbed in grief, their faces were turned from the light of day." The horrified letter writer explained that when a man inquired about purchasing one of the girls, they quickly turned their heads and he saw their faces swollen and disfigured from tears.⁴ Humanitas asserted

---

¹ "To the Editor of the Singapore Free Press," *The Singapore Free Press and Mercantile Advertiser*, January 19, 1837: p. 2; "To Anyone Who Has Perused the Account of Nias," *The Singapore Free Press and Mercantile Advertiser*, January 19, 1837: p. 3. Seow, *The Media Enthralled: Singapore Revisited*, pp. 6–8. According to Seow, the *Singapore Free Press* formed in 1830 in response to intense government censorship from the India Office (p. 7). It generated an intense competition that resulted in the closure of the *Singapore Chronicle*, which was the first newspaper published in Singapore in 1824 (p. 6). Parliament passed the Slavery Abolition Act in 1833, effective, January 1, 1834. For more see Major, *Slavery, Abolitionism and Empire in India, 1772–1843*, pp. 3–13.
² Munshi, *The Hikayat Abdullah*, pp. 181–5; Abdullah Bin Abdul Kadir was a "Malay scholar" who rose to a "position of importance as a member of the harbormaster's department under the Dutch" (pp. 6–7). Then, he eventually became "the youngest of a number of scribes and copyists whom Raffles employed in his office" and wrote extensively about the negotiations and events surrounding the birth of British Malaya (p. 9). Kadir's writings included a description of Singapore's slave markets as he remembered them in 1823 (pp. 181–3). "To the Editor of the Singapore Free Press," p. 2.
³ "To the Editor of the Singapore Free Press," p. 2.
⁴ Munshi, *The Hikayat Abdullah*, p. 182.

that he had "hoped and believed" the efforts of the British government had put an end to the slave trade in the Straits, or at least that which was carried on in open markets, but that he had been "wofully [sic] mistaken."[5] To his dismay, slavery persisted in the British Straits Settlements, despite British efforts to extinguish the "abhorred trade."

In that same January 19 issue, the editorial in the *Singapore Free Press* concurred with the descriptions of Humanitas and lamented that the peoples of "that fine island" were still vulnerable to the trade.[6] The editorial asserted that the "revolting and repine plunder" of the island of Nias for slaves "casts a stigma of the deepest dye on the Dutch government in Sumatra" whose ships were supposed to be in control of its entire coast line. As previously discussed, the Treaty of 1824 obliged the Dutch to join their effort at abolition and enforce antislavery legislation.[7] Moreover, the editor claimed that this trade was not simply a venture for the "petty rajahs," as Humanitas had assumed, but that Dutch vessels themselves still went on regular slaving expeditions to Nias from Padang.[8] It was one thing for native leaders, but a Dutch trade directly violated treaty stipulations. Nias was also not the only island along the western coast of Sumatra to have fallen prey to these slavers; many other islands within the archipelago were "endowed with all those qualities which render the possession of the Nias slaves so desirable—the beauty of the women, and the industry, ingenuity, and fidelity of the men."

However, Humanitas had overlooked one important detail; the editor reminded his readers that between 1820 and 1821, the rajas of the islands of Nias and Poggy had both "ceded their sovereignty" to the EIC and that neither of those islands could be "accounted dependencies of Sumatra," which was a Dutch territory.[9] He wrote that several of the rajas had been ready to agree to implement antislavery measures in 1820, but the profits were too appealing for others who did not want to let go of their stake in the lucrative trade.[10] He declared that it would be "no difficult accomplishment to our Government" to "check the external demand" for these slaves; then, he believed, it would be an even easier task to abolish the "revolting laws, which sanction the internal practice." Surely,

---

[5] "To the Editor of the Singapore Free Press," p. 2.
[6] Ibid., p. 3.
[7] Andaya and Andaya, *A History of Malaysia*, pp. 111–15; Hobhouse, *Returns*; Trocki, *Prince of Pirates*, pp. 66–7.
[8] "To the Editor of the Singapore Free Press," p. 3.
[9] Ibid. The Anglo-Dutch Treaty of 1824 split the Straits of Malacca down the middle; the British took control of the Malay states and the Dutch took the Sumatran coasts. For more see Trocki, *Prince of Pirates*, pp. 66–7; Andaya and Andaya, *A History of Malaysia*, pp. 121–4.
[10] "To the Editor of the Singapore Free Press," p. 3.

the editor asserted, the "object and attempt" of the British to liberate these slaves was "worthy of a nation which led the way in purifying Europe from the stain of that detested traffic." Like Resident Garling in Malacca almost a decade before, local Britons living in Singapore believed the EIC government should have been doing more to put an end to slavery in their settlements.

Technically, there should not have been any slaves in Singapore in 1837. Parliament passed the Slave Trade Act in 1807, the Felony Act in 1811, and Farquhar and Raffles had prohibited slavery when they acquired the island of Singapore from the Sultan of Johor in 1819.[11] Nonetheless, as we have seen, the Company was only marginally concerned with abolishing slavery in the east, and the trade in non-European slaves was even less important; their attentions were securely focused on the brutal inhumanity of the Atlantic system. The subject of antislavery ordinances in the newer settlements of Penang (est. 1780) and Singapore (est. 1819) was not like Malacca's political controversy over the loss of personal property. Since these two settlements had both prohibited slavery by 1820, the official and public discourse centered on the threat and persistence of the illicit slave trade dominated by indigenous chiefs, pirates, and the Chinese; the subject of slavery was maintained within the context of subversive and illegal behavior.

However, the incredible gender disparity within these colonial spaces—created by the floods of laboring, unattached, men and lack of immigrating women—was overwhelming motivation to begin refining legal terms and turn a blind eye to what was clearly a thriving trade in non-European slaves—women and girls brought into the Straits as domestic and sexual labor for the overwhelmingly male, predominantly transient, population. As we will see, in spite of clearly defined legal parameters, most officials were relatively indifferent to the illegal traffic of non-European women and girls, whom they often labeled as debtors, coming into the Straits. Examining the conflicting gender structures and slippery conceptions of slavery, debt, and free labor at odds within the British Straits Settlements at the turn of the nineteenth century makes us privy to the pliable definitions, competing agendas, and vague legislation that supported an inherently gendered system of global labor traffic and hobbled international antislavery efforts in these colonial cities. As the infamous case of

---

[11] Trocki, *Prince of Pirates*, pp. 107–9.

the confiscated slaves from Nias demonstrates, strongly held beliefs about gender roles, domesticity, and "native" behavior fundamentally shaped what officials believed was (and was not) slavery and were an additional factor preventing the complete abolition of slavery in the region.

Antislavery measures in Penang and Singapore were developed and administered quite different from the strategic negotiations in Malacca. Dubbed by administrators as "newly formed settlements," both Penang and Singapore began as small and, at the time inconsequential, trading ports within the Malay trading world.[12] While both had existing slave populations prior to British control, neither settlement had significant numbers of slaves, nor any substantial economic ties to the slave trade. In Penang, the oldest of Britain's settlements in the Straits, officials followed Malacca's example and created registries to make some accommodations to slave-owning residents. However, here, fewer slaves meant that the registry was negligible, and there were also fewer wealthy and powerful non-Europeans questioning the EIC's legal authority. So, theoretically, officials had more latitude—if they chose—to more rigorously enforce prohibitions within these communities.

Slavery was only legal for the first twenty years of British settlement, and Singapore was founded well after the prohibition of slavery. So by 1826, when they joined Malacca to form the Straits Settlements, these two colonies had already prohibited slavery and had—technically—begun to rely on convicts, "debtors" ("unfree"), and contracted ("free") labor.[13] Unfortunately, as scholars like Clare Anderson have demonstrated, while the terminology had certainly changed, the real, slave-like, experiences of those working had not.[14] Still, in the first decades of the nineteenth century, there were a plethora of convicted or contracted men available—few of whom were there with the intention to settle and start families—to assist the Company in their efforts to build their new Southeast Asian settlements.[15] However, at the turn of the nineteenth

---

[12] Hobhouse, *Returns*, pp. 107, 112; Lewis, *Jan Compagnie in the Straits of Malacca, 1641–1795*, pp. 116–17; John Cameron, *Our Tropical Possessions in Malayan India: Being a Descriptive Account of Singapore, Penang, Province of Wellesley, and Malacca; Their Peoples, Products, Commerce, and Government* (London: Smith, Elder, and Co, 1865), pp. 6–7.

[13] Ibid., pp. 107, 112.

[14] Anderson, "Convicts and Coolies: Rethinking Indentured Labour in the Nineteenth Century," p. 94.

[15] For more on British transportation and use of convict labor see Anderson, *Subaltern Lives*; Costello, *Botany Bay*; Thomas Keneally, *The Great Shame: And the Triumph of the Irish in the English-Speaking World*, 1st ed. (New York: Nan A. Talese, 1999); A. Shaw, *Convicts and the Colonies: A Study of Penal Transportation from Great Britain and Ireland to Australia and Other Parts of the British Empire* (London: Faber, 1966). Also, the following works discuss the rise in the migratory flows of cheap male labor during this period: Bayly, *The Birth of the Modern World, 1780–1914*, pp. 236–8; Manning, *Migration in World History*; Eric Williams, *Capitalism and Slavery* (Chapel Hill: University of North Carolina Press, 1994); Curtin, *Cross-Cultural Trade in World History*.

century, cultural prohibitions kept most Asian women from immigrating, which created a severe gender disparity, particularly in Singapore, that unsettled both EIC officials and local residents. As a result, colonial officials came to see the prevalence of women and girls within Southeast Asian slave markets as a lamentable, but convenient characteristic of the locale, to which many officials turned "a blind eye." While it is clear slave women labored in a multitude of ways—on plantations, in businesses, or in private households— and it is unlikely that any of them were dedicated to a single purpose, in general, slaves trafficked into Penang and Singapore were women and girls expected to provide domestic and sexual services to the swelling populations of convicted, contracted, and consigned male laborers pouring into these emerging commercial centers.

British ideas about gender and domesticity framed how officials saw the circumstances of the slave women and girls they encountered, while perceptions of the uncivilized, over sexualized "other," shaped how they understood these women's experiences, and then prioritized their response. So, when the editor of the *Singapore Free Press* asked in their 1837 editorial, why the slave trade, officially abolished in British colonial territories thirty years before, was able to thrive within the boundaries of what, by 1833, had been declared abolitionist territory, the answer was that in the Straits local officials found it easier to tolerate the enslavement of women and girls than to deal with the social unrest and economic blowback of immediate abolition and emancipation.

## Race, Class, Gender, and Domesticity in the Straits

Historians have established that attitudes and perceptions about race, gender, sex, and sexuality were fundamental to the British imperial project and influenced how officials perceived and reacted on colonial frontiers.[16] For Britons during this period, dominant perceptions of "civilized," and therefore

---

[16] Midgley, *Gender and Imperialism*, pp. 7–8; Ballantyne and Burton, *Bodies in Contact*, pp. 8–9; Gelman-Taylor, *The Social World of Batavia*, pp. 78–114; Hall, *Civilising Subjects*, pp. 84–170; Philippa Levine, ed., *Gender and Empire* (Oxford: Oxford University Press, 2004), pp. 136–7; Reid, *Charting the Shape of Early Modern Southeast Asia*, p. 189; Campbell, *The Structure of Slavery in Indian Ocean Africa and Asia*, pp. x–xiii.

productive, society consisted of two separate spheres: the public world of gainful employment, commerce, and politics for men, and the domestic sphere of home, hearth, and children for women.[17] Women, as Kathleen Wilson argues, were seen as "universal" "agents of progress."[18] Prevailing wisdom held that the domestic sphere, the realm of women, was vital to "the making of a healthy social body."[19] For contemporary British men, white women held the mantel of chaste and demure domestic angel, charged with cleansing away the corrupting influences of the outside world, rejuvenating a man's spirit, and maintaining the integrity of his household.[20] Ironically, in spite of such adoration, "women's work" was regularly devalued, trivialized, and considered nonessential.

When white women were not available, as in the East Indies, Asian women held an air of "female mystery" and exoticism that attracted several EIC officers who married and established large families of future Company servants.[21] However, as Wilson explains, some EIC officers like Joseph Collett, the deputy-governor at Fort Marlborough on the west coast of Sumatra, believed, "Malay men were 'addicted to women,'" and "native women were bestial, masculine, highly sexed, and oppressed by their men."[22] While Collett represents an extreme view, most Europeans during this period believed that those living in warmer climates, and farther down on the ladder of civilization, were hypersexual and lacked impulse control. Like at home, the British attempted to organize their colonial societies according to a patriarchal hierarchy in which white males levied "supreme authority" over both state and household, and, as Kathleen Wilson explains, "the household was the main unit of social order and indigenous reclamation."[23] After all, an orderly house brings an orderly life and obedient subjects. However, local administrators in British Malaya had a different challenge on their hands. They were not necessarily trying to solicit permanent residents; their goal was to create peace and stability in communities, like Singapore in particular, that were being overrun by working-class, and for the most part transient, men.

---

[17] Jennifer Morgan, "Male Travelers, Female Bodies, and the Gendering of Racial Ideology," in *Bodies in Contact: Rethinking Colonial Encounters in World History*, eds. Tony Ballantyne and Antoinette Burton (Durham: Duke University Press, 2004), p. 61; Catherine Hall, "Of Gender and Empire: Reflections on the Nineteenth Century," in *Gender and Empire*, ed. Philippa Levine (Oxford: Oxford University Press, 2004), pp. 56–7; Hall, *Civilising Subjects*, pp. 84–170; Linda Colley, *Britons: Forging the Nation 1707–1837* (New Haven: Yale University Press, 2005), pp. 238–9; Pateman, *The Sexual Contract*, pp. 10–11.

[18] Kathleen Wilson, "Empire, Gender, and Modernity," in *Gender and Empire*, ed. Philippa Levine (Oxford: Oxford University Press, 2004), p. 41.

[19] Hall, "Of Gender and Empire," p. 47.

[20] Colley, *Britons*, pp. 262–73.

[21] Wilson, "Empire, Gender, and Modernity," pp. 34–5.

[22] Ibid., p. 35.

[23] Ibid., p. 25.

Most middle- and upper-class British believed that the lower classes, like the rank and file soldiers, laborers, convicts, and seamen that made up the majority of the men in the Straits, did not possess the restraint and good character that might be expected from the more elite government or Company officers.[24] These men were not looking for wives; they simply needed services—domestic and sexual—during their stay. As Ann Stoler argues, European empires used the "legitimating rhetoric of civility and its gendered construals" to organize and police their settlements, but that little has been done to examine the "class tensions that competing notions of 'civility' engendered."[25] During this period in Europe, hierarchical notions of civility were entrenched in the formation of emerging class-based conflicts as the aristocracy separated itself from the laboring classes and the new middle class struggled for social position. Indeed, London's poor were regularly equated with colonial savagery and some elites even went "slumming" to catch sight of the beasts in their natural habitat.[26] The middle classes aspired to be aristocratic; both groups mistrusted and reviled the poor. By the 1820s, middle- and upper-class residents in the Straits worried that the dearth of women available for these irascible, lower-class men threatened the stability of their community.

Other than Malacca (1795), which was an established cosmopolitan community long before Europeans sailed into Southeast Asia, the purpose of the EIC factories of Penang (or Prince of Wales Island, 1786), Province of Wellesley (1800), and Singapore (1819) was to provide storage for British ships (Penang) and establish a free port at Singapore to challenge Dutch and Portuguese trade policies.[27] Most arriving in the Straits were neither aristocratic, nor European, and very few were looking to settle. The few resident Europeans were generally EIC administrators, officials, or clerks, missionaries, merchants, and sailors, many of whom would have come from European middle and working classes.[28] According to Robert Montgomery Martin's 1839 publication, *Statistics of the Colonies of the British Empire*, there were only 119 "Europeans" in Singapore among a total population of 20,880 in 1833.[29] The same report advises its readers to include 553 convicts and 600 "military and their followers" to the above total,

---

[24] Koven, *Slumming*, pp. 18–21, 103–12.
[25] Stoler, *Race and the Education of Desire*, p. 99.
[26] Koven, *Slumming*, pp. 26, 37, 39.
[27] Andaya and Andaya, *A History of Malaysia*, pp. 111–17.
[28] Levine, *Prostitution, Race, and Politics*, pp. 45–6.
[29] Robert Montgomery Martin, *Statistics of the Colonies of the British Empire: From the Official Records of the Colonial Office* (London: W.H. Allen and Company, 1839), p. 410.

who were not counted with the others.[30] As we know, colonies in the Straits relied heavily on convict, Indian indenture, and Chinese migrant labor, all of whom colonial authorities would have considered morally suspect in need of close supervision and control.[31] Of course, we should assume that at least some low- or working-class British soldiers made it to the brothels and gambling houses just like anyone else staying in the port. When discussing the peace and order of the community, both the government's and public's conversations regularly returned to how a lack of women affects the Malay and Chinese populations, but never about British or even European men. It would be unreasonable to believe that Europeans were not taking part in the debauchery, since we know from Philippa Levine, it was drastically different as early as the 1860s.[32]

The British men who established Singapore and Penang also came with strongly held ideas about social organization, gender roles, domesticity, and class.[33] Industrialization and the expansion of empire created a shift in the late eighteenth and early nineteenth British class and gender norms and initiated a period of cultural and social flux. New forms of wealth and poverty instigated the formation of middle- and working-class identities and, by the end of the eighteenth century, a struggle for citizenship as well.[34] Members of the middle class began to construct and utilize notions of masculinity, femininity, and domesticity as a way to distinguish themselves from the lower or working classes and, thus, obtain social legitimacy through suffrage.[35] By the mid-1820s, the dominant construction of a "civilized" society consisted of two separate spheres: the men's public world of commerce and politics, and the domestic sphere of home and children for women, and the "non productive woman" came to represent the ideal for British society.[36]

Included in this construction of civilized society were definitions of "true womanhood" that Carroll Smith-Rosenberg asserts "prescribed a female role bound by kitchen and nursery, overlaid with piety and purity, and crowned with

---

[30] Ibid.
[31] Levine, *Prostitution, Race, and Politics*, p. 35.
[32] Ibid., p. 49.
[33] The following are the most relevant works examining the connections between metropolitan and imperial ideology: Hall, *Civilising Subjects*, pp. 84–170. Stoler, *Carnal Knowledge and Imperial Power*; Stoler, *Race and the Education of Desire*, pp. 97–136; Stoler, "Making Empire Respectable," pp. 634–60; John M. MacKenzie, *Imperialism and Popular Culture* (Manchester: Manchester University Press, 1986), pp. 3–9; Sinha, *Colonial Masculinity*, pp. 2–3; Streets, *Martial Races*, pp. 1–2.
[34] Clark, *The Struggle for the Breeches*, pp. 2–7.
[35] Ibid., p. 7, pp. 139–42.
[36] This is how Carroll Smith-Rosenberg described middle-class woman who did not produce an income in *Disorderly Conduct: Visions of Gender in Victorian America* (Oxford: Oxford University Press, 1986), p. 13; Clark, *The Struggle for the Breeches*, p. 2; Kent, *Gender and Power in Britain, 1640–1990*, pp. 257–335.

subservience."[37] This is a particularly useful definition of "true womanhood," because it incorporates the three facets of women's roles and responsibilities necessary to achieve this lofty goal. First, she was responsible for maintaining the household and raising the children; second, she was to be the model of religious piety and female purity within the home, and third, she was subservient to the patriarch. While they were by no means considered equal, for the British, women were an essential element of a successful, civilized society.[38] Masculinity was also defined by this ideal; true patriarchs governed a frugal, orderly house with a deferent wife and obedient children.[39] Moreover, in a jab at the excesses of eighteenth-century libertines, this emerging middle class promoted sobriety and even temperament as critical attributes of British masculinity.[40] These images of true men and women stood in opposition to representations of the uninhibited poor with loose morals and "savage" behavior, as seen in the lower class sailors, workers, servants, and prostitutes found in the Straits.[41] Smith-Rosenberg argues that heterosexual marriage, patriarchal constructions of family, and "bourgeois sexual proprieties" were becoming recognizable and defining elements of middle-class respectability and were, by the 1820s, part of the dominant construct for British gender norms.

These middle-class constructions of ideal masculine and feminine roles during this period were their response to collective perceptions of exploitive excesses of the rich and the uncontrolled hedonism of the poor and led to the formation of a "cult of domesticity," which prevailed throughout the nineteenth century.[42] For the emerging respectable class, women's primary purpose was to maintain a domestic space that purified and civilized the men who had been corrupted by their time with the public.[43] Working-class reformers criticized the "aristocratic effeminacy" of elite males they claimed were responsible for Britain's political and economic troubles in the 1780s and 1790s.[44] As a result, popular opinion began

---

[37] Smith-Rosenberg, *Disorderly Conduct*, p. 13.
[38] Clark, *The Struggle for the Breeches*, p. 2.
[39] John Tosh, "Domesticity and Manliness in the Victorian Middle Class," in *Manful Assertions: Masculinities in Britain since 1800*, eds. Michael Rope and John Tosh (London: Routledge, 1991), pp. 44–8.
[40] Ibid., p. 50.
[41] Koven, *Slumming*, p. 7; Clark, *The Struggle for the Breeches*, p. 3.
[42] Notions of domesticity were crucial to early nineteenth-century British construction of gender norms. For a few of the more interesting analyses see Kent, *Gender and Power in Britain*, pp. 144–54; Clark, *The Struggle for the Breeches*, pp. 214–20; Ballantyne and Burton, *Bodies in Contact*, pp. 143–7; Sonya O. Rose, *Limited Livelihoods: Gender and Class in Nineteenth Century England* (Berkeley: University of California Press, 2004), pp. 131–3; Catherine Hall and Sonya O. Rose, *At Home with the Empire: Metropolitan Culture and the Imperial World* (Cambridge: Cambridge University Press, 2006), pp. 102–3; Levine, *Gender and Empire*, pp. 136–7; Walkowitz, *Prostitution and Victorian Society*, pp. 114–18.
[43] McClintock, *Imperial Leather*, pp. 168–72.
[44] Kent, *Gender and Power in Britain*, pp. 144–5.

to favor temperance and discipline as key attributes of ideal British masculinity.[45] In sum, at the turn of the nineteenth century, the ideal woman, regardless of race, was a civilizing force that tempered men's passions and brought harmony to both a household and society as a whole. White men were responsible for the stability and prosperity of the household and nation; native men and women, like Briton's poor, were like children in need of parental (patriarchal) guidance.[46] These concepts were ultimately embroiled in British national identity and, as we will see, determined the ways British officials perceived and reacted to what they saw on their colonial frontier.[47]

Attitudes and perceptions about sex and sexuality also played a foundational role in the formation of British identity during this early Victorian period. According to British perceptions, poor and working-class women continuously walked the line between respectability and the depravity of prostitution and, as Clark argues, mainstream society used the "double standard" to police women's behavior.[48] A working-class woman's survival in Britain was dependent upon the community's perception of her respectability and the threat of scandal—or even gossip of it—often kept women from challenging social norms. On the other hand, as Levine explains, uncontrolled male desire and extra-marital sex, although unsightly, was a normal exercise of male privilege, and British patriarchal society saw men's "natural" need for sexual release "as compelling as [their] appetite for food."[49] In fact, this desire was foundational to the "maintenance of empire" and assisted in the demarcation of maleness from femaleness.[50] British authorities often feared homosocial environments such as naval ships, military bases, labor camps, and imperial settlements like Penang and Singapore because they worried that men's need for sexual release might compel them to homosexuality, drunkenness, and violence.[51] British officials did not believe that the rank and file soldiers, Chinese laborers, Indian convicts, and Malay seamen that made up the majority of these settlements possessed the restraint that might be expected in its government or Company officers.

---

[45] Clark, *The Struggle for the Breeches*, pp. 66–7.
[46] Smith-Rosenberg, *Disorderly Conduct*, pp. 50–1; Kent, *Gender and Power in Britain*, p. 154; Tosh, "Domesticity and Manliness in the Victorian Middle Class," pp. 44–6.
[47] Smith-Rosenberg, *Disorderly Conduct*, p. 107.
[48] Clark, *The Struggle for the Breeches*, pp. 50–1; Kent, *Gender and Power in Britain*, pp. 144–5.
[49] Levine, *Prostitution, Race, and Politics*, pp. 196–7; Clark, *The Struggle for the Breeches*, pp. 66–8; Walkowitz, *Prostitution in Victorian Society*, p. 43; McClintock, *Imperial Leather*, pp. 79–80.
[50] Levine, *Prostitution, Race, and Politics*, p. 197.
[51] Suzanne J. Stark, *Female Tars: Women Aboard Ship in the Age of Sail* (Annapolis: Naval Institute Press, 1996), pp. 13–17; Levine, *Prostitution, Race and Politics*, pp. 292–3; Adele Perry, *On the Edge of Empire: Gender, Race, and the Making of British Columbia, 1849–1871* (Toronto: University of Toronto Press, 2002), pp. 36–47.

They thought even less of Asian temperment and had long fantasized about the sexual secrets of the "Orient"; colonists around the world believed non-westerners were, as Levine describes, "morally lax and sexually unencumbered."[52] British officials in the Straits would have considered a majority of the population to be wild, sexually uninhibited, violent, and in urgent need of control. Before the 1840s, when women's groups began to challenge the male double standard, authorities regularly expressed the needs of soldiers and seamen to have access to women's bodies in order to appease this masculine necessity and prevent "gross indecencies" without consideration for the circumstance of the women.[53] So the same emerging classist morality that assigned a life of private, secluded, and chaste domesticity (which some might describe as enslavement) for the wives and daughters of those who could afford it, prescribed heterosexual release for men—however they could arrange it— to prevent homosexuality and preserve British power and masculine industry.

These racialized and orientalist constructions of "native" behavior and sexuality were very much at play within the Anti-Slavery Project in colonial Southeast Asia. As we saw in the report from the Indian Law Commission, EIC officials viewed slaves and debtors in the east in similar ways to the "pauper classes in London."[54] We know that elites went on "slumming" tours in London to look at the "natives" in their own backyard.[55] The image of the "savage" poor was common by the early nineteenth century and women and middle-class domesticity were the prescribed cure.[56] By the nineteenth century, the British saw the "native states" they encountered as ancient and backward cultures in need of the civilizing influence of western values and institutions. There were regular articles in the *Singapore Chronicle* describing the "barbarity" of the surrounding tribes in Borneo, Sumatra, and Bali.[57] British officials assumed eastern cultures,

---

[52] Philippa Levine, "Sexuality, Gender, and Empire," in *Gender and Empire*, ed. Philippa Levine (Oxford: Oxford University Press, 2004), pp. 135–7.
[53] Wilson, "Empire, Gender, and Modernity," pp. 42–2; Stark, *Female Tars*, pp. 13–17; Levine, *Prostitution, Race and Politics*, pp. 292–3.
[54] Hobhouse, *Returns*, p. 189.
[55] Koven, *Slumming*, p. 4.
[56] Henry Mayhew, *London Labour and the London Poor: A Cyclopaedia of the Condition and Earnings of Those That Will Work, Those That Cannot Work, and Those That Will Not Work* (London: G. Woodfall and Son, 1851), p. 43; Smith-Rosenberg, *Disorderly Conduct*, 16–18.
[57] For more on European formation and maintenance of sexual, social, cultural, political, and economic distinctions between the colonized, indigenous Other and themselves, see Edward Said, *Orientalism* (New York, NY: Vintage Books, 1978); Stoler, *Carnal Knowledge and Imperial Power*; Anderson, *Imagined Communities*. The following works illustrate the British Empire's construction and zealous maintenance of racialized, gendered hierarchies as part of its colonial projects: Stoler, *Carnal Knowledge and Imperial Power*; Stoler, *Race and the Education of Desire*, pp. 97–136; Stoler, "Making Empire Respectable," pp. 634–60; Chaudhuri and Strobel, *Western Women and Imperialism*, pp. 1–34; Midgley, *Gender and Imperialism*, pp. 1–20; Gelman-Taylor, *The Social World of Batavia*, pp. 78–114. The following editions of the *Singapore Chronicle and Commercial Register* contained long editorials describing the despotism and barbarity of local chiefs on the surrounding islands: August 29, 1829; November 5, 1829; May 15, 1830; June 30, 1830.

like the poor, were less civilized "looser," unconcerned with western gender proprieties; slavery and the subjugation of women, they presumed, were an endemic part of non-European societies in the region.[58] Many saw the sale, suppression, and exploitation of these women as "evidence of their disorder."[59] As we will see, when colonial officials encountered women enslaved within British territories, many believed that the women were, as Governor Fullerton described, "satisfied with their situation."[60] The "interior frontiers" of gender were volatile points of interaction and most officials during this period were reluctant to become involved in disputes over women—particularly slaves.[61] As tenuously invited guests, it was important to affirm the notion that "the control of women's bodies fundamentally belonged to the men of that society" to exploit and control as they saw fit.[62] In the case examined below, of the slaves from Pulau Nias apprehended in Penang, colonial officials saw the Empire's territories as protected, safe, and civilizing spaces, where even illegal slaves had, at least as Superintendent Caunter contended, the "hope of redemption."[63] From the perspective of EIC officials and British authorities, the illicit traffic of women and girls coming into the Straits, slaves or not, destined for marriage, concubinage, or domestic servitude fit what was considered their "natural" role. For these British patriarchs, the women they encountered were indigenous and, therefore, like lower-class women, were meant to labor and satisfy the sexual needs of native or at least non-European men. These officials were convinced that women were naturally destined to serve men in a variety of domestic capacities—regardless of their station—and confident that even enslavement within the protecting arms of His Majesty's territories was better for everyone involved. It is not surprising then that colonial officials in the Straits either overtly promoted the migration of women and girls or overlooked the illegal importation of women all together to ensure the orderly behavior of the men within the community.[64] Just as in Malacca, antislavery efforts in Penang and Singapore were secondary to trade relationships and civil stability. Officials looked past what they knew to be a trade in women and girls, who they believed were arriving to fulfill their natural

---

[58] Philippa Levine, "'A Multitude of Unchaste Women': Prostitution in the British Empire," *Journal of Women's History* 15, no. 4 (2004): p. 159.
[59] Levine, "A Multitude of Unchaste Women," p. 159; Levine, "Sexuality, Gender, and Empire," pp. 150-1; Koven, *Slumming*, pp. 72-3.
[60] Evans, *Slave Trade (East India) Slavery in Ceylon*, p. 239.
[61] Stoler, *Carnal Knowledge and Imperial Power*, pp. 75-6.
[62] Ibid.
[63] "Slave Trade," IOR/F4/1130/30195/15.
[64] Levine, "Sexuality, Gender and Empire," p. 137.

destiny under what was, all things considered, the best possible circumstances: British protection.

## Penang

Elisha Trapaud, "Captain in the Engineer Corps on the Madras establishment," and "present at the hoisting of the flag" in April of 1786, tells us that Captain Light acquired "Pulo [sic] Penang" or Prince of Wales Island (a dedication to the prince on the eve of his birthday) and the Province of Wellesley from the Sultan of Quedah for the EIC as part of the dowry.[65] According to Trapaud, Light "assisted the above prince in quelling some troubles in his dominions," who in turn "bestowed upon him a princess of his blood in marriage, together with this island as her dower."[66] However, although Trapaud claims his account was "taken on the spot," it was written almost three years later and there are a few elements to his story that need further examination. First, his retelling presents Light's marriage to the princess as the valuable reward in this situation, when it is more likely—particularly considering the frequent attempts by various EIC officers to secure other strategic locations within the region—that the island was the Company's prize. The woman was, probably the daughter of a concubine or a slave connected to the Sultan's household, a gift for Light.

Trapaud also wrote that Light, "extremely beloved amongst the Malays, chose to marry her according to the fashions of her own country."[67] Such marriages of convenience, more like business contracts, were common in Southeast Asia but by the end of the eighteenth century respect for these "temporary wives" had disintegrated.[68] However, Marcus Langdon claims that before Light landed in Penang, he "spent many years based in Tha Rua on the east coast of Phuket," living with a woman named Martinha Rozells, with whom he had five children. Mary, Sarah, and William were born in Tha Rua, and the other two, Anne (Lukey) and Francis Lanoon, in Penang.[69] Langdon also writes that the pair "purportedly married according to local custom" but does not mention the "princess" Trapaud

---

[65] It should be noted that "Kedah" is the same as Queda or Quedah. ere are a variety of spellings throughout EIC correspondence, contemporary publications, and current literature for this Malay state. For no academic reason, this book uses "Quedah," unless directly quoting. Elisha Trapaud, *A Short Account of the Prince of Wales's Island, or Pulo Peenang, in the East-Indies; Given to Capt. Light, by the King of Quedah* (London: J. Stockdale, 1788), pp. 8–9.
[66] Ibid., p. 8.
[67] Ibid., p. 9.
[68] Andaya, "From Temporary Wife to Prostitute," p. 27.
[69] Marcus Langdon, *Penang: The Fourth Presidency of India, 1805–1830* (Penang, Malaysia: Areca Books, 2013), p. 191.

described.⁷⁰ A century later, a memorial written in the *Journal of the Straits Branch of the Royal Asiatic Society* contended that Light had

> allied himself in 1772 with Martina Rozells, but she was neither a Malay nor a Princess, but was apparently a Portuguese Christian of the Roman Catholic Mission at Kedah of Junk Ceylon. The old Junk Ceylon Mission removed about that time to Kedah, and in 1786 to Pulau Tikus village at Penang. She lived with him to his death, and inherited his house "Suffolk" and other property.⁷¹

It is highly likely that Trapaud's story conflated Light's acquisition of Penang with his non-European wedding, perhaps unaware of—or overlooking—the fact that Light had already fathered three of her children. Given the circumstances, it is apparent that the term "princess" was being used loosely. It is clear that Mrs. Light did not appear to be northern European; if she were Portuguese and lived on the coast, near the ocean, it would make sense for her to have dark skin and hair. Perhaps she was the daughter of a Malay "Princess" and Portuguese merchant from a generation before—it is hard to know. However, Trapaud's story was almost surely mistaken—Light and Rozell likely traveled together, and he had not married the Sultan's daughter. It is still worth noting that the idea of an EIC official marrying an indigenous woman as part of a trade deal was apparently still fine in 1788. This would not be the case by the 1810s with the arrival of Cornwallis and reform.

Negotiations for the settlement at Penang were also significantly more complex than Trapaud described. It is certainly true that, as part of continuing battles over power and territory, several Malay rulers during this period (those not aligned with the Dutch government at Batavia) had approached English traders like Captain Light—who spoke fluent Malay and was well liked—for protection against the Dutch.⁷² According to Diane Lewis, between 1786 and 1787, "every Malay and Bugis prince (except Siak's, who had submitted to Batavia in the 1760s) had been pressed by the VOC into new and more comprehensive treaties and called on 'their friends' the English to protect their independence."⁷³ Not wanting to embroil themselves in what they saw as the petty disputes of local chiefs, or illicit direct combat with the Dutch, the EIC soundly refused. By the end of the 1780s, the Company was looking for a trading port in the Straits of Malacca to curtail Dutch and French in the region and their options

---

⁷⁰ Langdon, *Penang*, p. 191.
⁷¹ A. M. S., "Memoir of Captain Francis Light," *Journal of the Straits Branch of the Royal Asiatic Society* 28 (August 1895): p. 13.
⁷² Lewis, *Jan Compagnie in the Straits of Malacca*, pp. 118–19.
⁷³ Ibid., p. 119.

were limited. According to Langdon, an eager Captain Light, convinced of the island's strategic benefits, arrived and began to develop Penang in July of 1786 with only a "verbal agreement of the terms of cession with the Sultan Abdullah Mukarram Shah of Kedah."[74] By November, in addition to the 100 or so soldiers and officers on duty and the original 58 that arrived with Light, there were an additional 250 residents—not including the large numbers yet to build their houses—who had moved to the island. Some were wealthy merchants and they immediately established a small market. Official approval for the settlement did not come from Bengal until 1790, when he was advised to continue on and maintain the place as a duty-free port. The Sultan demanded a monthly stipend of "SP$10,000 a year and protection of his coastline," as rent for their use of the island, but the India Office was unwilling to agree.[75] After a tense standoff and military skirmish, which the Sultan ultimately lost, Light informed the Company's government that the Sultan agreed to an annual payment of Sp$6000, "without any obligation to protect Kedah against regional invaders."[76] Nonetheless, while Light may have, as Langdon describes, sent "a pre-emptive strike force" and destroyed Kedah's fortifications, the Company still needed their cooperation; if they wanted to avoid constant attack from Malay and Bugis traders, they had to make some accommodations to the Sultan.[77] One of those provisions was the preservation of slavery. Both the original treaty (1791) and a renegotiated version managed by Sir George Leith (1800) stipulated that "all slaves be returned to their masters, for they are part of their property."[78] The same held true for "all servants of the Honourable Company, European or Indian, deserting, shall be delivered up, and the resident may send and officer, civil or military, [...] shall be empowered to search for and seize all such deserters."[79] Although Light's intention was to employ as many "free" laborers as possible, laboring bodies were difficult to come by, and neither the Sultan nor the EIC wanted to lose track of those they already had. In September of 1786, Light wrote to the governor-general at Bengal to tell him that there were so many people, "including women and children," immigrating to Penang that the concerned Sultan Abdullah "imposed a duty of 100 dollars upon every family leaving the place."

---

[74] Langdon, *Penang*, p. 192.
[75] Ibid., p. 195.
[76] Ibid., p. 196.
[77] Ibid., pp. 191–6.
[78] *Slavery in India*, pp. 419–20; Andaya and Andaya, *A History of Malaysia*, pp. 114–36; Langdon, *Penang*, p. 193.
[79] *Slavery in India*, pp. 420–1.

If Light was going to build a wealthy and stable port, he needed working bodies and, in Southeast Asia during this period, wage labor was nearly impossible to find because the few local Malay leaders willing to hire out their servants charged exorbitant prices.[80] In September of 1786, Light wrote to the governor-general in Bengal that "he had brought three carpenters and eight labourers, Chinese, who are of infinite service to us." He explained that he had "hired eight Chinese from Queda" but bemoaned that "they had been so long with the Malays that they [had] lost much of their native industry." The next month he sent a request for "100 Coolies as the price of labor here is enormous, one-quarter dollar per day for one man." Wanting to develop the agricultural output of the settlement, he added, "if they are husbandman, the better; they then may be employed occasionally in cultivating the ground."[81] In response, the governor-general wrote to officials at Fort Marlborough in Bencoolen explaining that their colleague, Superintendent Light, was in need of a "number of people for the purposes of cultivating the country, and assisting at the works carrying on there and other public services," and asked them to "hold 150 Caffrees, volunteers if possible, in readiness to be sent there." In January of 1787, the governor-general responded to Light telling him that he had requested Caffrees from Bencoolen and that they would entreat upon "the gentlemen at Canton to encourage the Chinese to resort to and settle on Prince of Wales Island." By July of 1787 the EIC had shipped "126 Caffrees" to "clear and cultivate the country" in Penang, and by June 1788 there are 857 people—EIC administrators, soldiers, and the original inhabitants—many of whom were slaves.[82] It is worth noting that many of those sent from Bencoolen were at the time "so old they [were] unfit for service Eventually, in 1809, the Company emancipated the few who remained that were "mostly old and infirm[ed], and young children incapable of maintaining themselves by their daily labor," and offered them an allowance with some land.[83]

In July of 1792, Light again sent word to his supervisors about a dispute he was having with the Sultan about who, exactly, held the title of slave and should be returned to Quedah, and the resulting exchange concretized the definition of a slave in the British Straits Settlements.[84] According to Light, the issue came about when several people whom the Sultan considered slaves had fled to Penang seeking refuge and "demanding protection." Although Light initially recognized the Sultan's request and made an attempt to return the refugees, he feared

[80] Reid, "The Decline of Slavery in Nineteenth Century Indonesia," p. 67.
[81] *Slavery in India*, pp. 421–2.
[82] Langdon, *Penang*, p. 195.
[83] *Slavery in India*, p. 439.
[84] Ibid., pp. 424–6.

they would be put to death in Quedah and refused their return. The situation placed Light in the position of arbiter, and he wanted to base his decision on the strictest sense of the term. As Light's letter to Bengal explained, for the British, "the term slave can only be applied to a person legally sold, or one condemned to slavery for crimes." However, the Sultan, he wrote, extended it "to such people as have taken refuge in his country from war, or famine, and to debtors to his merchants." Abdullah did not want to sacrifice any of his subjects, particularly those who were likely considered outsiders and performing the most arduous of tasks, to the encroaching European power. The Bengal government sent a response in August of 1793, clearly not in a rush, to advise Light that they thought it was a good idea to add an article to the treaty that would be "specifying precisely the class of persons coming in future under the description of slaves," and the Company's government wanted him to "receive the term in the most confined sense." The letter indicates that the Company's government was aware that Light would need to take care not to impinge upon the rights of the Sultan or overstep the treaty, but to afford "asylum from the oppression of the Queda government" would be appealing to people and "increase the population of the settlement under [his] superintendence." Both the Company and Light wanted to "fill the island with inhabitants and from their industry to provide provisions, refreshment, and succor for shipping," but Sultan Abdullah was adamant that he did not want the Company to draw from his subjects to do so.

As previously mentioned, during the first ten years in Penang's settlement, Soyad Hussein and Soyad Jaffer, the wealthy "Arabians" with "considerable property" and large families, immigrated to the city and requested the permission to "govern their own families, slaves, and dependents, with an independent power, and in all cases be judged by the Mahomedan [sic] laws."[85] Maintaining the EIC policy of noninterference, Superintendent Light told them that while "they could not have 'an entire independent authority,'" they could have reasonable independence as far as the "general welfare" of their families and dependents.[86] The official told them that "their religion, laws, and customs would be undisturbed" and that this included their right to maintain domestic slaves. Captain Light was the first superintendent of Penang and governed from 1786 until he died in 1794. He spoke fluent Malay and is rumored to have married a Malay princess and established his new settlement at a time when the Company held to its policy of noninterference. The new EIC's government in Penang,

---

[85] Ibid., p. 434.
[86] Ibid., p. 425.

like others throughout British territories in the East Indies during this period, honored the property rights of slave owners and enforced debtor obligations by returning slaves and debtors to their masters. Officials only intervened in the most extreme cases and, would continue to do so unchallenged, for another decade.

During his tenure, Light also created and maintained a quickly expanding tally of newly arriving inhabitants, "a registry of all slaves bought and sold" on the island, as well as "all transfers and sales of houses and lands."[87] This practice continued and Lieutenant Governor Sir George Leith reported that in 1802 the settlement boasted 723 property owners and estimated that there were between 1,200 and 1,400 slaves living in Penang. While the registries were a terrific tool to monitor the slave traffic in and out of the city, they also helped generate an additional stream of income for the struggling settlement. According to the governor-general in council in 1805, "[T]he number of male and female slaves now at that settlement [was] not inferior to five thousand"; this duty on such a large population of slaves would have generated a nice income for Company coffers.[88] A desire to transition to "free" labor did not prevent the British from collecting an opportune profit from the existing slave trade.

The matter came before the colony's Judge and Magistrate John Dickens, who addressed the governor-general in 1802 on the subject of "whether civil slavery, that is, a right in one man over the person and fortune of another, were to be considered as established at Prince of Wales Island."[89] The judge explained that those residents who had been allowed to maintain their slaves when they came to the settlement had initiated a necessity to develop regulations, and to define both the authority of the master over his slaves and the slaves' right to an opportunity for freedom.[90] Officials had too much difficulty attempting to detect newly imported slaves, who would have been illegal, from debtors and existing domestic servants, who were allowed. The magistrate told the government that the conditions of the slaves varied dramatically; some were in a position of "utter slavery," while others lived as beloved members of a wealthy household. Some, the judge explained, were in "the condition of those styled slave-debtors—people that voluntarily become slaves to their creditors until their debts are paid." With so many exceptions to their ordinance, the official sought clarification and assistance from the India Office deciding for whom and how antislavery laws

---

[87] Ibid., p. 434.
[88] Ibid., p. 422.
[89] Ibid., p. 420.
[90] Ibid., p. 429.

should be applied. The magistrate's request went unanswered until April of 1805, when the EIC board of directors expressed to the superintendent that they did not want to encourage the use of slave labor for any purpose. They would rather believe "the clearing of the lands and the cultivation of the pepper and other spices [...] be carried on by free people."[91] The Court of Director's felt the task of completely eliminating slave labor at Prince of Wales Island was neither unreasonable nor impossible, since it had only recently been settled. It seems that the Directors did not believe five thousand slaves was a significant number.

Increasing tensions with the French and the Dutch during the spring of 1805 made the protection of the sea trade in the Straits of paramount importance to Company officials. The following September 19, nineteen years after Captain Light had arrived with plans for building a new maritime trading center and dockyard, the Company elevated Penang to the level of fourth presidency in India, behind Madras, Bombay, and Calcutta. This meant that the seat of governance for the Straits Settlements was now in Penang. Penang's governor reported directly to the Court of Directors and was positioned among the top five in the Indian administration (behind the governor-general, his deputy, and the remaining three presidencies).[92] This remained the case until 1830, when the Court of Directors determined the government at Penang was too expensive and demoted them back to a residency of Bengal. All this is to say that, from 1805 to 1830, the Straits Settlements were given more latitude and less oversight to accomplish their goals for expansion.

In November of 1805, Lieutenant Governor Robert Townsend (R. T.) Farquhar proposed a "plan for the abolition of slavery" at Prince of Wales Island (Penang) that presumed an authority far beyond the EIC's ability to enforce, overlooked the entrenchment and sophistication of Southeast Asia's slave trade, and ignored the fact that the Company's government had been responsible for a fair number of the slaves at Prince of Wales Island. The plan was aggressive, proactive, and for the most part ignored until the 1811 Felony Act, which officially banned the slave trade in all British territories.[93] Not surprisingly, shortly after news of the Act's passage reached the Company's government, officials in Penang received notice that slavery "could not be necessary" in such a new colony and ordered them to develop a plan for its immediate extinction.[94]

A series of unfortunate deaths and administrative shuffling made Colonel Norman Macalister acting lieutenant governor in charge of Penang between

[91] Ibid., pp. 433–4.
[92] Langdon, *Penang*, p. 237.
[93] Major, *Slavery, Abolitionism and Empire in India*, pp. 59–69; Hobhouse, *Returns*, p. 108.
[94] Hobhouse, *Returns*, p. 108.

March of 1807 and October of 1810, which made him responsible for finding a way to implement the Company's new prohibition on slave trading.[95] In April of 1808, Governor Macalister wrote to the Court of Directors' "Public Department" with his plans for the abolition of slavery on the island. According to the letter, Penang's government had followed the Company's directive and prohibited "the future importation and transfer of slaves" and had taken the extra initiative and declared that all children born of slaves after the date of the proclamation would be considered free.[96] In fact, they asserted that if authorities apprehended someone bringing new slaves onto the island, they would immediately be freed. Captain Light's slave registries would also become a way to calculate tax income. The council proposed an annual duty of $5 for each male and $10 for each female slave registered; it would be due on the first of January each year and paid until the slave was either freed or died. If the "proprietors" were inclined to ignore the ordinance, as they had in years past, and the duty was not paid (or only a few of their slave population accounted for), those slaves were to be freed. The ordinance gave slave owners two months from the date of the proclamation to obtain "slave papers" from the collector's office for each of their slaves, "where an exact description roll of such slaves [was] kept." Finally, any unregistered slaves were "to be free and at liberty to go and come without molestation from their former masters or mistresses." As you might imagine, this would have been a devastating blow for those owning large numbers of slaves, and the local government received complaints from the Board of Planters and a few prominent Muslim families from the community. As a result, they had to back track a little, and took pains to create a plan "for freeing each class of slaves with the least pecuniary injury or domestic inconvenience to the proprietors."

Similar to propositions debated in London and bantered about in the Caribbean, Governor Macalister and Penang's Government in Council—despite warnings against potential abuses and exploitation of the system—felt that transferring slaves to debtors was their best option. In an attempt to affix a standard value and make transfers more efficient, the council wanted to establish a general amount that "would be fixed as nearly as possible at the cost or value, but so moderate that a debtor, in the event of wishing to leave his master, would not be likely to have any difficulty in procuring a loan of the amount from another."[97] Then, after explaining that the only slaves left on the island, aside from the Company's Caffrees, were "Malays, Battahs or Chuliahs,

---

[95] Langdon, *Penang*, p. 258.
[96] *Slavery in India*, pp. 437–8.
[97] Ibid., p. 442.

the former much more valuable that the latter," they proposed the sum of $50 (Spanish dollars) for each Malay slave and $100 for a family, "composed of a father and mother, or either of them, and all the children under nine years of age." The Caffrees, being more valuable, had to pay their masters (the Company) $100 for men, $50 for women, and $150 for a family. Any child above nine was considered at the rate according to their sex. So it was illegal to import any new slaves; slave owners had to register and pay a tax on all existing slaves (under penalty of emancipation); all children born to slaves after the date of the proclamation would be free, and officials had attempted to create a standard, affordable price that, theoretically, allowed slaves to purchase their "freedom" from their masters.

In order to regulate debtor contracts, the council recommended that local magistrates be given the authority to emancipate those "kept for prostitution, and slaves treated by their masters with inhumanity or cruelty."[98] Many of these regulations, officials also averred, prevented the parents from exploiting their children and young women from being, as one official argued, at the "absolute disposal and caprice of a private master, and their labors converted into the means of gratifying his lust or avarice."[99] Otherwise, the institution of slavery in Penang, according to the plan, would gradually die out with the last slave on the registry. All of these provisions certainly put on the air of a proactive effort around antislavery efforts and attempted to protect local women and girls. However, as we will see, traffickers had little trouble avoiding any serious consequences and the trade in slaves continued relatively undaunted.

While there may have been some administrators in the India Office at this time who wanted total and immediate abolition of all slavery, the majority of Company officials, recognizing the value in compromise, implemented provisions to accommodate the slave owners who were there. It is also important to remember how far the Straits were from both India and London.[100] Until the arrival of the first steamships in the 1840s, it could take months for the EIC government to respond and, in the meantime, officials had to improvise, strategize, and maintain order within their settlements. This distance also meant that help would also take a very long time, should a rebellion or conflict arise.[101]

[98] Hobhouse, *Returns*, p. 108.
[99] Ibid., p. 109.
[100] According to Henry Wise's *An Analysis of One Hundred Voyages to and from India, China. Performed by Ships in the Honorable East India Company's Service; with Remarks on the Advantages of Steam-Power* (London: J.W. Noire & Co., 1839), p. 22 it took more than five months to reach Penang from England and more than a month just to get from India to Penang.
[101] Many of the letters between local officials and the Straits government took as long as six months to receive a reply: Evans, *Slave Trade (East India) Slavery in Ceylon*, pp. 209–60, 309–36.

Consequently, it was both easier and more prudent to negotiate. Finally, on May 16, 1810, Penang's acting governor, Charles Andrew Bruce, received a letter from the Court of Directors approving their recommendations for the gradual abolition of slavery. In spite of a continuous rotation of administrators by the time this newly formed government at Penang had its colonial partners in crime, the Government in Council had hindered the foreign (European) trade in slaves to the Straits, initiated a transition toward debt-slavery, established regulations against the prostitution of slaves and debtors, and introduced the process of gradual abolition of slavery in the settlement. Aside from the remaining slaves on the registries, slavery was no longer legal in Penang by 1810—almost ten years before Raffles, then preparing to invade and take control of Java, laid the foundations for Singapore, the EIC's new duty-free port of call located at the mouth of one of the busiest commercial sea lanes in the world.

## Singapore

Raffles and Farquhar's negotiation for and the acquisition of Singapore from Abdul Rahman, Temenggong Sri Maharaja of Johor, in 1819 was a direct refutation of Dutch expansionism in Southeast Asia.[102] Despite a series of ineffectual administrators during its early years, as a successor to the thriving international Malaysian port of Riau, once established, Singapore connected Bugis, Malay, Kling, Arab, Chinese, and European traders, attracted pirates, and was a beacon to migrant laborers (voluntary and forced) from around the IOW. Although British country traders had been visiting these seas since the seventeenth century, and the Company had established its presence in the region by the 1780s, Singapore's duty-free trade policies made it a quick and convenient transfer point for commodities, both licit and illicit, traded between Asia and the Pacific, and the larger Indian Ocean World. Singapore's strategic value as a point to refresh and refuel became particularly apparent during the Opium Wars from 1839 to 1842 and then again from 1856 to 1860. Most ships entering or leaving the Straits landed at Singapore and, by 1850, it had become the seat of British power in Southeast Asia.[103]

---

[102] Carl A. Trocki, *Singapore: Wealth, Power and the Culture of Control* (New York: Routledge, 2006), p. 9.

[103] Trocki, *Singapore*, pp. 8–14, Trocki, *Prince of Pirates*, pp. 56–67; Andaya and Andaya, *A History of Malaysia*, pp. 115–19.

While many have asserted, mostly Anglophiles, that Singapore did not exist before the British, there is plenty of evidence to prove otherwise. Indeed, it is quite an act of hubris to believe that within such an archipelagic, trade-minded culture none of the myriad Malay societies within the region would have thought to settle there. However, as John Cameron explains in his 1865 descriptive work, *Our Tropical Possessions in Malayan India*, Singapore's "early history can possess but little interest to English readers as compared with its present condition."[104] As a result, Singapore's history, for the western world, begins with Stamford Raffles in 1819. However, we know from a variety of early works by EIC administrator/historians (and subsequently supported by Southeast Asian scholars) that there was more than just "a few Malay fisherman" on the island of "Singahpura" when the British arrived.[105]

Sources tell us that Singahpura was a Malay city, established as early as the 1160s, in opposition to the "powerful state of Java" and was prosperous enough that from its inception the colony sustained repeated attacks from Javanese forces until they eventually succeeded in taking it and evicting its "sturdy settlers" in 1252.[106] John Crawfurd explains that according to Malay history, after the above Javanese attack, the last king of Singahpura, Sri Iskandar Shah, fled north and a year later established the promising city of "Malaka," which, "under his wise government, became of considerable importance." But Crawfurd was suspicious of several sections of the Malay account because, having spent time in the Javanese court, he asserted that "the Javanese story is wholly silent" on the matter of the expulsion of Malays from Singahpura.

Of course, it is not all that surprising the Javanese Royal Court might have chosen not to discuss the unseemly matters of eradicating a rival port community and dispersing its inhabitants with impunity. Nonetheless, Crawfurd assures us, "[T]he main points may be relied upon, and we may conclude—that an extensive emigration took place from Sumatra to the extremity of the peninsula—that some Javanese drove the settlers from Singapura to Malacca—and that this event took place about the year 1276." However, this conflicts with later archeological evidence discussed in Chapter 5. As previously mentioned, Taylor argued that the Malay Prince, Parameśvara, went to the island of "Tumasik" in the 1390s in an effort to move away from the Javanese Court.[107] If you remember, Taylor's

---

[104] Cameron, *Our Tropical Possessions in Malayan India*, p. 6.
[105] Hobhouse, *Returns*, p. 118; Trocki, *Prince of Pirates*, pp. 56–62; Trocki, *Singapore*, p. 15.
[106] John Crawfurd, *History of the Indian Archipelago: Containing an Account of the Manners, Arts, Languages, Religions, Institutions, and Commerce of Its Inhabitants*, Vol. II (London: A. Constable and Co., 1820), pp. 372–5.
[107] Taylor, "The Early Kingdoms," p. 175.

study used Miksic's findings of earthenware and glass beads to illustrate that Tumasik, or the island of Singahpura, was an important trading center and experienced significant commercial prosperity at the end of the fourteenth century.[108] Although they are about a century apart, all the sources agree that the former inhabitants of Singapore emigrated north and established Malacca, and for our purposes here, we will error on the side of archeology and say this happened around 1390.[109]

Crawfurd argues that Singahpura, Malacca, and Johor "colonized the islands Lingga and Bintan, Kampar and Aru on Sumatra, Borneo [...] and all the states which exist on the Malay Peninsula."[110] This tells us that Singahpura was not just a fishing village when the British arrived. After the expulsion of Paramesvara, because of its vulnerability, the island spent the next three hundred years in Malacca's shadow. Still, Singahpura remained an esteemed part of the kingdom of Johor and a small vacation island for the Temenggong, a quasi "minister of justice" to the Sultan, until it was leased to Raffles in 1819.[111] At first glance, the above history might not seem relevant to our discussion of slavery and abolition in the Straits. However, the early history of Singahpura is evidence that, rather than being an empty backwater village, with potential unnoticed by indigenous leaders for millennia, the island had proven to be a sleeping dragon with the promise of both profit and war. The British were not the first to discover Singahpura, but their increasingly advanced military power protecting the surrounding waterways over the course of the nineteenth century gave the dragon a chance to emerge as one of the world's most vibrant and influential centers for commerce, a title it continues to hold as I write this exactly two hundred years later. More important to our discussion here, there were almost certainly slaves living in this Malay port.

British Singapore was founded in 1819, well after the Company's Regulation X in 1811, which made the importation of slaves into the British East Indies a felony. According to EIC records Farquhar and Raffles prohibited slavery on the island when they acquired it from the Sultan of Johor; they also followed Penang's lead and encouraged any emigrating slave owners to convert their slaves to debtors in an effort to eliminate the existing legal slave population on the island. Technically, to bring a slave to Singapore, unless documented on one

---

[108] Ibid.
[109] For more on Malacca, see Harry Miller, *A Short History of Malaysia* (New York: F.A. Praeger, 1966); Leonard Andaya, *Leaves of the Same Tree Trade and Ethnicity in the Straits of Melaka* (Honolulu, HI: University of Hawai'i Press, 2008); Donald Freeman, *The Straits of Malacca Gateway or Gauntlet?* (Montreal: McGill-Queen's University Press, 2003).
[110] Crawfurd, *History of the Indian Archipelago*, Vol. II, pp. 376.
[111] Trocki, *Prince of Pirates*, pp. 6–10; Reid, *Charting the Shape of Early Modern Southeast Asia*, pp. 240–5; Trocki, *Singapore*, p. 9.

of the accepted registries, was illegal. And yet the description by Abdullah Bin Abdul Kadir offered in the introduction of this book is evidence that there was a viable and visible slave trade on the island of Singapore as late as 1823.[112] Kadir had personally seen a Bugis trader lead "fifty or sixty slaves, male and female" around town, hitting them with a cane when he liked. Then, upon further inquiry, the EIC assistant discovered a ship filled with women and girls of all ages, both Malay and foreign, openly for sale. He described the "tear-stained eyes" of the women groped and fondled by the "hundreds of Chinese [who] came to make purchases," explaining that the slaves were given "rice in coconut shells and water in bamboo scoops, just as one gives food to dogs," and the slave dealers behaved in "a savage manner devoid of any spark of feeling." There were a few men roped and fastened to the side of the boat, but Kadir's writings made it clear that most of the slaves were women and that he had been overwhelmed by what he had seen inside the ship. When he relayed his horror to Governor Raffles, Raffles assured Kadir that the EIC and the British government planned to eliminate such "wicked" practices in the region.

Although Raffles's private letters in fact clearly expressed his disdain for slavery, as well as his intentions to abolish it in Britain's eastern territories, they were likely written for public consumption, and there are other sources starkly contradicting his heroic image as the benevolent founder of Singapore.[113] Another of Raffles biographers, C. E. Wurtzburg, wrote that among the many things that dissatisfied him about Farquhar was that he was seemingly unaware of the Company's law against slave trading. According to Wurtzburg, Raffles was a staunch abolitionist and lost all respect for his colleague when he learned that under his watch a slave trade existed in Singapore. In spite of the Company's 1807 prohibition and early efforts to regulate conditions for slave-debtors, when approached, Farquhar reportedly told Raffles that because the colony was so young, he felt it "unwise to be too particular."[114] This is certainly plausible, since it rings true to prevailing EIC policy and sentiment. However, Hannigan explains that Raffles's firm stance on slavery became most vocal while serving under Lord Minto, a battle-proven abolitionist, and together they made plans to set an example for the rest of the Empire by "freeing the slaves of the Dutch

---

[112] Munshi, *The Hikayat Abdullah*, pp. 181–5.
[113] These letters were assembled posthumously by his wife, Lady Sophia Raffles, *Memoir of the Life and Public Services of Sir Thomas Stamford Raffles, F.R.S. &c: Particularly in the Government of Java, 1811–1816, and of Bencoolen and Its Dependencies, 1817–1824; with Details of the Commerce and Resources of the Eastern Archipelago, and Selections from His Correspondence* (London: John Murray, 1830), p. 285.
[114] Wurtzburg, *Raffles of the Eastern Isles*, pp. 728–9, 613.

East Indies."¹¹⁵ These plans also included appointing Raffles lieutenant governor of Java and giving him ultimate authority over Company business on the island.

However, when the British arrived in Batavia in the fall of 1811, freeing the slaves was not on Raffles's mind, and he eventually acquired several of his own. After they learned the extent of European slave ownership in Java, the newly appointed lieutenant governor began to sound like so many other EIC officials and asserted that slavery in Java was purely domestic and could not be eliminated immediately. Java, like Malacca, and Penang would work toward a gradual abolition. Unfortunately, Minto and Raffles were not able to liberate Java's slaves after all. Moreover, Lieutenant-Governor Raffles' zealously liberal ideology did not translate into personal behavior. In addition to around twenty-six salaried European and Indonesian servants, Raffles kept eight personal slaves and had seventy-seven at his grand white house in Buitzenburg.¹¹⁶ As we can see, even the EIC officials who were the most vocal proponents of antislavery legislation behaved ambiguously when actually confronted with Asian slavery. It is not hard to imagine that an illicit trade in slaves was flowing through the Straits with impunity, when regardless of the law, EIC officials were either outright complicit or, like Farquhar, wanted to maintain good diplomatic relationships to ensure the growth of prosperous and stable settlements.

In spite of his apparent disregard for the Company's antislavery ordinances, according to his memoirs, between 1819 and 1823, Raffles drafted several laws attempting to regulate the abuse of vulnerable populations from what he saw as despotic exploitation from unscrupulous indigenous chiefs.¹¹⁷ Due to health reasons, Raffles returned to London in 1823; however, before leaving, he made one last effort to implement antislavery measures in the Straits and drafted regulations stipulating the legal parameters for "slave-debtors" in Singapore.¹¹⁸ To ensure that local customs of indenture did not devolve into unbridled slavery, these regulations limited all contracts for servitude to a maximum of three years. Additionally, the ordinance attempted to limit the profits of slave traffickers and declared that when purchasing "debtors" from boats, a nakhoda, or captain of a Chinese junk, could charge no more than "$20 dollars, what may be considered as an equivalent for passage money of the party."¹¹⁹ The contracts were to be registered with the magistrate, and a debtor's services could not be transferred to

---

[115] Hannigan, *Raffles and the British Invasion of Java*, p. 128.
[116] Ibid., pp. 131, 244.
[117] Raffles, *Memoir of the Life and Public Services of Sir Thomas Stamford Raffles*, pp. 77–9.
[118] "Extract from Raffles' Regulations," CO273/79/99-100; *Singapore Local Laws and Institutions, 1823*, pp. 12–16.
[119] Ibid., p. 100; *Singapore Local Laws and Institutions, 1823*, p. 14.

another party. Despite his complicated past, while he was in Singapore, Raffles did work diligently to establish laws that he believed would ensure the eventual extinction of slavery in the Company's territories in the East Indies. However, while Raffles may have told Kadir that he hoped to "see all the slaves gain their freedom" he clearly had not considered (or was arrogantly ignorant of) the enormity of the task.[120] Nevertheless, by the time he was back in London in 1823, Raffles had proclaimed slavery and the slave trade was illegal in Singapore, for everyone, and established guidelines for the expectations and duration of slave-debtor contracts. Officially, the EIC government in Singapore had taken a hard stance on slavery from its inception. The Company would need to tap into its resources of convicts and indentured and contracted labor from India to build this new settlement. However, the success of that venture created an entirely new demand, which formed the foundations of what, eventually, became an illicit traffic in women and girls for the purposes of domestic and sexual labor that has persisted for the past two hundred years.

By the time Penang and Singapore joined with Malacca in 1826 to form the British Straits Settlements, there was a surplus of men, many of them hungry and desperate, ready to contract themselves to work on the Company's projects. Extant research has established that due to famine and an increase in impoverished populations during this period, there were abundant supplies of male labor desperately looking for work in the Straits Settlements.[121] In fact, Reid tells us that slavery began a natural decline in Indonesia because, by the beginning of the nineteenth century, the costs of maintaining slaves and a growing population of cheap labor offered alternatives to the life-long commitment of traditional slave ownership.[122] Additionally, as discussed, there were shiploads of convicts, sailors, deckhands, soldiers, and merchants making their way from ports around the world to Britain's newest frontier in the eastern Empire.[123] These two new

---

[120] Minshu, *The Hikayat Abdullah*, p. 183.
[121] The most relevant works explaining labor migrations, as well as the political and social constructions that made this era so vital to imperial expansion and the development of the modern world: Manning, *Migration in World History*; Williams, *Capitalism and Slavery*; Bayly, *Imperial Meridian*; Bayly, *The Birth of the Modern World, 1780-1914*; Tony Ballantyne, *Moving Subjects: Gender, Mobility, and Intimacy in an Age of Global Empire* (Urbana: University of Illinois Press, 2009); Curtin, *Cross-Cultural Trade in World History*.
[122] Reid, "The Decline of Slavery in Nineteenth Century Indonesia," p. 69.
[123] The following provides evidence that the British regularly used convict and emancipated slave labor in Singapore: Evans, *Slave Trade (East India) Slavery in Ceylon*, pp. 20-1. However, the following secondary sources have established that this was a common practice for the British during this period. In fact, in a letter to the colonial office in India on February 9, 1859, the governor of the Straits Settlements asked the British government to stop sending convict labor to Singapore because it was turning it into a "penal settlement," CO273/2/432.

colonies teemed with men who were either far from their wives or were too poor to afford the cost of having wives at all.[124] So while there were abundant supplies of cheap male labor during these first forty years of the nineteenth century, as we will see below, there was a dramatic shortage of women and many EIC officials saw the gradual emancipation of slavery as a "convenient compromise."[125]

---

[124] Warren, *Pirates, Prostitutes and Pullers*, pp. 209–15; Reid and Brewster, *Slavery, Bondage, and Dependency in Southeast Asia*, p. 26.
[125] Evans, *Slave Trade (East India) Slavery in Ceylon*, p. 241.

8

# The Wild, Womanless East Indies

At the end of the monsoon season, it was likely raining on February 15, 1827, when that day's edition of the *Singapore Chronicle* complained of the murder and mayhem that prevailed in the settlement. Residents living in Singapore had become weary of the street brawls and late-night parties, indicative of the uncivilized savagery of the poorer classes residing by the docks. A resident voicing their concerns in the local paper worried that there were not enough women to quell jealousies between the swelling number of lawless and violent men arriving almost daily.[1] The editorial announced that "within the last fortnight, no less than two murders have been committed, one of a man by a Chinese, and another of a young woman by a Malay" and that the culprits had not been found.[2] The author asserted they were aware that "a large portion of the murders committed at Singapore [had] originated in jealousy or revenge of which women [had] been the source and sometimes the victims." They lamented the fact that there was "too great a disparity in the numbers of the sexes in the settlement, the male being much more numerous than the females" and that this dramatic disproportion between the sexes would "excite rivalry for the smiles of the fair." The difference was so great that it caused "rivalry" and "dissent," which was "inimical to the peace and good order of the community."

As curmudgeonly comical as this editorial might seem almost two centuries later, a number of interesting clues about contemporary perceptions can be drawn from this colonist's complaints. This resident believed that the large population

---

[1] The following works, all published in the 1830s, perpetuate this image of a lawless and dangerous environment in the Straits Settlements: Elijah C. Bridgman and Samuel W. Williams, *The Chinese Repository, Volume 4* (Tokyo: Maruzen Kabushiki Kaisha, 1836), p. 524; James Silk Buckingham, *The Oriental Herald and Colonial Review Volume 7*, ed. J. S. Buckingham (London: Sanford Arnot, 1825), p. 160; Thomas John Newbold, *Political and Statistical Account of the British Settlements in the Straits of Malacca: Viz. Pinang, Malacca, and Singapore, with a History of the Malayan States on the Peninsula of Malacca* (London: J. Murray, 1839), p. 52; John Phipps, *A Practical Treatise on the China and Eastern Trade: Comprising the Commerce of Great-Britain and India Particularly Bengal and Singapore with China and the Eastern Islands* (London: Allen, 1836), p. xxiii.

[2] *The Singapore Chronicle*, February 15, 1827.

of Chinese and Malay laborers filling the settlement were not civilized enough to maintain themselves in a mature and sober manner. Their savagery threatened the stability and (from the British perspective) prosperity of the colony, and the editorial suggested that the presence of more women would alleviate their problems of violence and crime. The author's frustrations articulated common nineteenth-century descriptions/stereotypes and rested on the classed, gendered, and racialized identities Europeans were working so hard to construct during this period. Since the victims and perpetrators in the editorial remain unnamed and overgeneralized, we can assume that they are likely among the poorer class of laborers in Straits who at that point were predominantly made up of soldiers and convicts from India, and indentured Chinese.[3] In essence, these poor Asian men were without access to women's bodies and receiving neither the civilizing effects of domesticity nor the distracting pleasures of sex; not to mention, the few women who were there became the subject of "uncivilized" competition. There is no question that women (slave and free) performed myriad labors within the British Straits Settlements (and everywhere else in the world) since the formation of each individual factory. However, at this moment, in this place, women providing domestic and sexual labor were incredibly valuable and important commodities and Company officials believed these lawless fraternities needed the domesticating influence of women or at least more of their bodies for a distraction.

## The Slaves from Nias

In early June of 1828, Superintendent Caunter summoned eight "passengers" from Pulau Nias into the police office to answer a few questions about the circumstances of their arrival at Penang.[4] They had allegedly been aboard three detained Chinese junks and, according to a complaint received from a Portuguese missionary Reverend Boucho, were sold into slavery in the community. Correspondence from Resident Councilor Ibbetson had ordered Caunter to investigate the complaint by Boucho, which claimed "not less than 80 captives" had been imported to the island "a few days before."[5] After having located some

---

[3] There is a long discussion about slaves in Bencoolen in Evans, *Slave Trade (East India) Slavery in Ceylon*, pp. 20–1; Hobhouse, *Returns*, pp. 107–9 explains the prominence of convicts and Chinese labor within the Straits; and Allen's, "Satisfying the 'Want for Labouring People,'" pp. 45–6; Allen, "Suppressing a Nefarious Traffic," pp. 874–5.
[4] "Slave Trade," IOR/F4/1130/30195/15.
[5] Ibid., p. 5.

of the "captives" in houses within the community, local authorities took four women, a girl, and three boys to the superintendent's office for questioning. The captives explained to the superintendent how they had been the last of a much larger shipment of slaves collected by the nakhodas, or commanders, of three Chinese junks. They told the officer that they spent "some weeks" on board before they sailed from Nias, about ten days before.[6] While many of these slaves may have been from Nias, some were clearly from stops the nakhodas made before they reached that island; therefore, they could have been from any one of a string of islands within the archipelago, Siam (modern Thailand), or China.[7]

Having already deposed the constable, George Godfrey, the superintendent knew that the three junks in question belonged to influential local Chinese merchants and that the nakhodas were believed to have "brought away from thence upwards of 100 persons," whom they "purchased or procured" with cloth.[8] Francisco, a local "Nias man of the Christian faith," presumably provided by Reverend Boucho, told Caunter that he "questioned the Nias people" who were found and brought here in the Chinese junks. Francisco told Caunter that he had "every reason to believe what they say is true, as they are too young and too ignorant to fabricate stories of this kind." Upon further investigation the superintendent learned that Maj Teejah, a Siamese woman living in a nearby district, had also "purchased the little Nias boy, Boodee Boodee, here present about 20 days ago, for 23 dollars," as her adopted son. According to testimony, the nakhodas unloaded two other boys, Lama and Dalooah, in "different Achinese ports they touched at." Dalooah and Rakhye, one of the young women, were working in the houses of one of the nakhodas when police took them.

Caunter described Nahoo as "one of the most intelligent of the Nias girls" and used her statements to establish the timeline and route of their voyage. While the report does not indicate where she had come from, Nahoo told the superintendent that she had been on board the Hoh Hoatheen for weeks "with 70 or 80 others" before sailing to the island and that they made several stops along the way. Nahoo, Noora, Luklye, and Jenooah were "put by the nakhoda in the house of a Chinaman, by whom they were compelled to prostitute themselves every night to different men." In his report to Ibbetson on June 19,

---

[6] Ibid., p. 23.
[7] This is where both primary and secondary literature say the majority of slaves during this period came from: Evans, *Slave Trade (East India) Slavery in Ceylon*, pp. 20–1; Hobhouse, *Returns*, pp. 107–9; Allen, "Satisfying the 'Want for Labouring People,'" pp. 44–5; Allen, "Suppressing a Nefarious Traffic," pp. 874–5; Reid and Brewster, *Slavery, Bondage, and Dependency in Southeast Asia*, pp. 11–24.
[8] "Slave Trade," IOR/F4/1130/30195/22-28.

the superintendent noted that the girls all corroborated each other's stories and that "their ears and hair were cut and trimmed to improve their appearance." Presumably, this was a recognizable method of adornment and perhaps verification of the women's stories. However, in his report, the official noted at the end of his interviews with each of the witnesses that "the foregoing Nias boys and girls appear quite ignorant of the nature of an oath, consequently cannot be sworn to their information." Since these slaves were not Christian, Caunter believed they could not understand the meaning of "swearing before God," and therefore their statements could not be trusted.[9] As a result, their testimony was disregarded, which ultimately prevented the full prosecution of the case. Nevertheless, Caunter agreed that Reverend Boucho's complaint "appear[ed] to be well founded."[10] In response, Ibbetson ordered the junks detained, and on June 27 Master Attendant C. W. H. Wright reported to the resident that the three Chinese junks in question had been "taken charge of."[11] Wright made sure that the ships were incapacitated and awaited further orders.

Meanwhile, on June 26, the superintendent also interrogated the accused nakhodas, Too Kung, Picklow Lim, and Jooey Sim, or "Yooey," who all denied "having been at all concerned in slave-dealing."[12] Kung claimed he had not even been to Nias. Lim and Sim told Caunter that they had sailed from Nias but had taken on the persons in question as debtor servants in exchange for their passage. Each of the men claimed some of the women to be their personal concubines or servants, while others, apparently, had been servants promised to adoptive families. Additionally, the owners of the junks, Seong Sim and Cheong Cheah, claimed they had no knowledge of slave dealing on their junks and would never have sanctioned such a venture. Moreover, Ticklow Sim, the merchant who Nahoo, Noora, Luklye, and Jenooah all accused of forcing them to work as prostitutes, said that two of the women who were taken from his house were sent to him as domestic servants from a man named Choo. The other three were the concubines of crew members who had asked the merchant to allow them to stay there "whilst the junk hauled on shore to careen and repair." He unequivocally denied having compelled any of them to prostitute themselves or that they had "ever been intended for such a life."

We know from Chapter 2 that Secretary John Anderson perceived the case too "hazardous for the prosecutor to proceed to trial" and that the case

---

[9] Evans, *Slave Trade (East India) Slavery in Ceylon*, p. 227.
[10] "Slave Trade," IOR/F4/1130/30195/7.
[11] Ibid., p. 13.
[12] Ibid., pp. 28–33.

was dismissed until further evidence could be collected.[13] Ultimately, the EIC officials did keep the girls; they went to stay with Reverend Boucho in the local nunnery.[14] But the owners were only required to pay a small fine, and the harbor master returned the junks to their owners on August 14.[15] However, though the punishment was slight, this case ultimately initiated a thorough investigation of slavery in the Straits that eventually led the government's overall ban on debt-slavery in 1830. However, just as before, the preservation of political and economic relationships was paramount, and efforts to maintain stable trade and profits circumscribed the authority of the British Navy and inhibited the enforcement of antislavery measures. Rear Admiral Gage told Resident Ibbetson that unless he had irrefutable proof that a vessel sailing under His Majesty's flag was trafficking slaves, there was very little he could do to search and seize arriving ships.[16] But the Straits government did not want a public discussion about their inadequacies and worked to stifle the public conversation. Secretary to the Governor in Council John Patullo claimed the *Chronicles*' articles that discussed the local slave trade "tended to destroy the peace, harmony, and good order of the settlement" and ordered Singapore's Resident Murchison to prevent any further discussion of the matter.[17]

So although there were laws in place that initiated the investigation in the first place, Caunter's preconceived, racialized notions of gender, class, and domesticity shaped the way he behaved. For Caunter, the statements of slaves (or debtors)—especially women and children—did not carry the same weight as those of wealthy business*men*. The word of wealthy merchants or the captains of ships held far more weight than that of a slave. Thus, when the assertions of nine poor women and children were pitted against six influential men, it is not difficult to see why Superintendent Caunter claimed that he did not believe that they were slaves or that they were "ever intended as such, and insisted they were debtors."[18] Moreover, as the superintendent explained, he did not see their circumstance as all that tragic; these women and girls were only brought in to do what he would have believed women were supposed to do and what they

---

[13] Ibid., p. 16.
[14] Ibid., p. 17; this archive did not indicate that these specific women were introduced to native Christian men as wives; however, this was practice that the following scholars address: Hall, *Civilising Subjects*, pp. 65–70; Eliza F. Kent, *Converting Women: Gender and Protestant Christianity in Colonial South India* (Oxford: Oxford University Press, 2004), pp. 165–91.
[15] Evans, *Slave Trade (East India) Slavery in Ceylon*, p. 240.
[16] Ibid., p. 37.
[17] Ibid., p. 234.
[18] "Slave Trade," IOR/F4/1130/30195, p. 14.

would have done anywhere else. On top of that, he believed they were in a better situation, regardless of their status. It is safe to assume that had the reverend not reported it, the importation of Nahoo, Noora, Luklye, Jenooah, and the others would have gone unnoticed.

When authorities were confronted with an undeniable case of slave trading, they were not always able to, or chose not to, discern the difference between slaves, debtors, and free people. Convicting these wealthy men of a felonious offense they likely did not agree was criminal in the first place, and confiscating their property, would have caused unwelcome controversy, which as officials suggested was "too hazardous for the prosecutor to proceed to trial."[19] There is not any further explanation as to what officials thought would happen—we simply know that the case ultimately fizzled away and the owners of the junks paid a minimal fine for their neglect to report the "debtors" to the magistrate right away.[20]

It seems quite clear that officials also chose to overlook key elements of the Nias testimony: the girls told Caunter that Picklow had "put them in the house of a Chinaman" who forced them "every night to prostitute themselves to different men."[21] Though Caunter believed Nahoo's story enough to use her statements to establish timelines and routes, the fact that he deemed them unable to swear to their testimony made it convenient for officials to disregard their assertions that the merchants and nakhodas had illegally trafficked and sold them as slaves within the settlement—clearly a felony. If the superintendent knew the slaves' statements were inadmissible at the beginning, authorities would not even have had to go through the effort of investigating and trying to prosecute. But they did proceed and were quickly confronted with conflicting, potentially incendiary, stories. While officials never explicitly said so, it is possible that the compelling nature of the women's stories was the reason officials were able to keep custody of the slaves—who the nakhodas claimed were debtors—without resistance. If they truly were their wives, servants, or concubines it is hard to believe their husband or employers would not have asked for their return. Since we know, both from articles as well as from Secretary Patullo's threats, that this case was being covered in the *Malacca Observer* and the *Singapore Chronicle*, to do any less might have caused a scandal that, regardless of the vast distances between the two, would most certainly have eventually reached London.[22]

---

[19] Ibid., p. 16.
[20] Evans, *Slave Trade (East India) Slavery in Ceylon*, p. 234.
[21] IOR/F4/1130/30195, p. 26.
[22] This is in fact what Secretary Patullo was worried about and he expressed as such in his communication to Resident Murchison on November 30, 1829; Evans, *Slave Trade (East India) Slavery in Ceylon*, p. 235.

However, colonial officials did not seem to be appalled after learning that the girls had been forced into prostitution. According to official correspondence and parliamentary records, slavery "for the purpose of prostitution" represented the basest form of the trade; EIC officials repeatedly professed that the elimination of it should be the primary focus of antislavery legislation.[23] No doubt, perceptions of indigenous sexuality would have dulled the sense of outrage. They would certainly have felt differently had the women been white Europeans. Some studies have indicated that British colonial officials did very little to prohibit the illegal traffic in women and girls they encountered in various regions around the Empire.[24] Local authorities understood women and girls were being trafficked into their districts and that prostitution was a problem, but as we already know, the British considered the profession a necessary and convenient civilizing force for large groups of uncivilized men.[25] Caunter admitted the nakhodas had likely purchased the women but was apparently not convinced they had been forced to work as prostitutes. Perhaps he believed them so savage that they did not understand the difference between the domestic and sexual obligations expected of a wife or concubine from those of a prostituted slave.

Governor Fullerton's and Superintendent Caunter's actions made it clear that they saw the importation of these women as an acceptable price to pay for the "gradual advancement" of the settlement's civilization and also that they chose to ignore evidence of slavery to avoid legal conflict.[26] At the same time, even if they truly believed these women were concubines, as part of the patriarchal order and "sexual contract" between British men and their male colonial subjects, officials would have been reluctant to interfere with these men's access to women's labor or bodies.[27] Certainly, if Caunter believed the women were in fact concubines, he would have thought the women obligated to stay with the nakhodas. The confiscation of these women would have been a transgression of both the Company's policy of noninterference and of this contract, but a far more acceptable compromise in order to avoid a potentially damaging public legal proceeding. At the same time, whether or not these women were truly slaves or debtors was likely a question of semantics. For these officials, being a slave

---

[23] This opinion is expressed in a variety of ways, from a multitude of officials; see *Slavery in India*, pp. 435, 440, 453; Evans, *Slave Trade (East India) Slavery in Ceylon*, pp. 4, 68; Hobhouse, *Returns*, pp. 87–9, 99, 154, 109, and in that same publication a "Copy of the Report from the Indian Law Commissioners" also addresses the issue of using slaves for the purpose of prostitution, pp. 208–9.
[24] Chatterjee, *Gender, Slavery, and Law in Colonial India*, pp. 218–19; Levine, *Gender and Empire*, p. 136.
[25] Levine, "A Multitude of Unchaste Women," p. 159.
[26] Hobhouse, *Returns*, p. 109.
[27] Pateman, *The Sexual Contract*, p. 6.

in HM Empire was a step up the evolutionary ladder! Caunter even asserted to Ibbetson that "they are certainly, in general, benefited by the change."[28] This, despite the fact that Noora had testified and the others corroborated that she, Luklye, Tenaaloo, and Naha were all slaves and had been forced to work as prostitutes.[29]

To be fair, Caunter admitted to Ibbetson that "some of the females brought here have no doubt been improperly disposed of," but he maintained that their importation, regardless of the circumstance, was to their advantage.[30] He and other colonial officials conveniently ignored the reality that not all of the women imported into the colonies could be, as Secretary Anderson described to the EIC Government in Council, "comfortably settled" as the "wives of opulent Chinese merchants."[31] We know from Indrani Chatterjee that "in the face of abolition, the simple reduction of the complex and different grades of slavery into 'marriage' relations, [...] absolved the Company of any responsibility to legally end slave-concubinage."[32] A quick glance at official correspondence and newspaper discourse proves that officials understood the majority of men in Singapore were seamen, migrant laborers, or simply too poor to afford marrying or setting up a household and, as we have learned, the majority of slave traffic in the Straits were of women and girls.[33] Officials overlooked the felonious importation of these women because they were an unintended but convenient compromise that offered domestic and sexual labor for the laboring masses when those services were at a premium.

We see the clearest expression of the EIC's understanding of its predicament in Governor Fullerton's March 12 address to the Straits Government in Council at Singapore in 1830.[34] After receiving the results of the investigation from Lewis, Fullerton announced that there was, indeed, a "clandestine" slave trade in the Straits and that the system of debt-slavery that all three settlements had come to depend upon was just a ruse for "pure slavery." Then, he took the opportunity to state that "they must not omit the mention of its few redeeming qualities." As

---

[28] IOR/F4/1130/30195, p. 8.
[29] IOR/F4/1130/30195, p. 16; Evans, *Slave Trade (East India) Slavery in Ceylon*, pp. 237–8.
[30] IOR/F4/1130/30195, p. 9.
[31] This is what John Anderson told the council in his article in *Quarterly Review* that the editor of the *Singapore Chronicle* took such offense to, April 26, 1827.
[32] Chatterjee, *Gender, Slavery, and Law in Colonial India*, p. 21.
[33] Evans, *Slave Trade (East India) Slavery in Ceylon*, p. 239. The following articles in the *Singapore Chronicle* offer examples of local demographics and populations discussed: *The Singapore Chronicle*, March 1, 1827; *The Singapore Chronicle*, February 26, 1829; *The Singapore Chronicle* November 15, 1829; *The Singapore Chronicle*, June 23, 1831; *The Singapore Chronicle*, November 8, 1932; *The Singapore Chronicle*, February 7, 1833.
[34] Evans, *Slave Trade (East India) Slavery in Ceylon*, pp. 238–9.

expected, Fullerton explained that aside from the arguments that slavery was entrenched within the social customs of the region, the "service was entirely domestic and not partaking in the severe labor extracted from the slaves of our West India colonies." He also wanted to explain why there seemed to be so many women and girls within this "nefarious traffic" coming in to their ports. The governor explained:

> The emigration of females from China is not allowed; from India it is repugnant to Hindoo ideas; of indigenous Malays the proportion between the sexes is nearly equal. It is only, therefore, from females imported under the present system that the population can arise out of the progressive addition of new settlers; and it will be recollected that the female slaves imported into Penang from Pulo [sic] Nias, before the operation of slave laws, are the mothers of the whole indigenous population of the Prince of Wales' Island.[35]

Then, he reminded the council of their very limited authority to enforce antislavery measures in the region. The governor asserted that the British were doing "all that [could] reasonably be done for the amelioration of the habits of our people, and their gradual advancement in the scale of civilization." While Fullerton did not support the institution of slavery, he clearly understood that before the slave laws women like Nahoo, Noora, Luklye, and Jenooah were a valuable supply of wives and concubines for immigrants who wanted to stay permanently, as well as a source of temporary services for those just passing through.

In a summary letter to Resident Councilor Ibbestson, Superintendent Caunter wrote that the captives did not have enough understanding of their circumstance to obtain "precise information" but that they all "appear happy and healthy, and not to wish to return to their own country."[36] He explained that one woman, "Kafeeha," was with one of the nakhodas and did "not wish to leave him." Although we know the women testified that they worked in the houses of the nakhodas during the day and were "compelled every night to prostitute themselves to different men," we do not know if they saw themselves as slaves or how they felt about their circumstance. We know that they asked to be returned to their own communities, so they were not in the port voluntarily. Did they indenture themselves? Were they sold involuntarily? There is no evidence that any of the captives were scared, abused, or wanting to escape. We also do not know what these women felt about being sent to a nunnery with Reverend

---

[35] Ibid., p. 239.
[36] Ibid., p. 224.

Boucho. If the nakhoda, Khung Too, purchased Kafeeha as a slave, but married or made her a concubine, did that mean she was no longer a slave? The report seems to intimate that she was content with her situation because she did not want to leave Khung. Maybe she was happy, perhaps even in love; or it is possible that previous personal experiences might have made her suspicious of foreign officials; or maybe he has some connection to other members of her family? We have no way of knowing why this woman chose to stay and neither did the police. More to the point, it is worth asking, once the women were ostensibly "freed" (sent to the nunnery), what were they free to do as young indigenous women and children within this overwhelmingly patriarchal society? Were *they* free to dispose of themselves as they saw fit? Could they leave the nunnery at will? What expectations did the reverend, or the church, have for them? Were they expected to labor for the church? If they stayed, it is safe to assume that they were at least asked to participate in the domestic duties to maintain the facility. Assuming that the nunnery did not prostitute them out in the evenings, the colonial government's apprehension and detention of the slaves from Nias had a similar appearance to their situation with the Chinese—the Company just had not paid for them. There is no evidence to indicate whether or not their lives in the nunnery were any more or less arduous than with the nakhodas. Colonial officials simply transferred them from one patriarchal system to another.

As late as 1842, in response to an inquiry about the "slave question" in his settlement, then assistant resident to Prince of Wales Island Lewis wrote that "since the English settled here it has been free from slavery" and that he believed no one could "dispute the right of anyone to dispose of himself in any way he might think proper."[37] Yet, in the following paragraph, he also explains that

> amongst the better class of Natives, including Chinese, Malay, and Kling it is well known that they have in their houses many women but these are kept as far as I can discover as concubines they do the work of the house which must naturally fall on the female inmates whether they are wives daughters or concubines.[38]

Once again, whether or not these women were purchased as slaves was not part of the discussion—they were considered wives or concubines and, therefore, were not slaves. Lewis assured Garling that these women or any debtor/indentured servant on the island understood their rights and knew they could seek out the police for redress.

In response to that same inquiry on "the slave question" in Singapore, Resident Councilor Thomas Church reported that while there were no "true" slaves, a

---

[37] IOR/F4/1960, p. 42.
[38] Ibid., p. 43.

number of debt-slaves were still on the island and, because they are incredibly difficult to identify, cases were rarely prosecuted.[39] Nonetheless, he reported that to his knowledge, "no European since 1834" had "been even suspected of purchasing slave debtors brought from the adjacent native states." However, his language is telling. Church asserted that none were accused of *purchasing* debtors. This implies that there is a market where one can find people with liquid, transferrable debt, which essentially equates to establishing a monetary value for that person and their liberty. As we have discussed, by the nineteenth century, that market was generally controlled by the Chinese. Later in that same correspondence, Church explained that most debtors in the settlement were "women and children from Bali, Celebs, East Coast of Sumatra, and Borneo, they are employed as domestic servants and are generally well treated."[40] According to Church, this benevolent system was assured based in the understanding that should a debtor "quit the house in displeasure," there was no way to compel them to return. The resident explained that most of these women "did not get any regular money allowance," which motivated many "to become the wives of Chinese and other Settlers." If they were not being paid, they were slaves, but, he contended that since disparity between sexes was so great (in December 1842 there were 26,240 men and only 7,729) that a "marriageable female, if so disposed, has no manner of difficulty in obtaining a protector." The fate of unmarriageable women, or those not so disposed, was less secure. For Lewis and Church, the law was broken when someone forced a *man* to work against his will or without compensation. For women, the line was less clear. We know from correspondence, private records, government publications, and submitted reports that most drew the line at forced prostitution. However, as we saw with the case of the Nias slaves even when confronted with direct testimony that women had been forced to prostitute themselves, Caunter still chose to identify them as debtors, labeled them as concubines and domestic servants, and reported back to the council that they were never intended to be slaves. Lewis knew there were many women held in the private quarters of wealthy Chinese and Muslim residents. Not only does he reduce them to debtors (not eligible for the protection of antislavery laws), he either naively or disingenuously asserted that because they were legally free, if anything nefarious happened, they could seek police protection. Of course, this completely ignored the vulnerability that placed these women in that circumstance in the first place. Resident Church, like the others,

[39] Ibid., p. 48.
[40] Ibid., p. 50.

reported that there were no slaves in Singapore. There were, however, debtors who were generally women and girls working in households as domestic servants that rarely received monetary compensation for their work. By Church's logic, these women were not slaves because the ones who could find a husband, or someone else to pay their debt (purchase them), could easily do so. Except they *were* slaves—they had already been purchased, taken far outside their communities, not allowed to freely choose where they went or worked, and forced to provide both domestic and sexual labor—the vast majority without direct compensation. For Caunter, Lewis, Church, and so many others, gendered presumptions about the type of labor these women were expected to provide eradicated their slave status, vis-à-vis their right to legal protection from enslavement.

Keeping in mind that contemporary British saw an abundance of "unchaste women" in the east, and that officials did not believe domestic labor was real slavery, it is highly probable that under normal circumstances, most simply ignored the illicit traffic of women and girls they encountered. A system bringing in non-European women to accommodate the island of men would likely have been perceived as a convenient solution, which helped to promote the success and stability of the colony.[41] This time, a local citizen reported directly to the colonial government and, perhaps more importantly, landed on the ear of someone sympathetic to the abolitionist cause; an investigation was necessary. Nonetheless, it seems clear that stopping the non-European slave trade was not the Company's priority. Considering what we know about British gendered and orientalist perspectives by this point, it is not unreasonable to assume that these officials saw the importation of these women as an acceptable cost for the "gradual advancement" of the settlement's civilization.[42] As a part of the "sexual contract" between British men and male colonial subjects in Singapore, in order to maintain the patriarchal order colonial officials were reluctant to interfere with these men's access to women's labor or their bodies.[43] At the same time, they saw them as the potential mothers for the settlement's future indigenous population, which would likely have become the next generation of laborers. It is very likely that EIC officials perceived the women and girls who were illegally imported into the Straits as an expedient, but unavoidable, tragedy. They offered an avenue to domesticate those laborers who immigrated to the settlement and wanted to stay permanently, as well as provided temporary services for those

---

[41] Levine, "'A Multitude of Unchaste Women,'" pp. 159–63.
[42] Hobhouse, *Returns*, p. 109.
[43] Pateman, *The Sexual Contract*; Pateman's argument is that there is an implicit, sometimes explicit, contract about women, but between men, and secures the transformation of man's "natural right over women into the security of civil and patriarchal right" (p. 6).

just passing through. The EIC government was not interested in compromising lucrative trade relationships or aggravating temperamental political arrangements to change the fate of poor, indigenous, and Chinese women, whom officials believed were ultimately getting a step up in life. True, they did intervene and took the Nias "slaves" from their "masters," but there is not any indication within the correspondence of what happened to these women after they went to the nunnery under the supervision of Reverend Boucho. However, since they had been purchased as slaves and were not likely returning home, it is safe to assume they would have either stayed in the nunnery or married a local man. Had they chosen not to marry, as previously discussed, British ideas of domesticity would have almost certainly prescribed them a life of domestic, household servitude within the convent or perhaps, if they were lucky (sarcasm intended), a Company official.

## Too Many Men and Not Enough Women

The likelihood that authorities disregarded antislavery ordinances in the Straits to facilitate the importation of women into their colonies increases when considered in light of the concern local colonists expressed over the tremendous disparity in numbers of women and men. According to a census published in the *Singapore Chronicle*, on July 15, 1830, there were 12,213 men and 4,121 females on the island. Only three years later, another census recorded 15,161 men and just 5,797 women; 4,262 of them were Chinese, Malay, or "natives" of the western Indian coasts of Coromandel.[44] By 1835, a lengthy article in *The Singapore Free Press* asserted that the "abundance of working hands can never be wanting here so long as the means of supporting life may be easier than in India or China."[45] This letter to the editor detailed the differences between hiring debtors versus free laborers and explained that "there is plenty to choose out of, a selection is made of the most efficient men." Over the same five years, there were frequent articles published in the *Singapore Chronicle* of residents complaining of violence, drunkenness, and other criminal behavior.[46] A census published on January 21, 1841, illustrates that there were still very large differences between

---

[44] *The Singapore Chronicle*, July 15, 1830; "Comparative Statement of the Census Taken on the 1st of January," *The Singapore Chronicle*, February 7, 1833.
[45] "Correspondence," *The Singapore Free Press and Mercantile Advertiser*, October 20, 1835, p. 2.
[46] *The Singapore Chronicle*, September 10, 1830; *The Singapore Chronicle*, February 3, 1831; *The Singapore Chronicle*, June 23, 1831; *The Singapore Chronicle*, March 1, 1832; *The Singapore Chronicle*, May 17, 1832.

the number of men and women in the colony. This count in the *Singapore Free Press* demonstrates that there were only 7,729 women and 26,240 men, and residents continued to complain about the violence and lawlessness within the settlements.[47] An underground trade in women and girls offered the promise of civilized, domestic stability, which might have been a reasonable motive to overlook the fact that in spite of their pronouncements about living lives as pampered wives, local official knew that many, if not most, of them were destined to be domestic slaves and public prostitutes.

## Singapore's Continuing Problem with Prostitution

Indeed, by the 1850s, ships loaded with cargo from around the world sailed into Singapore's harbors looking for bargains. Slave traffickers continued to bring more women and girls to work in the growing number of brothels, gambling houses, and opium dens that filled the growing entrepôt. Not only did Chinese merchants make large profits from their portion of the trade from China, the money prostitutes made was regularly injected back into their communities in the form of local purchases or remitted to families at home. In a very real sense, the commercial sex trade in the Straits—particularly Singapore—helped finance European expansion, Chinese trade, and Japanese industrialization.[48]

Until the 1870s—nearly thirty years after the abolition of slavery in the Straits—the bulk of the women smuggled into Southeast Asia came from China and Japan; some were also bought or kidnapped from villages in the surrounding islands by local pirates and traffickers. As the colony expanded, so did the diversity of the women in the market. Urbanization, drought, famine, and poverty during the late nineteenth century compelled many families in China and Japan to either sell their daughters to avoid starvation or "pawn them" and send them to work in brothels. At the same time, brokers, many of them former prostitutes themselves, deceived families into believing their daughters would work as servants for wealthy families, barmaids, or peddlers. Once they had the children away from their families, they sold them again to brothel owners as

---

[47] "Census of Singapore Taken in the Month of December 1840," *The Singapore Free Press and Mercantile Advertiser*, January 21, 1841, p. 3.
[48] Shawna Herzog, "Selling Sex in Singapore: The Development, Expansion, and Policing of Prostitution in an International Entrepôt," in *Selling Sex in the City: A Global History of Prostitution, 1600s–2000s*, eds. Magaly Rodriguez Garcia, Lex Heerma van Voss, Elise van Nederveen Meerkerk (Leiden: Brill, 2017), pp. 594–620.

soon as they docked in Singapore. By taking them far away from their homes and communities, traffickers reduced the risk of family intervention.[49]

Under similar economic pressures, women in Europe also became vulnerable to traffickers who proposed marriage or promised employment opportunities to lure them from their homes; once in Southeast Asia, there was little these women could do to escape from their captors. Although only a small segment of Singapore's sex market, women imported from France, Germany, Hungary, Poland, and Russia serviced the local European residents keen on avoiding intimacies with Asian women. However, colonial officials strictly enforced a ban that prevented British women form working as prostitutes. While European women endured similar experiences as the Chinese and Japanese, they resided in another section of the city and lived under slightly better conditions. There were indeed social hierarchies within the system; regardless of ethnicity, the younger and more beautiful women were reserved for colonial officers and rich merchants, while the older and less attractive women appeased the masses of sailors, laborers, and tradesmen.

Of course, not all prostitutes were coerced, trafficked, or duped into the business; there were significant numbers of women who traveled to Singapore on their own, hoping to earn a better living or at least enough to send home to their families. A strictly controlled system of trafficking and brothel ownership insured a direct stream of capital for powerful Chinese secret societies based in Singapore, and the money sent back to Japan ultimately funded its industrial revolution at the end of the nineteenth century. Many, once they became too old to work as prostitutes, became brothel owners, brokers, or traffickers themselves and continued to make and send money home. Singapore's booming economy promised opportunity for everyone, and for local administrators, the grossly disproportionate sex ratio within the colony made the maintenance of a commercial sex industry a "necessity."[50]

Local prostitutes became a vital commodity as the port rapidly became an international entrepôt, and, as local inhabitants, prostitutes, and brothels were also regular consumers of imported commodities, food, and clothing and made use of other local services.[51] Beautiful gowns, makeup, perfume, and spirits were all important elements for prostitutes and business owners in their efforts to temporarily provide the "comforts of home" and appease the swell of male

---

[49] Tagliacozzo, *Secret Trades, Porous Borders*, p. 231.
[50] Ibid., p. 230.
[51] James Francis Warren, *Ah Ku and Karayuki-san: Prostitution in Singapore, 1870–1940* (Singapore: Oxford University Press, 1993), pp. 80–4.

migrant labor, traders, and soldiers flowing in and out of its port. By the end of the nineteenth century, Singapore had become a key transfer point for the international sex trade in the region; traffickers from around the world brought women to Singapore, where owners of opium dens, pubs, hotels, and brothels from throughout the region came to bargain for fresh supplies of girls.

## Conclusion

In 1845, an article in the *Singapore Free Press* titled "Slave Trade in the Indian Archipelago" reminded its readers that slavery and the slave trade still existed in the British Straits Settlements.[52] The piece focused on the plight of a widow, another young woman, and her child and described the extent of the local trade. The author asserted that an "active system of kidnapping and slave-dealing prevails in the Island of Bally [Bali]" and inferred that women from this island comprised a large portion of those trafficked into the settlements. After describing the system of indigenous and Chinese slaving, the author blamed Dutch authorities for their lack of effort to stop slavery in their colonies and pointed a finger at the French buying "young and handsome" women from Malay rajas. The article insisted that the British must demand the rajas within their influence prohibit slavery in their territories so that the Chinese and Bugis slave dealers would no longer find a market and made it clear that efforts to abolish the slave trade to that point had been largely reactionary and useless.

The Anti-Slavery Project officially began in the British Straits Settlements with the Slave Trade Act in 1807. Though the Company still used slaves during the first twenty years of the settlement for agriculture and construction, by 1820 the EIC Board of Control expected local officials to emancipate all Company slaves and eliminate the institution within its eastern territories. As a transitional measure, the governments of Malacca and Penang encouraged slave owners to convert their slaves to debtors and developed registries to accommodate the property rights of the few existing slave-owning families who had immigrated with their slaves.[53] Otherwise, those seeking labor needed to engage free laborers or debtors, whose contracts were regulated by the local magistrate. By 1826—aside from a few who remained on the registries—slavery was illegal throughout the Straits. However, the EIC considered the wealthy Chinese, Arab, and Malays

---

[52] "Slave Trade in the Indian Archipelago," *The Singapore Free Press and Mercantile Advertiser*, November 8, 1845, p. 2.
[53] Evans, *Slave Trade (East India) Slavery in Ceylon*, p. 246.

a formidable presence in these settlements; we know from the statements of Governor Fullerton and Rear Admiral Gage that the British understood the limits to their power in the region. It seems quite clear that non-European slave trades were simply not a priority for colonial officials, who were more concerned with curtailing European slavers and maintaining amicable trade relationships in the region. Eventually, abolitionism and antislavery legislation became a useful tool that created a pretense to monitor and regulate those whom the British perceived as key competitors in the region; in this case, it was usually the Chinese. Nonetheless, in spite of a string of antislavery ordinances, the trade continued through the first half of the nineteenth century and beyond.

As the 1827 *Singapore Chronicle* article described, the increasingly lawless and violent environment in Singapore alarmed some colonists. There were too many men and not enough women, and many believed this disproportion threatened the peace and order of the community. The importation of young women and girls emerged as an obvious solution. At the same time, the ambiguity of debt and bondage in Southeast Asia, combined with orientalist perceptions of uncivilized, hypersexual Asian women, freed officials from guilt and gave them leeway to label the women as slaves or debtors. Either way, they were sure that those brought into the Empire's territory were better off because of their proximity to Britain's civilizing influence. British notions of gender constructed women as both subservient to men and as managers of domestic spaces. So while there is no explicit evidence that officials consciously facilitated an illicit traffic of women and girls into their male-dominated settlements, it seems clear that they were willing to "turn a blind eye" to it to ensure the peace and stability of the colony.[54] Ultimately, in spite of a professed effort to abolish the slave trade throughout the Empire, even as late as 1845, thirty-four years after the Slave Trade Felony Act, the trade persisted. Indeed, the trade remained an issue even after these colonies gained their independence from the Empire a little more than a century later.[55]

---

[54] Levine, *Prostitution, Race, and Politics*, p. 126.
[55] Jin Hui Ong, "Singapore," in *Prostitution: An International Handbook on Trends, Problems, and Policies*, ed. Nanette Davis (Westport: Greenwood Press, 1993), p. 245.

# Conclusion: In the Wake of Abolition

In 1879, his Honor Chief Justice Sir John Smale of the Hong Kong Supreme Court presided over the case of Siu Ahing, a fourteen-year-old Japanese girl; both Keung Ato and Li Akak, local residents of Hong Kong, were criminally charged with buying and selling her for the purpose of prostitution.[1] Ahing testified to the court that she had been "sold to a Chinaman"—she did not remember his name—in Kobe, Japan, when she was eleven years old. She said she was brought to Hong Kong and then sold again as a "female servant" on Lan Kwai Fong Lane to Pan Chee Wan, a Chinese merchant whose wife had beaten her. Ahing explained that she had been the Wans' servant for three years, but that one night, after a particularly severe thrashing, she ran away. As she sat on the side of the street crying, an older woman approached. This woman, Li Akak, was a seasoned procuress who saw an opportunity and consoled the girl. She offered to take Ahing to her house. Ahing explained that "the second defendant" (Akak) told her the next morning that she planned to sell her "to be a prostitute." After breakfast, Akak sold her for $60 to "the first defendant" (Keung Ato)—another trader in women and girls—who took her to be groomed and trained to serve. Plied with "good clothing and jewelry," Ahing was "treated kindly" by those in Ato's house. However, she testified, "[A]fter two or three days, the first prisoner's wife took me to Singapore in a large Steamer." According to testimony, Ahing spent "five or six months" in Singapore, where she was "placed in a brothel as a servant." She told the court that when she returned to Hong Kong, she lived with the first prisoner's wife until a dispute about her, which she did not hear, caused the police to interfere. Akak and Ato both disputed the girl's story, claiming that she lied about going to Singapore and that she had only been threatened because she had misbehaved. Nevertheless, in his closing arguments the Attorney General Honorable J. Russell argued that

---

[1] *Correspondence Respecting the Alleged Existence of Chinese Slavery in Hong Kong: Presented to Both Houses of Parliament by Command of Her Majesty* (London: Her Majesty's Stationary Office, 1882), pp. 37–49.

> [t]he whole of the surrounding circumstances showed that the intention was to keep the girl here as a prostitute or to send her to Singapore, and if the jury believed that the object was to send her to Singapore, knowing as they did the traffic that had been going on, they would have little difficulty in determining that the purpose for which she was to be sent there was an immoral one.[2]

The prosecutor was aware of the flourishing traffic in women and girls supplying the local sex trade in the region and believed that this young girl had fallen victim to the system of procuresses, traffickers, and brothel owners who worked to maintain it. Singapore had developed a notorious reputation for its many brothels and the litigator relied upon his audience's understanding "that Singapore, Australia, and San Francisco are supplied from Hong Kong with prostitutes, kept women, and concubines."[3] However, Ahing had only testified that she worked as a servant in a brothel. The attorney general laid the entire fate of the case on his belief (and he was betting the jury would agree with him) that the only reason someone might take a young Japanese girl to Singapore—or even threaten to—was for "immoral" purposes. As chief law enforcement officer for that district, Russell would have had his finger on the pulse of the Asian traffic in women and girls, and his prosecution of Keung Ato and Li Akak allowed contemporary colonial administrators and modern researchers a glimpse into the illicit slave-trading networks that still existed with the larger British territories as late as the 1880s—more than forty years after Abolition.

Ahing's parents had sold her into an ancient and global system and her story is one among thousands who validate the assertion that the abolition of slavery has been more of a perpetual project than a concrete accomplishment. As has been discussed, slavery and the slave trade were important parts of most indigenous societies in Southeast Asia when Europeans arrived and most embraced it. Slave trading not only provided large amounts of capital for indigenous states, but it was also an important part of the social welfare system in many Southeast Asian societies. People regularly bound themselves in servitude voluntarily to pay off debts. The victims of violent slave raids and captives of warfare were also among these enslaved populations, but indigenous Southeast Asian societies did not differentiate these slaves from any other hereditary servants, debtors, or bondsmen.

Europeans took full advantage of this established system and used it to expand and operate their imperial outposts in Africa and Asia. As Britain's Southeast

---

[2] Ibid., p. 49.
[3] Ibid., p. 104.

Asian settlements grew, tensions over slaves absconding to British settlements and seeking asylum motivated the Sultan of Quedah to broaden the definition of those considered slaves to his kingdom in 1791 and, therefore, obliged to be returned. The EIC, however, recommended that Captain Light use the narrowest of definitions, which they felt might encourage a larger number of people to immigrate and increase tensions with local leaders. Their goal was to attract people, both wealthy and working class, to finance and build a prosperous new settlement. Constructing Britain's newest outpost in the Straits would require a significant amount of labor, but they had hoped the "clearing of the lands and the cultivation" would be done by a force of free laborers. Instead, they settled for boatloads of the Company's transported convicts, indentured laborers from India, and contracted "debtors" from China to erect the city and extract the surrounding resources. The 1807 Slave Trade Act prohibited slave trading in British territories, and by 1824, the Company had criminalized all European slave trading in the east. However, they had also significantly increased the value of slaves, the profitability of slaving, and left the slave markets open to Malay and Chinese distributors. The Slave Act had not eliminated slave trading, nor had they freed any slaves, it had only reduced the presence of Europeans in the system.

Antislavery policies did, however, create a liminal phase that was ended by the Emancipation Act in 1834, during which neither the Company's government nor local administrators had a clear understanding of their role or responsibilities in the enforcement of the Empire's agenda. Moreover, in anticipation of abolition, profit-minded officials developed registration systems that identified slave owning as a luxury, narrowed the definition of a *slave* to only those "person[s] legally sold, or one condemned to slavery for crimes," established a tax on all registered slaves, and encouraged slave owners to convert their slaves to debtors. At the same time, in spite of increasing antislavery measures, EIC authorities continued to recognize and enforce slave status by punishing them and returning registered slaves to their masters.[4] As those on the India Law Commission described, these early measures essentially placed the colonial state in the position of overarching patriarch charged with managing the stability and productivity of their societies/households. Becoming the arbiter of disputes between slave owners and slaves, and assuming the right as administer of "justice"/punishment usurped the power of masters within their own estates. In addition to being a direct transgression into the private spaces, and challenge to the power of wealthy elites, the increase in

---

[4] Reid, "The Decline of Slavery in Nineteenth Century Indonesia," p. 68.

slaves absconding to British territories after Captain Light's regulations and offers of paid positions, increased tensions between the Company and the trading elite. Asian slave owner/traders demanded an explanation of the EIC's authority to make such demands, but, as the Nias case illustrated, they had not been convinced—slave trading persisted in the Straits; only Europeans had been legally barred from profiting from it.

Once defined, EIC governments organized, categorized, and established alternatives that helped them negotiate the implementation of continuously encroaching antislavery legislation. Debt-slavery offered an attractive avenue toward the "gradual abolition" of local slavery that became EIC policy in the east. However, as officials soon learned, debt-slavery was, more often than not, just a different name for the same circumstance. In the end, in spite of the zealous desires of a few, EIC administrators relied on negotiation, diplomacy, and the official registries to bring an end to legal slavery in the Straits. It was the Malaccan residents, brokered by Superintendent Lewis in 1837, who finally agreed to the December 31, 1841, deadline—eight years after the Emancipation Act in 1834. However, as Lewis explained to Resident Ibbetson, it is more than likely many locals simply ignored the regulations and continued to maintain their slaves as before; as long as no one complained, authorities maintained the status quo.[5]

Immediate abolition of all slavery in the East Indies was neither a priority for either the British government or EIC officials. Similar to slavery apologists in the west, slave owners and British officials in Straits argued that slaves were ill equipped for freedom, could not support themselves, and many were likely to starve without the protections of their master. The more pressing concerns, however, were that, the economic and political consequences of immediate abolition would likely have devastated profits and seriously impeded expansion efforts in the region. In established trading ports such as Malacca, because slaves were considered such valuable property, the Company was on shaky legal ground and had to accommodate the rights of its wealthy and influential residents. However, even in places like Penang and Singapore, where they ostensibly had more power and control, officials continued to recognize the rights of non-European slave owners in order to develop and maintain a peaceful and prosperous settlement. Such a direct invasion into indigenous cultural practice also flew in the face of the EIC's long-established and sworn policy of noninterference. For a time, officers chose to ignore local slave systems and focused on the "foreign" or European trade. The British competed fiercely in the Indian and Pacific Oceans for imperial dominance and antislavery measures

[5] Evans, *Slave Trade (East India) Slavery in Ceylon*, pp. 217–21.

were another way for them to take a jab at their European adversaries. As a result, treaties with local rajas generally made exceptions for indigenous trades and local slave populations. Sometimes, as with the imam of Muscat, the cost of abolition was more than the British were willing to sacrifice and officials walked away, happy to have at least limited the European networks. Since the British were primarily concerned with inhibiting French, Dutch, and Portuguese access to sources of cheap labor, the promise of a gradual abolition of Malay and Chinese trades was an acceptable accommodation, but left internal networks intact and bolstered demand. Consequently, an illicit trade was allowed to thrive.

However, it is crucial we consider the limitations to British power and authority in Southeast Asia during this period. Although the Straits were under the direct rule of the Bengal presidency, their distance from the colonial center, in an age when it took almost a month to travel from Bengal to Penang, required that Company officials rely on the support of their local allies. Moreover, EIC authority in the East Indies was limited by the parameters set within their established treaties. For instance, the king of Quedah insisted that British authorities recognize the property rights of slave owners in his kingdom and that EIC authorities in Penang return runaway slaves to their masters. Britain's quasi-legal conquest of these territories meant that restrictions on slavery had to be negotiated, rather than legislated. Even by 1830, as Rear Admiral Gage explained, unless British authorities had indisputable proof that a vessel subject to *British* authority was trading slaves, he could do nothing about it. This meant that the Arab, Chinese, and Malay ships in the area, those with the majority of ships and most frequently cruising the waters of the region, were immune to regulation. Even as late as 1879, seventy-two years after the slave trade had been completely criminalized and forty-five years since the status *slave* was no longer recognized, the British still did not have the political or military power, or the administrative capabilities to completely abolish slavery in the Straits of Malacca.

The need for women was also a significant inhibitor to antislavery enforcement in the Straits. Both the cities of Malacca and Penang had relied on slave women for both their physical and reproductive labor. However, antislavery legislation and cultural prohibitions on emigration for Hindu and Chinese women meant emigrating laborers were not travelling with their wives, girlfriends, sisters, or mothers. Although early population numbers of non-European men and women were relatively equal, the swelling force of labor arriving in Penang and Singapore was overwhelmingly male and, by the 1830s, there was a dramatic dearth in available women. As we saw, local officials were willing and able to engage in intellectual and linguistic gymnastics to avoid the conflict that rigorous enforcement of antislavery policy would no doubt have instigated.

In addition to racist and orientalist attitudes, gendered perceptions about the role of women were key reason why British antislavery measures were not successful at the beginning of the nineteenth century. EIC officials contended that the systems in the east were not "true slavery" at all. EIC officials asserted that slavery was purely domestic in nature and even scholars later described the trade of women and girls in Southeast Asia as a "large scale marriage market."[6] Contemporary officials, and subsequent historians, maintained the presumption that, unless they were publicly prostituted, once women obtained the title of domestic servant, wife, or concubine—regardless of who they were before they obtained that title or how they obtained it—they were no longer slaves. Of Course, Company officials believed that slaves living in British domain would be living better lives than they would have otherwise. Once a woman was purchased and brought into the household—her "natural" habitat—her labor was somehow no longer forced. Consequently, there is no way to know how many slave women were imported into the Straits. If Caunter was any indicator of common procedure, and we have seen evidence that he was, EIC authorities saw the non-European slave women they encountered on Chinese junks and in local houses and businesses as the domestic and sexual property of the men they were with or intended for. Officials honored the sexual contract between men and did not questions the legal status of the women they encountered; if the nakhodas said those were their concubines and servants, then that is what they were. Abolitionism was intended to free men from the bondage of other men, not to liberate women from their position as the servant of man.

Before publications such as the aforementioned *Slavery and the Slave Trade in British India* in 1841 informed the British public of the true nature of slavery in the East Indies, there was a general perception in London that slavery in the east was entirely domestic, mild in nature, and beneficial to the lower classes of society. Additionally, some officials, such as Superintendent Caunter, did not think that it should have been prohibited at all. He believed that the lives of slaves would automatically be better, just by serving within the folds of His Majesty's protection—such as it was. The beginning of the nineteenth century saw a rise in liberalism and an increase in impoverished populations that initiated a natural decline in male slavery in the region. At the same time, ideas of freedom, liberty, and self-determination ricocheted around the globe and placed the institution of slavery in direct opposition to conceptions of modernity, capitalism, and the progress of humanity.[7] It eventually became cheaper to hire temporary labor

---

[6] Trocki, "Opium as a Commodity in the Chinese Nanyang Trade," pp. 88–94; Levine, *Prostitution, Race, and Politics*, p. 25; Warren, *Pirates, Prostitutes and Pullers*, pp. 148–50; Reid, *Charting the Shape of Early Modern Southeast Asia*, p. 207.

[7] Reid, "The Decline of Slavery in Nineteenth Century Indonesia," p. 69.

than to maintain the cost of a large population of slaves for a lifetime. Colonial officials began to use convicts and contracted labor, which quickly deteriorated into what essentially became *slave-like* conditions. So, either by destiny or design, systems of large-scale male enslavement had been curtailed by the end of the eighteenth century. However, as we know from decades of feminist scholarship, those liberal ideas of freedom and self-determination did not necessarily apply to women during this period and men's demand for women's bodies persevered over a woman's right to self-determination.[8]

According to contemporary British constructions of civilized society, women and children belonged in the domestic sphere and a male patriarch dictated their lives. EIC officials regularly explained away the importation of women and girls into the settlements by asserting that they were intended only to be the servants, concubines, and wives of the wealthy. Technically, provisions had been made to free those used for the purpose of prostitution. Superintendent Caunter contended that even though these women and girls may have been bought or traded as slaves, their life of domestic servitude was not really slavery at all.[9] Both he and Fullerton admitted that some of the girls were used "improperly," but they argued that it was not a cause for concern.[10] Officials would certainly have understood that most of the male population in both Penang and Singapore were not wealthy and very likely could not have afforded the expense of a wife, servant, or concubine—most were convicts, indentured labor, or sailors just there to do a job and leave. In fact, we know that some colonists were concerned about the violence and lawlessness due to a lack of women. Concerns proliferated that without access to women's bodies, these lower-class men could not be trusted to live civilly. Whether they believed they might instill a domesticating influence or simply offer a sexual release, it is clear that authorities saw the lack of women as a problem in their community. Officials saw a "multitude of unchaste women" around them and ignored what was at that point an illicit trade in women and girls to accommodate what they perceived as a necessity for the success and prosperity of the colony.[11]

Slavery scholars like Seymour Drescher tell us that the 1830s were the beginning of a "zenith" for British abolitionist's campaign against slavery in the West Indies; we see that EIC efforts in the east were still haphazard at best.[12]

[8] Kent, *Gender and Power in Britain, 1640–1990*, pp. 172–5; Clark, *The Struggle for the Breeches*, pp. 142–5.
[9] IOR/F4/1130/8.
[10] Ibid., p. 9.
[11] Levine, "A Multitude of Unchaste Women," pp. 159–63.
[12] Drescher, *Abolition*, p. 267.

British Parliament had left abolition in the east to the discretion of the EIC, and the Company as a whole was not specific in its expectations regarding the enforcement of ordinances. The creation and enforcement of local policies depended on the ideological perspective of governing officials and enforcing authorities. As a result, rather than actually bringing an end to slavery and the slave trade in the East Indies, British antislavery measures at the beginning of the nineteenth century simply accelerated the transition of this ancient institution into its next phase, which developed into a sophisticated black market that continues to supply vulnerable people to labor for the wealthy, in slave-like conditions. In the case of the British Straits Settlements, this new trade became an illicit traffic in women and girls that brought women like Nahoo, Nora, Luklye, Jenooah, and Ahing to colonial centers for the purpose of domestic and sexual labor throughout the nineteenth and well into the twentieth century.

# Bibliography

## Primary and Archival Sources

### The British National Archives

*Colonial Office Records (CO):*

CO273/1 Colonial Office: Straits Settlements Original Correspondence, 1838–1946
CO273/2
CO273/3
CO273/79

### The British Library

India Office of Records (IOR)
Series:
E/4 East India Company: Correspondence with India, 1703–1858
F/4 Records of the Board of Commissioners for the Affairs of India, 1620–1859
G/34 Factory Records for the Straits Settlements (Malay Peninsula), 1769–1830

## Published Materials

A. M. S. "Memoir of Captain Francis Light." *Journal of the Straits Branch of the Royal Asiatic Society* 28 (August 1895): pp. 1–17.

Anderson, John. *Mission to the East Coast of Sumatra: In M.DCCC.XXIII, under the Direction of the Government of Prince of Wales Island: Including Historical and Descriptive Sketches of the Country, an Account of the Commerce, Population, and Customs of the Inhabitants, and a Visit to the Batta Cannibal States in the Interior.* London: W. Blackwood, 1826.

Bates, Mary. *The Private Life of John C. Calhoun: A Letter Originally Addressed to a Brother at the North, Communicated to the "International Magazine," and Now Reprinted at the Request of Many Personal Friends.* Charleston: Walker, Richards & Co., 1852.

Behn, Aphra. "The False Count; or, a New Way to Play an Old Game." In *The Plays, Histories, and Novels of the Ingenious Mrs. Aphra Behn, Volume III*. London: J. Pearson, 1700, pp. 150–1.

Bigelow, John and Alexis de Tocqueville. *Democracy in America: Volume I*. New York: D. Appleton, 1899.

Bridgman, Elijah C., and Samuel W. Williams. *The Chinese Repository, Volume 4*. Tokyo: Maruzen Kabushiki Kaisha, 1836.

Buckingham, James Silk. *The Oriental Herald and Colonial Review, Volume 7*, edited by J. S. Buckingham. London: Sanford Arnot, 1825.

Calhoun, John Caldwell and Robert Mercer Taliaferro Hunter. *Life of John C. Calhoun: Presenting a Condensed History of Political Events from 1811 to 1843. Together with a Selection from His Speeches, Reports, and Other Writings Subsequent to His Election as Vice-President of the United States, Including His Leading Speech on the Late War Delivered in 1811*. New York: Harper & Brothers, 1843.

Cameron, John. *Our Tropical Possessions in Malayan India: Being a Descriptive Account of Singapore, Penang, Province of Wellesley, and Malacca; Their Peoples, Products, Commerce, and Government*. London: Smith, Elder, and Co, 1865.

Chandler, Elizabeth. *Essays, Philanthropic and Moral, Principally Relating to the Abolition of Slavery in America*. Philadelphia: T.E. Capman, 1845.

*Correspondence Respecting the Alleged Existence of Chinese Slavery in Hong Kong: Presented to Both Houses of Parliament by Command of Her Majesty*. London: Her Majesty's Stationary Office, 1882.

Crawfurd, John. *History of the Indian Archipelago: Containing an Account of the Manners, Arts, Languages, Religions, Institutions, and Commerce of Its Inhabitants. Volumes I-III*. London: A. Constable and Co., 1820.

Earl, George Windsor. *The Eastern Seas: Or, Voyages and Adventures in the Indian Archipelago, in 1832-33-34, Comprising a Tour of the Island of Java—Visits to Borneo, the Malay Peninsula, Siam …* London: W. H. Allen, 1837.

*East-India Sugar: Papers Respecting the Culture and Manufacture of Sugar in British India: Also Notices of the Cultivation of Sugar in Other Parts of Asia: With Miscellaneous Information Respecting Sugar. Printed by Order of the Court of Proprietors of the East-India Company*. London: E. Cox and son, 1822.

Evans, Williams. *Slave Trade (East India) Slavery in Ceylon: Copies or Abstracts of All Correspondence between the Directors of the East India Company and the Company's Government in India, since the 1st Day of June 1827, on the Subject of Slavery in the Territories under the Company's Rule: Also Communications Relating to the Subject of Slavery in the Island of Ceylon*. London: Great Britain Foreign Office, 1838.

*Hansard's Parliamentary Debates, William IV Vol. LXV. July 12 to August 12. Vol. VI*. London: Thomas Curson Hansard, 1842.

Hobhouse, John. *Returns: Slavery (East Indies)*. London: Great Britain Foreign Office, 1838.

Lushington. *Return to an Order: A Continuation to the Present Time of the Papers Respecting Slavery in the East Indies, Which Were Printed by the Order of This House on the 31st Day of July 1838*. London: Great Britain Foreign Office, 1841.

Marsden, William. *The History of Sumatra Containing an Account of the Government Laws, Customs, and Manners, of the Native Inhabitants with a Description of the Natural Productions, a Relation of the Ancient Political State of that Island*. London, UK: Thomas Payne & Son, 1784.

Martin, Robert Montgomery. *Statistics of the Colonies of the British Empire: From the Official Records of the Colonial Office*. London: W.H. Allen and Company, 1839.

Mayhew, Henry. *London Labour and the London Poor: A Cyclopaedia of the Condition and Earnings of Those That Will Work, Those That Cannot Work, and Those That Will Not Work*. London: G. Woodfall and Son, 1851.

Munshi, Abdullah. *The Hikayat Abdullah*. Translated by A. H. Hill. London: Oxford University Press, 1970.

Newbold, Thomas John. *Political and Statistical Account of the British Settlements in the Straits of Malacca: Viz. Pinang, Malacca, and Singapore, with a History of the Malayan States on the Peninsula of Malacca*. London: J. Murray, 1839.

O'Byrne, William R. *A Naval Biographical Dictionary: Comprising the Life and Services of Every Living Officer in Her Majesty's Navy, from the Rank of Admiral of the Fleet to That of Lieutenant, Inclusive*. London: The Admiralty, 1849.

Phipps, John. *A Practical Treatise on the China and Eastern Trade: Comprising the Commerce of Great Britain and India Particularly Bengal and Singapore with China and the Eastern Islands*. London: Allen, 1836.

Raffles, Lady Sophia. *Memoir of the Life and Public Services of Sir Thomas Stamford Raffles, F.R.S. &c: Particularly in the Government of Java, 1811–1816, and of Bencoolen and Its Dependencies, 1817–1824; with Details of the Commerce and Resources of the Eastern Archipelago, and Selections from His Correspondence*. London: John Murray, 1830.

Raffles, Stamford. *The History of Java: In Two Volumes*. London: Black, Parbury, and Allen and John Murray, 1817.

*Singapore Local Laws and Institutions, 1823*. London: Cox and Baylis, 1824.

*Slavery and the Slave Trade in British India: With Notices of the Existence of These Evils in the Islands of Ceylon, Malacca, and Penang*. London: Thomas Ward and Co., 1841.

*Slavery in India: Return to an Address of the Honorable House of Commons, Dated 13th of April 1826, Presented June 1827*. London: House of Commons, 1828.

Tocqueville, Alexis De. *Democracy in America. Vol. 1. United States*, Francis Bowen and Henry Reeve, trans. Cambridge: Sever and Francis, 1863.

Trapaud, Elisha. *A Short Account of the Prince of Wales's Island, or Pulo Peenang, in the East-Indies; Given to Capt. Light, by the King of Quedah*. London: J. Stockdale, 1788.

Wise, Henry. *An Analysis of One Hundred Voyages to and from India, China. Performed by Ships in the Honorable East India Company's Service; with Remarks on the Advantages of Steam-Power*. London: J.W. Noire & Co., 1839.

## Newspapers and Journals

*The Asiatic Journal and Monthly Register for British and Foreign India, China and Austrailasia* (1830–1834).
*Journals of the House of Lords.* Vol. LXXIII. London (1841).
*The London Quarterly Review* (1826–1846).
*Simmond's Colonial Magazine and Foreign Miscellany* (September–December 1845).
*The Singapore Chronicle and Commercial Register* (1827–1835).
*The Singapore Free Press and Mercantile Advertiser* (1835–1846).
*The Straits Times* (1837–1840).

## Unpublished Materials

Klinkers, Ellen. "Op Hoop van Vrijheid: van Slavensamenleving Naar Creoolse Gemeenschap in Suriname, 1830–1880." PhD diss., University of Utrecht, 1997.
Trocki, Carl A. "The Temenggongs of Johor, 1784–1885." PhD diss., Cornell University, 1976.

## Secondary Sources

Abu-Lughod, Janet. *Before European Hegemony: The World System A.D. 1250–1350.* New York: Oxford University Press, 1989.
Allen, Richard B. "Licentious and Unbridled Proceedings: The Illegal Slave Trade to Mauritius and the Seychelles." *Journal of African History* 42, no. 1 (2001): pp. 91–116.
Allen, Richard B. "The Mascarene Slave-Trade and Labour Migration in the Indian Ocean during the Eighteenth and Nineteenth Centuries." *Slavery & Abolition* 24, no. 2 (2003): pp. 33–50.
Allen, Richard B. "A Traffic Repugnant to Humanity: Children, the Mascarene Slave Trade and British Abolitionism." *Slavery and Abolition* 27, no. 2 (2006): pp. 219–36.
Allen, Richard B. "The Constant Demand of the French: The Mascarene Slave Trade and the Worlds of the Indian Ocean and Atlantic during the Eighteenth and Nineteenth Centuries." *The Journal of African History* 49, no. 1 (2008): pp. 43–72.
Allen, Richard B. "Suppressing a Nefarious Traffic: Britain and the Abolition of Slave Trading in India and the Western Indian Ocean, 1770–1830." *The William and Mary Quarterly* 66, no. 4 (2009): pp. 873–94.

Allen, Richard B. "Satisfying the 'Want for Labouring People': European Slave Trading in the Indian Ocean, 1500–1850." *Journal of World History* 21, no. 1 (March 2010): pp. 45–73.

Allen, Richard B. *European Slave Trading in the Indian Ocean, 1500–1850*. Athens: Ohio University Press, 2014.

Allen, Richard B. "Slavery in a Remote but Global Place: The British East India Company and Bencoolen, 1685–1825." *Social and Education History* 7, no. 2 (2018): pp. 151–76.

Alpers, Edward A. "The African Diaspora in the Northwestern Indian Ocean: Reconsideration of an Old Problem, New Directions for Research." *Comparative Studies of South Asia, Africa, and the Middle East* 17, no. 2 (1997): pp. 62–81.

Andaya, Leonard. *Leaves of the Same Tree Trade and Ethnicity in the Straits of Melaka*. Honolulu: University of Hawai'i Press, 2008.

Anderson, Benedict. *Imagined Communities*. London: Verso, 1983.

Anderson, Clare. "'The Ferringees Are Flying—The Ship Is Ours!': The Convict Middle Passage in Colonial South and Southeast Asia, 1790–1860." *The Indian Economic and Social History Review* 42, no. 2 (June 2005): pp. 143–86.

Anderson, Clare. *The Indian Uprising of 1857–8: Prisons, Prisoners, and Rebellion*. London: Anthem Press, 2007.

Anderson, Clare. "Convicts and Coolies: Rethinking Indentured Labour in the Nineteenth Century." *Slavery and Abolition* 30, no. 1 (March 2009): pp. 93–109.

Anderson, Clare. *Subaltern Lives: Biographies of Colonialism in the Indian Ocean World, 1790–1920*. Cambridge: Cambridge University Press, 2012.

Armitage, David. *The British Atlantic World, 1500–1800*. New York: Palgrave Macmillan, 2002.

Armitage, David and Sanjay Subrahmanyam. *The Age of Revolutions in Global Context, C. 1760–1840*. New York: Palgrave Macmillan, 2010.

Ballantyne, Tony. "Introduction: Debating Empire." *Journal of Colonialism and Colonial History Special Edition* 3, no. 1 (Spring 2002).

Ballantyne, Tony. *Moving Subjects: Gender, Mobility, and Intimacy in an Age of Global Empire*. Urbana: University of Illinois Press, 2009.

Ballantyne, Tony and Antoinette Burton, eds. *Bodies in Contact: Rethinking Colonial Encounters in World History*. Durham: Duke University Press, 2005.

Bayly, C. A. *Imperial Meridian: The British Empire and the World, 1780–1830*. London: Longman Group, 1989.

Bayly, C. A. *The Birth of the Modern World, 1780–1914: Global Connections and Comparisons*. Hoboken: Wiley, 2004.

Bender, Thomas. *The Antislavery Debate: Capitalism and Abolitionism as a Problem in Historical Interpretation*. Berkeley: University of California Press, 1992.

Best, Geoffrey. *War and Society in Revolutionary Europe*. New York: St. Martin's Press, 1982.

Blackburn, Robin. *Overthrow of Colonial Slavery, 1776–1848*. London: Verso, 1988.

Blythe, Wilfred and Royal Institute of International Affairs. *The Impact of Chinese Secret Societies in Malaya: A Historical Study*. London: Oxford University Press, 1969.

Bowen, H. *The Worlds of the East India Company*. Rochester: D.S. Brewer, 2002.

Breman, Jan. *Taming the Coolie Beast: Plantation Society and the Colonial Order in Southeast Asia*. 2nd ed. Delhi: Oxford University Press, 1990.

Breunig, Charles. *The Age of Revolution and Reaction, 1789–1850*. New York: W. W. Norton, 1977.

Brown, Christopher and the Omohundro Institute of Early American History & Culture. *Moral Capital: Foundations of British Abolitionism*. Chapel Hill: University of North Carolina Press, 2006.

Cain, P. J., and A. G. Hopkins. *British Imperialism: Crisis and Deconstruction, 1914–1990*. London: Longman, 1993.

Campbell, Gwyn, ed. *The Structure of Slavery in Indian Ocean Africa and Asia*. Portland: Frank Cass, 2004.

Campbell, Gwyn, Suzanne Miers and Joseph Calder Miller, eds. *Women and Slavery: The Modern Atlantic*. Columbus: Ohio University Press, 2007.

Cannadine, David. *Ornamentalism: How the British Saw Their Empire*. London: Penguin Books, 2001.

Cassels, Nancy Gardner. *Social Legislation of the East India Company: Public Justice versus Public Instruction*. New Delhi: Sage Publications India, 2010.

Chatterjee, Indrani. *Gender, Slavery, and Law in Colonial India*. Oxford: Oxford University Press, 1999.

Chaudhuri, Nupur and Margaret Strobel, eds. *Western Women and Imperialism*. Bloomington: Indian University Press, 1992.

Chew, Emry. "The Naning War, 1831–1832: Colonial Authority and Malay Resistance in the Early Period of British Expansion." *Modern Asian Studies* 32, no. 2 (1998): pp. 351–87.

Chew, Sing C. "The Southeast Asian Connection in the First Eurasian World Economy, 200 BCE–CE 500." *Journal of Globalization Studies* 5, no. 1 (May 2014): pp. 82–109.

Clarence-Smith, William Gervase. *The Economics of the Indian Ocean Slave Trade in the Nineteenth Century*. London: Frank Cass, 1989.

Clarence-Smith, William Gervase. *Islam and the Abolition of Slavery*. Oxford: Oxford University Press, 2006.

Clark, Anna. *The Struggle for the Breeches: Gender and the Making of the British Working Class*. Berkeley: University of California Press, 1995.

Cohn, Bernard S. *Colonialism and Its Forms of Knowledge: The British in India*. Princeton: Princeton University Press, 1996.

Colley, Linda. *Britons: Forging the Nation 1707–1837*. Yale: Yale University Press, 1992.

Collier, Richard. *The Great Indian Mutiny: A Dramatic Account of the Sepoy Rebellion*. 1st ed. New York: Dutton, 1964.

Collini, Stephan, Richard Whatmore and Brian Young. *History, Religion, and Culture: British Intellectual History, 1750-1950*. Cambridge: Cambridge University Press, 2000.

Cooper, Frederick and Ann Laura Stoler. *Tensions of Empire*. Berkeley: University of California Press, 1993.

Costello, Con. *Botany Bay: The Story of the Convicts Transported from Ireland to Australia, 1791-1853*. Cork: Mercier Press, 1987.

Curtin, Philip. *Cross-Cultural Trade in World History*. Cambridge: Cambridge University Press, 1984.

Davis, David Brion. *The Problem of Slavery in the Age of Revolution, 1770-1823*. Oxford: Oxford University Press, 1999.

Davis, David Brion. *In the Image of God: Religion, Moral Values, and Our Heritage of Slavery*. New Haven: Yale University Press, 2001.

Davis, David Brion. *Inhuman Bondage: The Rise and Fall of Slavery in the New World*. Oxford: Oxford University Press, 2006.

Davis, Mike. *Late Victorian Holocausts: El Nino Famines and the Making of the Third World*. London: Verso, 2001.

Drescher, Seymour. *Econocide: British Slavery in the Era of Abolition*. Pittsburgh: University of Pittsburgh Press, 1977.

Drescher, Seymour. *Abolition: A History of Slavery and Antislavery*. Cambridge: Cambridge University Press, 2009.

Drescher, Seymour. "The Shocking Birth of British Abolitionism." *Slavery & Abolition* 33, no. 4 (December 2012): pp. 571-93.

Dunn, Ross. *The Adventures of Ibn Battuta, a Muslim Traveler of the Fourteenth Century*. Berkeley: University of California Press, 1986.

Dunn, Richard S. *Sugar and Slaves*. New York: W. W. Norton, 1972.

Edgerton-Tarpley, Kathryn. *Tears from Iron: Cultural Responses to Famine in Nineteenth-Century China*. Berkeley: University of California Press, 2008.

Emmer, P. C. *The Dutch Slave Trade, 1500-1850*. New York: Berghahn Books, 2006.

Engels, Frederick. *The Origin of the Family, Private Property and the State*. Elenore Burke Leacock, ed. New York: International Publishers, 1972.

Engerman, Stanley L., Seymour Drescher and Robert L. Paquette. *Slavery*. Oxford: Oxford University Press, 2001.

Farr, Kathryn. *Sex Trafficking: The Global Market in Women and Children*. New York: Worth Publishers, 2005.

Finn, Margot. "Slaves Out of Context: Domestic Slavery and the Anglo-Indian Family, c. 1780-1830." *Transactions of the Royal Historical Society* 6, no. 19 (December 2009): pp. 181-203.

Foster, Shirley. "Colonialism and Gender in the East: Representations of the Harem in the Writings of Women Travellers." *The Yearbook of English Studies* 34 (2004): pp. 6-17.

Foucault, Michael. *The Archaeology of Knowledge*. New York: Tavistock Publications, 1972.
Freeman, Donald. *The Straits of Malacca: Gateway or Gauntlet?* Montreal: McGill-Queen's University Press, 2003.
Garcia, Magaly Rodriguez, Lex Heerma van Voss and Elise van Nederveen Meerkerk, eds. *Selling Sex in the City: A Global History of Prostitution, 1600s–2000s*. Leiden: Brill, 2017.
Gelman-Taylor, Jean. *The Social World of Batavia: Europeans and Eurasians in Colonial Indonesia*. Madison: University of Wisconsin Press, 2004.
Getz, Trevor R., and Heather Streets-Salter. *Modern Imperialism and Colonialism: A Global Perspective*. Boston: Prentice Hall, 2011.
Ghosh, Durba. "Gender and Colonialism: Expansionism of Marginalization?" *The Historical Journal* 47, no. 3 (2004): pp. 737–55.
Hall, Catherine. *Civilising Subjects: Colony and Metropole in the English Imagination, 1830–1867*. Chicago: University of Chicago Press, 2002.
Hall, Catherine and Sonya O. Rose. *At Home with the Empire: Metropolitan Culture and the Imperial World*. Cambridge: Cambridge University Press, 2006.
Hannigan, Tim. *Raffles and the British Invasion of Java*. Singapore: Monsoon Books, 2012.
Headrick, Daniel R. *Tools of Empire: Technology and European Imperialism in the Nineteenth Century*. Oxford: Oxford University Press, 1981.
Headrick, Daniel R. *Power over Peoples: Technology, Environments, and Western Imperialism, 1400 to the Present*. Princeton: Princeton University Press, 2012.
Hibbert, Christopher. *The Great Mutiny: India, 1857*. New York: Viking Press, 1978.
Hillemann, Ulrike. *Asian Empire and British Knowledge: China and the Networks of British Imperial Expansion*. New York: Palgrave Macmillan, 2009.
Hobsbawm, Eric. *The Age of Capital 1848–1875*. New York: Pantheon Books, 1979.
Hobsbawm, Eric. *The Age of Empire 1875–1914*. New York: Pantheon Books, 1987.
Hobsbawm, Eric. *The Age of Revolution 1789–1848*. London: Orion, 2010.
Hopkins, B. D. "Race, Sex and Slavery: 'Forced Labour' in Central Asia and Afghanistan in the Early 19th Century." *Modern Asian Studies* 42, no. 4 (July 2008): pp. 629–71.
Howell, Philip. *Geographies of Regulation: Policing Prostitution in Nineteenth Century Britain and the Empire*. Cambridge: Cambridge University Press, 2009.
Hua, Hsieh Bao. *Concubinage and Servitude in Late Imperial China*. London: Lexington Books, 2014.
Hui, Ong Jin. "Singapore." In *Prostitution: An International Handbook on Trends, Problems, and Policies*, edited by Nanette Davis. Westport: Greenwood Press, 1993, pp. 243–72.
Husni, Ronak and Daniel L. Newman. *Muslim Women in Law and Society: Annotated Translation of Al-Tahir Al-Haddad's Imra Tuna Fi L-Sharia Wa L-Mujtama, with an Introduction*. New York: Routledge, 2007.

Hussin, Nordin. *Trade and Society in the Straits of Melaka: Dutch Melaka and English Penang, 1780–1830*. Copenhagen: NIAS Press, 2007.

Jones, Eric. *Wives, Slaves, and Concubines: A History of the Female Underclass in Dutch Asia*. DeKalb: Northern Illinois University Press, 2010.

Jones, Jeremy. *Oman, Culture and Diplomacy*. Edinburgh: Edinburgh University Press, 2013.

Kale, Madhavi. *Fragments of Empire*. Philadelphia: University of Pennsylvania Press, 1998.

Keneally, Thomas. *The Great Shame: And the Triumph of the Irish in the English-Speaking World*. 1st ed. New York: Nan A. Talese, 1999.

Kent, Eliza F. *Converting Women: Gender and Protestant Christianity in Colonial South India*. Oxford: Oxford University Press, 2004.

Kent, Susan Kingsley. *Gender and Power in Britain, 1640–1990*. London: Routledge, 1999.

Killingray, David, Margarette Lincoln and Nigel Rigby, *Maritime Empires*. Suffolk: Boydell Press, 2004.

Klein, Herbert. *The Atlantic Slave Trade*. Cambridge: Cambridge University Press, 1999.

Klein, Martin A. ed. *Breaking the Chains: Slavery, Bondage, and Emancipation in Modern Africa and Asia*. Madison: University of Wisconsin Press, 1993.

Knapman, Gareth. *Race and British Colonialism in Southeast Asia, 1770–1870: John Crawfurd and the Politics of Equality*. New York: Routledge, 2017.

Kolfin, Elmer. *Van de Slavenzweep En de Muze: Twee Eeuwen Verbeelding van Slavernij in Suriname*. Leiden: KITLV, 1997.

Koven, Seth. *Slumming: Sexual and Social Politics in Victorian London*. Princeton: Princeton University Press, 2004.

Kumar, Ashutosh. *Coolies of the Empire; Indentured Indians in the Sugar Colonies, 1830–1920*. Cambridge: Cambridge University Press, 2017.

Langdon, Marcus. *Penang: The Fourth Presidency of India, 1805–1830*. Penang: Areca Books, 2013.

Lasker, Bruno. *Human Bondage in Southeast Asia*. Chapel Hill: University of North Carolina Press, 1950.

Levine, Philippa. "Orientalist Sociology and the Creation of Colonial Sexualities." *Feminist Review, Reconstructing Femininities: Colonial Intersections of Gender, Race, Religion and Class*, no. 65 (Summer 2000): pp. 5–21.

Levine, Philippa. *Prostitution, Race and Politics: Policing Venereal Disease in the British Empire*. New York: Routledge, 2003.

Levine, Philippa. "'A Multitude of Unchaste Women': Prostitution in the British Empire." *Journal of Women's History* 15, no. 4 (Winter 2004a): pp. 159–63.

Levine, Philippa, ed. *Gender and Empire*. Oxford: Oxford University Press, 2004b.

Levine, Philippa. "What's British about Gender and Empire? The Problem of Exceptionalism." *Comparative Studies of South Asia, Africa and the Middle East* 27, no. 2 (2007): pp. 273–82.

Lewis, Dianne. *Jan Compagnie in the Straits of Malacca, 1641–1795*. Athens: Ohio University Press, 1995.

Lockard, Craig. *Southeast Asia in World History*. Oxford: Oxford University Press, 2009.

Lockard, Craig. "Chinese Migration and Settlement in Southeast Asia before 1850: Making Fields from the Sea." *History Compass* 11, no. 9 (September 2013): pp. 765–81.

Loos, Tamara. "A History of Sex and the State in Southeast Asia: Class, Intimacy and Invisibility." *Citizenship Studies* 12, no. 1 (February 2008): pp. 27–43.

Lovejoy, Paul E. *The Ideology of Slavery in Africa*. Beverly Hills: Sage Publications, 1981.

Lovejoy, Paul E. *Transformations in Slavery: A History of Slavery in Africa*. Cambridge: Cambridge University Press, 1983.

MacKenzie, John M. *Imperialism and Popular Culture*. Manchester: Manchester University Press, 1986.

Major, Andrea. *Slavery, Abolitionism and Empire in India, 1772–1843*. Liverpool: Liverpool University Press, 2012.

Malarek, Victor. *The Natashas: Inside the New Global Sex Trade*. New York: Arcade Publishing, 2003.

Manning, Patrick. *Slavery and African Life: Occidental, Oriental, and African Slave Trades*. Cambridge: Cambridge University Press, 1990.

Manning, Patrick. *Migration in World History*. New York: Routledge, 2005.

Mathieson, William. *British Slavery and Its Abolition, 1823–1838*. London: Longmans, Green, and Co., 1926.

McClintock, Anne. *Imperial Leather: Race, Gender, and Sexuality in the Colonial Contest*. New York: Routledge, 1995.

McKeown, Adam. *Melancholy Order: Asian Migration and the Globalization of Borders*. New York: Columbia University Press, 2008.

Mendelson, Sarah E. *Barracks and Brothels: Peacekeeping and Human Trafficking in the Balkans*. Washington: Center for Strategic & International Studies, 2005.

Midgley, Claire, ed. *Gender and Imperialism*. Manchester: Manchester University Press, 1998.

Miers, Suzanne. *Slavery in the Twentieth Century: The Evolution of a Global Problem*. New York: Alta Mira Press, 2003.

Miksic, John N. *Archeological Research on the "Forbidden Hill" of Singapore: Excavation at Fort Canning 1984*. Singapore: The National Museum of Singapore, 1985.

Miller, Harry. *A Short History of Malaysia*. New York: F.A. Praeger, 1966.

Mintz, Sidney. *Sweetness and Power: The Place of Sugar in Modern History*. New York: Viking Penguin, 1986.

Morgan, Philip D., and Sean Hawkins. *The Black Experience and the Empire*. Oxford: Oxford University Press, 2004.

Mui, Hoh-cheung. *The Management of Monopoly: A Study of the English East India Company's Conduct of Its Tea Trade, 1784–1833*. Vancouver: University of British Columbia Press, 1984.

Northrup, David. *The Atlantic Slave Trade*. 2nd ed. Boston: Houghton Mifflin Co., 2002.

Nwulia, Moses. *Britain and Slavery in East Africa*. 1st ed. Washington: Three Continents Press, 1975.

Oostindie, Gert. *Fifty Years Later: Antislavery, Capitalism and Modernity in the Dutch Orbit*. Pittsburgh: University of Pittsburgh Press, 1996.

Osterhammel, Jurgen and Niels Petersson. *Globalization: A Short History*. Princeton: Princeton University Press, 2009.

Pateman, Carol. *The Sexual Contract*. Stanford: Stanford University Press, 1988.

Patnaik, Utsa and Manjari Dingwaney. *Chains of Servitude: Bondage and Slavery in India*. India: Sangram Books Ltd., 1985.

Patterson, Orlando. *Slavery and Social Death: A Comparative Study*. Harvard: Harvard University Press, 1982.

Perry, Adele. *On the Edge of Empire: Gender, Race, and the Making of British Columbia, 1849–1871*. Toronto: University of Toronto Press, 2002.

Philips, C. *The East India Company, 1784–1834*. Manchester: Manchester University Press, 1961.

Pomeranz, Kenneth. *The Great Divergence: China, Europe, and the Making of the Modern World Economy*. Princeton: Princeton University Press, 2000.

Pomeranz, Kenneth and Steven Topik. *The World That Trade Created: Society, Culture, and the World Economy, 1400 to the Present*. 2nd ed. Armonk: M.E. Sharpe, 2006.

Quirk, Joel. *The Anti-Slavery Project: From the Slave Trade to Human Trafficking*. Philadelphia: University of Pennsylvania Press, 2011.

Ransmeier, Johanna S. *Sold People: Traffickers and Family Life in Northern China*. Cambridge: Harvard University Press, 2017.

Ray, Himanshu Pragha and Edward A. Alpers, eds. *Cross Currents and Community Network: The History of the Indian Ocean World*. Oxford: Oxford University Press, 2007.

Reid, Anthony and David G. Marr. *Perceptions of the Past in Southeast Asia*. Ann Arbor: University of Michigan, 1979.

Reid, Anthony and David G. Marr. *Southeast Asia in the Age of Commerce 1450–1680, Volume One: The Lands below the Winds*. New Haven: Yale University Press, 1993a.

Reid, Anthony and David G. Marr. *Southeast Asia in the Age of Commerce, 1450–1680, Volume Two: Expansion and Crisis*. New Haven: Yale University Press, 1993b.

Reid, Anthony and David G. Marr. *Charting the Shape of Early Modern Southeast Asia*. Chiang Mai: Silkworm Books, 1999.

Reid, Anthony and Jennifer Brewster, eds. *Slavery, Bondage, and Dependency in Southeast Asia*. New York: St. Martins, 1983.

Reynolds, Jonathan and Erik Gilbert. *Trading Tastes: Commodity and Cultural Exchange to 1750*. New Jersey: Prentice Hall, 2005.

Risley, Ford. *Abolition and the Press: The Moral Struggle against Slavery*. Evanston: Northwestern University Press, 2008.

Rope, Michael and John Tosh, eds. *Manful Assertions: Masculinities in Britain since 1800*. London: Routledge, 1991.

Rose, Sonya O. *Limited Livelihoods: Gender and Class in Nineteenth Century England*. Berkeley: University of California Press, 2004.

Roukis, George. "The British East India Company 1600–1858: A Model of Transition Management for the Modern Global Corporation." *Journal of Management Development* 23, no. 10 (December 2004): pp. 938–48.

Roy, Tirthankar. *The East India Company: The World's Most Powerful Corporation*. New York: Penguin Books India, 2012.

Said, Edward W. *Orientalism*. New York: Vintage Books, 1978.

Scarr, Deryck. *Slaving and Slavery in the Indian Ocean*. London: Macmillan Press, 1998.

Searight, Sarah. "The Charting of the Red Sea." *History Today* 53, no. 3 (March 2003): pp. 40–6.

Seow, Francis T. *The Media Enthralled: Singapore Revisited*. Boulder: Lynne Rienner Publishers, 1998.

Shaw, A. *Convicts and the Colonies: A Study of Penal Transportation from Great Britain and Ireland to Australia and Other Parts of the British Empire*. London: Faber, 1966.

Shelley, Louise I. *Hearing before the Subcommittee on International Terrorism, Nonproliferation and Human Rights of the Committee on International Relations House of Representatives, Trafficking in Persons Report* on June 25, 2003, 108th Cong., 1st session: pp. 108–53.

Sinha, Mrinalini. *Colonial Masculinity: The "Manly Englishman" and the "Effeminate Bengali" in the Late Nineteenth Century*. Manchester: Manchester University Press, 1995.

Smith-Rosenberg, Carroll. *Disorderly Conduct: Visions of Gender in Victorian America*. Oxford: Oxford University Press, 1986.

Stark, Suzanne J. *Female Tars: Women Aboard Ship in the Age of Sail*. Annapolis: Naval Institute Press, 1996.

Stoecker, Sally and Louise Shelly, eds. *Human Trafficking and Transnational Crime: Eurasian and American Perspectives*. Lanham: Rowman & Littlefield Publishers, Inc., 2002.

Stoler, Ann Laura. "Making Empire Respectable: The Politics of Race and Sexual Morality in 20th-Century Colonial Cultures." *American Ethnologist* 16, no. 4 (November 1989): pp. 634–60.

Stoler, Ann Laura. *Race and the Education of Desire: Foucault's History of Sexuality and the Colonial Order of Things*. Durham: Duke University Press, 1995.

Stoler, Ann Laura. *Carnal Knowledge and Imperial Power: Race and the Intimate in Colonial Rule*. Berkeley: University of California Press, 2002.

Streets, Heather. *Martial Races: The Military, Race and Masculinity in British Imperial Culture, 1857–1914*. Manchester: Manchester University Press, 2004.

Tagliacozzo, Eric. "Ambiguous Commodities, Unstable Frontiers: The Case of Burma, Siam, and Imperial Britain, 1800–1900." *Comparative Studies in Society and History* 46 (2004): pp. 354–77.

Tagliacozzo, Eric. *Secret Trades, Porous Borders: Smuggling and States along a Southeast Asian Frontier, 1865–1915*. New Haven: Yale University Press, 2005.

Tagliacozzo, Eric and Wen-chin Chang, eds. *Chinese Circulations: Capital, Commodities, and Networks in Southeast Asia*. Durham: Duke University Press, 2011.

Tarling, Nicholas. *British Policy in the Malay Peninsula and Archipelago, 1824–1871*. Oxford: Oxford University Press, 1957.

Tarling, Nicholas, ed. *The Cambridge History of Southeast Asia, Volume One Part One: From Early Times to c. 1500*. Cambridge: Cambridge University Press, 1999a.

Tarling, Nicholas, ed. *The Cambridge History of Southeast Asia, Volume One Part Two: From c. 1500 to c. 1800*. Cambridge: Cambridge University Press, 1999b.

Tarling, Nicholas, ed. *The Cambridge History of Southeast Asia, Volume Two Part One: From c.1800 to the 1930s*. Cambridge: Cambridge University Press, 1999c.

Testart, Alain. "The Extent and Significance of Debt Slavery." *Revue Française de Sociologie* Annual English Selection 43, no. 1 (2002): pp. 173–204.

Thornton, John. *Africa and Africans in the Making of the Atlantic World, 1400–1680*. Cambridge: Cambridge University Press, 1992.

Tinker, Hugh. *A New System of Slavery: The Export of Indian Labour Overseas, 1830–1920*. 2nd ed. London: Hansib, 1993.

Trocki, Carl A. *Prince of Pirates: The Temenggongs and the Development of Johor and Singapore, 1784–1885*. Singapore: Singapore University Press, 1979.

Trocki, Carl A. *Opium, Empire, and the Global Political Economy: A Study of the Asian Opium Trade, 1750–1950*. London: Routledge, 1999.

Trocki, Carl A. "Borders and the Mapping of the Malay World." Paper presented at the *Annual Meeting of the Association for Asian Studies*, San Diego, March 9, 2000.

Trocki, Carl A. *Singapore: Wealth, Power and the Culture of Control*. London: Routledge, 2006.

Turley, David. *Slavery*. Oxford: Blackwell Publishing, 2000.

United Nations Office on Drugs and Crime (UNODC) 2018. *Global Report on Trafficking in Persons*. New York: United Nations, 2018.

Vink, Markus. "'The World's Oldest Trade': Dutch Slavery and Slave Trade in the Indian Ocean in the Seventeenth Century." *Journal of World History* 14, no. 2 (June 2003): pp. 131–77.

Wade, Geoff. "An Early Age of Commerce in Southeast Asia, 900–1300 CE." *Journal of Southeast Asian Studies* 40, no. 2 (June 2009): pp. 221–65.

Walkowitz, Judith. *Prostitution and Victorian Society: Women, Class, and the State*. Cambridge: Cambridge University Press, 1980.

Ward, Kerry. *Networks of Empire: Forced Migration in the Dutch East India Company*. New York: Cambridge University Press, 2009.

Warren, James Francis. *The Sulu Zone, 1768–1898: The Dynamics of External Trade, Slavery, and Ethnicity in the Transformation of a Southeast Asian Maritime State*. Singapore: Singapore University Press, 1981.

Warren, James Francis. *Ah Ku and Karayuki-san: Prostitution in Singapore, 1870–1940*. Singapore: Oxford University Press, 1993.

Warren, James Francis. *Pirates, Prostitutes and Pullers: Explorations in the Ethno- and Social History of Southeast Asia*. Crawley: UWA Press, 2008.

Watson-Andaya, Barbara. "From Temporary Wife to Prostitute: Sexuality and Economic Change in Early Modern Southeast Asia." *Journal of Women's History* 9, no. 4 (Winter 1998): p. 11.

Watson-Andaya, Barbara. *Other Pasts: Women Gender and History in Early Modern Southeast Asia*. Honolulu: University of Hawaii Press, 2000.

Watson-Andaya, Barbara and Leonard Y. Andaya. *A History of Malaysia*. Honolulu: University of Hawaii Press, 2001.

Webster, Anthony. *Gentleman Capitalists: British Imperialism in Southeast Asia, 1770–1890*. London: I.B. Tauris, 1998.

Webster, Anthony. *The Twilight of the East India Company: The Evolution of Anglo-Asian Commerce and Politics, 1790–1860*. Rochester: Boydell Press, 2009.

Wilbur, Marguerite. *The East India Company and the British Empire in the Far East*. New York: R.R. Smith, 1945.

Williams, Eric. *Capitalism and Slavery*. Chapel Hill: University of North Carolina Press, 1994.

Wurtzburg, C. E. *Raffles of the Eastern Isles*. London: Hodder and Stoughton, 1956.

Yang, Anand. "Indian Convict Workers in Southeast Asia in the Late Eighteenth and Early Nineteenth Centuries." *Journal of World History* 14, no. 2 (June 2003): pp. 179–208.

## Web-Based Sources

*2017 Global Estimates of Child Labour and Modern Slavery: Asia and the Pacific Regional Brief*. Accessed May 31, 2019. https://www.ilo.org/wcmsp5/groups/public/@ed_norm/@ipec/documents/publication/wcms_597873.pdf.

"Early Beginnings." Government of India Law Commission of India: Ministry of Law and Justice. Accessed May 15, 2013. http://lawcommissionofindia.nic.in.

"Map of Southeast Asia." Accessed May 13, 2013. http://asiasociety.org/countries/traditions/introduction-southeast-asia.

United States Department of State. *2018 Trafficking in Persons Report—Singapore*. June 28, 2018. Accessed July 9, 2019. https://www.refworld.org/docid/5b3e0a8a4.html.

United States Department of State. *2018 Trafficking in Person Report—Malaysia*. June 28, 2018. Accessed July 9, 2019. https://www.refworld.org/docid/5b3e0ae1a.html.

# Index

Abdul Rahman 168
Act V (1843) 88
Allen, Richard 7, 38, 42, 44, 48, 50, 51, 81
Alpers, Edward 15
America. *See* United States
American Revolution 77
Andaya, Leonard 111, 113
Anderson, Clare 88, 150
Anderson, John 97, 178, 182
Anglo-Dutch Treaty (1824) 79, 115, 116, 148
Anglo-Indian families 49
antislavery
    laws/legislation 2, 3, 5, 6, 8, 9, 15, 17, 19–21, 23, 29–33, 37–41, 46–50, 57, 59, 60, 64, 70–7, 79, 81, 85, 86, 88, 89, 91–4, 100, 105, 109–11, 116, 118–20, 123, 125, 132, 137, 143–5, 148, 151, 164, 172, 179, 181, 183, 187, 191, 196, 197, 200
    movement 38
    policies 15, 17, 20, 37, 46, 47, 52, 71, 73, 91, 107, 110, 125, 197
    reform 19
Anti-Slavery Project 16, 20, 21, 23, 33, 85, 95, 110, 117, 128, 144, 145, 157, 190
*Anti-Slavery Project, The* (Quirk) 14
Arab Chief of Wadi 60, 72
Arab Muslims 46

Baring, B. 3
Bayly, C. A. 17
Behn, Aphra 24
Bencoolen 9, 31, 38, 44
Bengal 29, 38, 41, 68, 84, 91, 93, 110
black market 21, 76, 107
Britain 16, 21, 28, 32, 33, 36, 37, 40, 51, 57, 73, 74, 77–80, 106, 107, 110, 114–15, 118, 156, 194–5
    colonies 1, 75
    government 1, 16, 28, 37, 95, 148, 171
    Parliament 128, 147, 200
    superiority on indigenous rulers 59

British Anglophiles 169
British Library's India Office of Records 30
British Straits Government in Council 118, 120, 123, 125, 130, 133, 141, 166, 168, 182
British Straits Settlements 2, 6, 9, 12, 15, 23, 33, 39, 47, 57, 61, 69, 72, 77, 85–9, 92–4, 96–103, 105, 106, 110, 116, 125, 126, 130, 131, 134, 148–59, 162, 165, 173, 176, 190, 195, 200
Brooke, James 19
Bruce, Charles Andrew 168
Buginese 52, 53

Cameron, John 169
Cannadine, David 73
Cape of Good Hope 94, 95
Captain Phillip 130
Caunter, Richard 96, 100, 104, 106, 158, 176–84, 186, 198, 199
Charter Act (1833) 61 n.13
Chatterjee, Indrani 41, 45, 182
Chew, Emrys 20
Chew, Sing 37
China 80–1, 112, 188
Chinese labor 44, 76, 81
Chinese merchants 4, 5, 26, 31, 43, 47, 80, 92, 177
Chinese secret societies 80, 89, 189
Church, Thomas 184–6
civility 153
civilized society 154, 155
Clarence-Smith, William 46
Clark, Anna 156
class 72, 151–2, 154–9, 179
    based conflicts 153
    pauper 73, 74, 136, 157
Collett, Joseph 152
colonial authorities 6, 11, 16, 33, 118, 122, 129, 154
colonialism 16, 18, 19, 24, 26, 76, 82

concubinage/concubines 5, 6, 12, 17, 21–3, 25, 27, 28, 41, 92, 96, 178, 181, 182, 184, 185, 198, 199
"coolies" 17, 81
Court of Judicature 100
Crawfurd, John 17–20, 23, 80, 82, 83, 128, 169, 170
Criminal Procedure and the Penal Code 61 n.13
cultural exchanges 43, 80

*Dar al-Islam* 46
Davis, David Brion 77
de Albuquerque, Afonso 113
debt-slaves/debtors 4, 10, 11, 13, 14, 25, 29, 42, 68, 78, 79, 83, 85–7, 92, 93, 95–8, 100, 102–6, 137, 150, 157, 164, 166–8, 171, 172, 178–80, 182, 185, 186, 190, 195, 196
dehumanization 78, 147
*Democracy in America* (de Tocqueville, Alexis) 64
de Tocqueville, Alexis 64
Dickens, John 164
discourse 67
    popular 31, 53 n.74, 65
    public 5, 8, 149
domesticity 151–9, 176, 179, 187
domestic labor 5–7, 13, 23, 25
Drescher, Seymour 69, 77, 199
Dutch Asia 26
Dutch Burghers 117
Dutch East India Company 25, 48, 114, 115, 117, 121, 122, 160
Dutch expansionism 79, 168

East India Company (EIC) 1–9, 15–18, 20, 21, 23, 28–32, 38, 41, 48, 57, 64, 65, 73, 75, 80, 85, 99, 105, 138, 148, 195, 200
    Board of Control 19, 35, 36, 109, 110, 135, 140, 143, 190
    Court of Directors 67, 91, 142, 143, 165, 166, 168
    expansion 128
    factory in Penang 115
    government 37, 40, 49, 57, 60, 71, 76, 87, 94, 125, 131, 141, 143, 145, 149, 163, 165, 167, 173, 187, 196

Law Commission 70
    officials 2, 8, 9, 15, 23, 29, 32, 33, 35–7, 39, 40, 44, 58, 60, 61, 71–6, 81, 83, 84, 87, 88, 91–3, 106, 109, 115, 116, 123, 132, 136, 141–4, 151–3, 157, 158, 167, 172, 174, 179, 181, 186, 196, 198, 199
    policy on slavery 126
    role in Britain's Empire 57
East Indies 5, 7, 8, 15, 19, 29, 30, 33, 40, 59–63, 65, 67, 68, 71–3, 75, 76, 84, 91, 93, 94, 110, 111, 128, 136, 138, 143, 152, 164, 170, 172, 173, 196–8, 200
Emancipation Act (1834) 3, 15, 21, 195, 196
English Court Justice 110
Enlightenment Liberalism 17
Europe 78, 99, 153
Europeans in Singapore 153–4, 176
Evans, William 28

Farquhar, William 85, 86, 118, 122, 123, 145, 149, 165, 168, 170–2
Felony Slave Trade Act (1811) 8, 20, 32, 38, 40, 57, 76, 118, 129, 149, 165, 191
Finn, Margot 48, 49
forced labor system 138
Foreign and British Anti-Slavery Society 107
free labor/laborers 2, 20, 21, 56, 60, 75, 83, 86, 93–5, 106, 120, 149, 150, 164, 190
free trade 2, 86–7, 94, 168
Fullerton, Robert 97, 100–5, 109, 119, 120, 123, 125, 129–43, 158, 181–3, 191, 199

Gage, William Hall 97–8, 106, 179, 191, 197
Garling, Samuel 72, 109, 110, 125–36, 138–40, 142, 143, 145, 149, 184
gender 40, 73, 151–9, 179
    of abolition 21–8
    concepts 6, 7
    disparity 149, 151, 175, 185, 187–8, 191
    norms 154, 155
geopolitical economy 36, 179

Godfrey, George 177
Governor Phillips 91

Haitian revolution 65
Hannigan, Tim 18, 171
Hastings, Warren 38
'Head Money' 120
Hindu-Javanese social hierarchies 45
*History of the Indian Archipelago* (Crawfurd) 82
Hobhouse, John 29
homosexuality 157
House of Commons (HoC) 28, 29, 61, 86
"Humanitas" 147, 148
humanity 38, 97, 137, 140, 141, 198
human trafficking 21, 60, 96, 98, 151, 181–3
Hussin, Nordin 48, 117

Ibbetson, Robert 96, 97, 176–9, 182, 183, 196
imam of Muscat 37, 72, 197
"imperial meridian" 17, 80
imperial policy 5, 17, 23, 77, 80
indentured laborers 88, 94, 199
India 40, 61, 65, 69, 83, 84, 87, 88, 92, 93, 173
Indianization 44
Indian Law Commission/Commissioners 29, 30, 39–41, 61–6, 68, 72, 73, 78, 136, 157
India Office 84, 161, 164, 167
indigenous labor 89
indigenous societies 10, 33, 62, 79, 82, 194
Indonesia 15, 46, 50, 52, 53, 93, 114, 173

Japan 188
Java 19, 45, 172
Javanese Royal Court 169
Johor 114, 115, 170
Jones, Eric 26
Jones, Jeremy 35
*Journal of the Straits Branch of the Royal Asiatic Society* 160

Kadir, Abdullah Bin Abdul 1–6, 79, 147, 171, 173
Kent, Susan Kingsley 21–2
Keung Ato 193, 194

King of Queda 85, 91, 116, 134, 197
Knapman, Gareth 17, 19, 82
Kock, Daniel 127–9
*kongsis* 47, 80–1

Langdon, Marcus 159, 161
legal injury 70
Leith, George 161, 164
Levine, Philippa 23, 154, 157
Lewis, Diane 113, 160
Lewis, W. T. 72, 105, 109, 113, 118, 119, 125–9, 131–5, 137, 138–43, 145, 182, 184–6, 196
Li Akak 193, 194
liberalism 198
Light, Francis 44, 85, 91, 159–66, 195
linguistic gymnastics 88, 197
Loch 100
Lockard, Craig 9, 45, 46
Lockett 59
London 28, 57, 60, 62, 75, 76, 84, 136, 140, 153, 157, 166, 167, 198
Lord Minto 18, 171, 172

Macalister, Norman 165–6
Macaulay 61 n.13
Macnaughten, W. H. 59
Maddock, T. H. 39
Major, Andrea 3, 8, 15, 20, 38, 84, 92, 117, 149
Malacca 109–10, 125, 128, 130, 131, 140, 141, 150, 170, 172, 173, 190, 196, 197
  and its heirs 111–16
  slaves in 109–10, 116–23, 126, 127, 131–3, 137, 142–4
*Malacca Observer* 75, 95, 98, 99, 102, 180
Malagasy of Madagascar 8
Malaya 16, 79, 111, 112, 115, 152, 170
Malaysia 52, 53, 81, 111, 114
male laborers 22, 174–6
Manuel (king) 113
marriage market 12, 24, 28, 198
Marsden, William 82
Martin, Robert Montgomery 153
masculinity 154–7
men and sexual release 156, 157
Miksic, John 112
"Minute by the President" 100

monetary compensation 185, 186
Morgan, Jennifer 23
*Morning Chronicle* 75
Murchison, Kenneth 99

nakhodas 97, 98, 177, 178, 180, 181, 183
Naning War (1831–2) 20
national identity 156
*Networks of Empire* (Ward) 51
New Poor Law 66
Niemeijer, Hendrik 26
noninterference policy 36, 37, 40, 47, 58, 122, 123, 128, 130, 132, 136, 163, 181, 196

opium markets 81
Opium Wars (1839–1842) 168
oppression 68, 69, 73, 74, 163
*Ornamentalism* (Cannadine) 73
*Our Tropical Possessions in Malayan India* (Cameron) 169
ownership 13, 26, 122, 126, 172, 173

Pacific Ocean 16, 30, 39, 60, 117, 168
Parameśvara (Malayan prince) 111, 112, 169
Pateman, Carol 22
patriarchy 21–5, 72, 73, 152, 156, 181, 184, 186
Patullo, John 99, 102, 106, 140, 141, 179, 180
pauperism 63, 66
Pearson, John 142, 143
Penang 3, 31, 32, 44, 85, 86, 91, 95–8, 100, 102, 104, 115, 118, 125, 130, 131, 150, 151, 154, 158–68, 172, 173, 190, 196, 197, 199
personal freedom 14, 77
pirates/piracy 11, 16, 53, 75, 89, 105, 112, 144, 149, 168, 188
Pires, Tomé 113
Political Department in London 60
Portuguese 113, 114, 117
Presgrave, E. 103–5
Prince of Wales Island. *See* Penang
property rights 22, 70, 87, 110, 123, 164, 190, 197
prostitution 28, 46, 70, 81, 96, 177, 178, 180, 181, 183, 185, 188–90, 193, 198, 199

protocapitalism 80
public controversy 98–101
Pulau Nias 96–9, 101, 104, 106, 147, 148, 150, 158, 176–87

Quirk, Joel 9, 14, 21, 194

race 69, 72, 73, 151–9
Raffles, Stamford 2, 4, 6, 13, 17–19, 79, 82, 83, 85–7, 104, 106, 128, 149, 168–73
Raffles Regulations. *See* Regulation V
Raj of Borneo 118
Regulation V 86
Regulation X 20, 32, 57–9, 85, 86, 170
Reid, Anthony 10, 11, 41–3, 45, 84, 117, 144
Reverend Boucho 95, 96, 102, 176–9, 183–4, 187
Rozells, Martinha 159, 160
Russell, J. 193, 194

Sammee, Renga 126
sexual contract 22–3, 181, 186
sexuality 6, 41, 151, 156, 157, 181
  Asian 13
  women 23
Singapore 1, 4, 5, 13, 16, 19, 32, 79, 85–6, 95, 97, 106, 115, 125, 131, 147, 149–51, 153, 154, 158, 168–75, 184, 186, 188–91, 194, 196, 199
*Singapore Chronicle* 75, 94, 98, 99, 102, 106, 144, 157, 175, 180, 187, 191
Singapore Consultations 100
*Singapore Free Press* 144, 147, 148, 151, 187, 188, 190
Siu Ahing 193–4
slave markets 1, 8, 16, 23, 26, 39, 53, 95, 147, 151
slavery 2, 6, 7, 29, 30, 41, 86, 129. *See also* slave(s); slave trade
  agricultural 63
  American 78
  in Asia 68, 93, 172
  Atlantic 10, 13, 33, 40, 57, 78, 84, 149
  chattel 9–10, 45, 69
  concept 95, 149
  discourse 133

in east 5, 6, 57, 60–5, 68, 69, 72–4, 94, 132, 136–8, 198
European 3, 48, 57, 60, 65, 71, 72, 93, 98, 104, 116
Indian Ocean 7, 10, 11, 15, 16, 30, 32, 39, 40, 43, 48, 50, 52, 57, 60, 68, 71, 72, 78, 82, 116, 117, 168
in Islam 46
plantation 84
redefining 81–5
in Straits Settlements 75, 77–81, 103, 105 (*see also* British Straits Settlements)
voluntary 40, 63, 68, 104
in west 62, 67, 69, 133
*Slavery, Abolitionism and Empire in India* (Major) 3, 15
*Slavery, Bondage, and Dependency in Southeast Asia* (Reid) 41
Slavery Abolition Act 29, 147
*Slavery and the Slave Trade in British India* 75, 198
slave(s) 43. *See also* slavery; women
African 64, 84
children 4, 14, 70, 120, 122, 135, 145, 162, 179
classification 20
compensation to owners 69–70
definition 9–10
in Dutch settlements 48
economic advantage of 42
emancipation 60, 63, 65, 66, 76, 91–4, 106, 110, 111, 117, 118, 122, 123, 125–6, 129–32, 134, 136–7, 139, 140, 142, 145, 151, 162, 167, 171, 172, 174
experiences of 11, 68, 78, 93
import/export of 123, 134, 136, 164, 166, 170, 176–7, 186
in Indian archipelago 84
laws 60, 104, 109, 126
in Malacca 109–10, 116–23, 126, 127, 131–3, 137, 142–5
male 2, 4
marriage 70
owners 121, 126, 127, 129–31, 134, 135, 137, 138, 141, 164, 166, 167, 170, 195–7
from Pulau Nias 176–87

punishment 66, 67, 70, 73, 122, 125, 136, 139
raiding 78–9
registries 85, 91, 92, 94, 95, 103, 110, 118–23, 128–9, 134–9, 144, 145, 150, 166–8, 171, 190
revolts 65
status 6, 13, 26, 28, 62, 63, 66, 71, 86, 93, 98, 106, 123, 126, 131, 145, 195, 197
taxable 121, 167
treatment 23, 25, 38, 84, 100, 101, 122, 131–4, 136, 171
West-India 68
slave trade 4, 5, 30, 78–9, 156, 165, 171, 179, 180. *See also* slavery
abolishing 1–3, 6, 7, 14–16, 21, 29–32, 36, 38, 49, 56, 59, 65, 71, 72, 76, 77, 87, 88, 91–3, 106, 111, 117, 118, 123, 127, 128, 130, 132–4, 136, 138, 141, 143, 145, 149–51, 165–8, 170, 171, 191, 194, 196, 198, 200
African 23, 57, 88
Bugis and Sulu in 53
Chinese 8, 96–9, 104, 176–8, 198
clandestine 182
European 15, 16, 20, 39, 48, 50–2, 56, 76, 195
foreign 116
French 49–50
by Indians 44–5, 59, 106
indigenous 8, 11, 15, 16, 31, 41, 43, 48, 52–3, 59, 71, 77, 84
legal and illegal 16, 85–7, 96–8, 102, 106, 121, 126, 136, 143, 145, 149, 151, 164, 167, 170, 172, 173, 186, 194, 197
networks 51, 52, 57–8, 76, 89, 110
non-European 57, 58, 76, 186, 191
trans-Atlantic 14, 15, 39
underground 75, 95, 188
Slave Trade Act (1807) 3, 4, 38, 88, 116, 149, 171, 190, 195
*Slave Trade (East India)—Slavery in Ceylon* (Evans) 28
"Slave Trade in the Indian Archipelago" 190
Smale, John 193
Smith 125, 126, 135, 140

Smith-Rosenberg, Carroll 154, 155
Southeast Asia 2–4, 10–12, 14, 16–17, 21, 22, 24–6, 31, 58, 68, 71, 72, 76, 79, 80–5, 87, 89, 93, 95, 110, 112, 113, 115–17, 119, 120, 123, 150, 151, 157, 159, 162, 165, 168, 188, 189, 191, 194, 197, 198
    slaveholding and trading in 40–56
*Southeast Asia and the Age of Commerce* (Reid) 42
*Southeast Asia in World History* (Lockard) 9
Sri Iskandar Shah (King) 169
*Statistics of the Colonies of the British Empire* (Martin) 153
Stecher, J. H. 121
Stoler, Ann 153
Straits of Malacca/Melaka 7, 9, 16, 30, 31, 41, 44, 46, 48, 53, 58, 72, 80, 85, 86, 95, 97, 111, 138, 144, 160
sugar production 67–8
Sultan Abdullah Mukarram Shah of Kedah 161, 163
Sultan Mahmud 113, 114
Sultan of Johor 149
Sulu Sultanate 52
*Sulu Zone, 1768–1898, The* (Warren) 52
Sumatra 7, 12, 47, 50, 51, 83, 96, 97
Supreme Government 138–40
sweeping reform 118

Taylor, Jean Gillman 25
Taylor, Keith 112, 169–70
Thyssen, J. S. Timmerman 117, 119
Townsend, Robert 165
Trapaud, Elisha 159, 160
Trocki, Carl 47
"true womanhood" 154–5
Trunkerrah, Abdullah 126
Turley, David 10
"the tyranny of the Atlantic" 15

United Company of Merchants of England Trading to the East Indies 67
United States 15, 33, 37, 62, 64, 69, 78, 80, 84, 94

van der Capellen, Godert Alexander Gerard Phillip Baron 119
Van San, H. 122
*Vereenigde Oost-Indische Compagnie* (VOC). *See* Dutch East India Company
vertical bonding 11, 41, 42, 45

Ward, Kerry 51
Ward, Thomas 75, 76
Warden 35, 36
Warren, James 11, 52, 89, 144
Watson-Andaya, Barbara 24, 25, 111
West Indies 84, 94, 95, 111, 138, 199
Wilson, Kathleen 13, 22, 23, 152
*Wives, Slaves and Concubines* (Jones) 26
women. *See also* sexuality
    Asian 150, 152, 189
    bodies 21, 27, 95, 157, 158, 176, 181, 186, 199
    Chinese 187, 188
    for domestic and sexual servitude 76, 81, 96, 100, 151, 153, 158, 173, 176, 178, 181, 182, 185, 186, 188, 198, 200
    emancipation 24, 91, 184
    European 189
    exploitation 6, 9, 158
    labor 25, 76
    as men's property 22, 23
    non-European 21, 22, 149, 186
    for reproductive abilities 26–7
    roles and responsibilities 155, 156
    sexual relationship with 24, 25, 27
    slaves/slavery 1–2, 4, 5, 9, 11–14, 17, 21–8, 32, 41, 57, 59, 70, 75, 76, 81, 100, 106, 127, 149, 151, 158, 167, 171, 179, 180, 183–5, 188, 198–200
    trafficking 98, 181–3, 186–91, 193–4, 200
    white 152
    working-class 156
    in zinanas 91
Wright, C. W. H. 96, 178
Wurtzburg, C. E. 18, 19, 171

www.ingramcontent.com/pod-product-compliance
Lightning Source LLC
Chambersburg PA
CBHW072232290426
44111CB00012B/2061